DUBLIN

A CULTURAL AND LITERARY HISTORY

Siobhán Kilfeather

the
liffey
press

Published by
The Liffey Press Ltd
Ashbrook House, 10 Main Street
Raheny, Dublin 5, Ireland
www.theliffeypress.com

A catalogue record of this book is
available from the British Library.

ISBN 1-904148-69-7

Drawings by Wendy Skinner Smith
Cover Design: Sin É Design
Cover images courtesy of Fáilte Ireland (Trinity Library);
National Photographic Archive (Custom House and Ulysses Book);
Sin É Design (Spire); Dublin City Library (Map of Dublin)

Printed in Malaysia.

CONTENTS

CHAPTER THREE

A Promenade on the South Side   71

CHAPTER FOUR

From the Union to the Famine   105

CHAPTER FIVE

Kilmainham   132

CHAPTER SIX

Dublin after the Famine   141

CHAPTER SEVEN

PARNELL SQUARE 188

CHAPTER EIGHT

THE CAPITAL SINCE INDEPENDENCE 201

CHAPTER NINE

NEVER GET OLD: CULTURE AND COUNTER-CULTURE 229

EPILOGUE

Foreword

The days when being Irish seemed an affliction second only to being stricken by typhoid are now irrevocably behind us. Given its history of mass emigration, Ireland was once a nation which seemed to exist in order to be abandoned. These days, however, it is a country which is being eagerly joined—literally so, as immigrants arrive in bulk on its shores for the first time, but also spiritually, for those captivated by its culture and life-style. For the first time in its plagued, fractured modern history, this "afterthought of Europe", as James Joyce brutally dubbed it, is once again a name to be conjured with in cosmopolitan circles— just as it was in the Middle Ages, when it was monks, scholars and missionaries, rather than advertising executives and computer scientists, whom it despatched to the four corners of Europe for the enlightenment of its inhabitants. And most of these come from the oversized village known as Dublin, a city of gossip, drink and story-telling where everyone seems to know everyone else, and which has been said to have marvellous acoustics.

It is not hard to see why the Irish should have regained their popularity in a postmodern age. For one thing, postmodernism is much preoccupied with ethnicity; and ethically speaking the Irish are sufficiently close to the British to be unthreatening, while sufficiently different from them to be charming or intriguing. For another thing, culture lies close to the centre of postmodern thought, and Ireland, most unusually, is a nation which has made an international name for itself through culture rather than through politics or military power. It is Van Morrison, Sinéad O'Connor, U2, Riverdance, Christy Moore, the films of Neil Jordan and the drama of Brian Friel that Ireland exports to the rest of the world, not armaments or oil tankers. Modern Ireland has never fought a war, and is not even part of NATO. As in the Middle Ages, its global influence today is largely a matter of artefacts and ideas, not high-powered diplomacy or military alliances. Dublin, as Siobhán Kilfeather shows in this brilliantly informative survey, was for centuries a seat of power; but the power in question was never Irish.

All this makes the country an attractive proposition to those jaded cosmopolitans in search of a spot of tradition and locality. Ireland has for a long time been a locus of sentiment and nostalgia; indeed, its role in the age of Enlightenment rationalism, like that of Scotland, was to supply the "sensibility", imagination, feel for kinship, sense of history and sense of place which that brand of reason largely excluded. The country became "exoticized", and was not at all slow in reaping the benefits of this image of itself. In its admirably detailed portrayal of modern Dublin, this book shows how this is still a significant feature of Irish life. Yet if one aspect of postmodern thought is about the distinctiveness of place, the other aspect is a full-blooded cosmopolitanism—and the marvellous convenience of contemporary Ireland is that it meets both requirements at the same time. As Kilfeather demonstrates, this is a country where statues of freedom fighters can be found cheek-by jowl with fast food joints, and traditional music can be heard in the shadow of corporate office blocks.

This book is a history of Dublin, with a remarkable feel for the way the past is embodied in bridges and alleyways, sculpture and slums. But in classical Dublin manner it also ambles and diverges, pausing to illuminate the reader about a whole range of subjects from duels to theatres, maternity hospitals to prisons, *The Book of Kells* to Bono. Politics, industry, painting, architecture, feminism, poetry, famine, armed insurrection: these are a mere handful of the topics explored in this extraordinarily rich account. Like all the finest surveys, it combines a deep affection for its subject with an astutely critical eye. There are a good many guides to contemporary Dublin, and a shelf-load of histories of the place; but to combine the two, as Kilfeather has done in this book, is a rare achievement.

Terry Eagleton

Preface and Acknowledgements

The seeds of my romance with Dublin were sown long before I was born. In the late 1940s my mother, a working-class Ulster Protestant girl, moved to Dublin for a year. It was probably the biggest adventure of her life before marriage and she was lucky to be befriended independently by two of the most interesting writers living in the city at that time. The poet and novelist Patrick Kavanagh lived in a cold, bare flat on the Pembroke Road. My mother wrote him a fan letter. The first time he took her out for lunch he had to hunt through pockets and under chairs for enough coins to buy two bowls of soup and a pot of tea. She met Seosamh Mac Grianna's partner, Peggy, in a bakery. They became friends and eventually Peggy took her to meet the writer, who was living separately from his partner and son because of the social stigma attached to unmarried couples. Mac Grianna was an Irish language writer who depended on translation work and on the socially conservative world of Irish language publishing, where he believed that the influence of the Catholic Church put him under threat. He was also struggling in terrible poverty and under that pressure had begun to show symptoms of the mental illness that enveloped the second half of his life. Perhaps if they had been wealthier and more successful, Kavanagh and Mac Grianna would have had less time for a girl who had left school at fourteen and spent most of her working life as a shop assistant. But my mother was also intelligent, very well read, and innocently enthusiastic about everything to do with literature.

My mother came back to Belfast, became a Catholic as much through political as religious conversion, married my father, and spent most of my childhood talking about how much happier we would be if we could afford to escape the brutal philistinism (as she saw it) of Belfast, move to Dublin and live the life of the mind. A trip to Dublin was our favourite day out. We did not have a car, so we would take the Enterprise train from Belfast to Connolly Station, determinedly love the bad coffee and biscuits, and be thrilled when we crossed the border and the money changed. If I were pressed I would have to concede that Connolly is one of the ugliest railway stations in the world, but my heart lifts whenever I arrive there, and descend the steps to Amiens Street. I cannot really remember all that we did on those days out or why we enjoyed them so much.

My mother, who had been a child evacuated to the countryside during the war, associated Dublin with good food (!) and she always bought sausages, tea and cakes to take home with us. We walked about the main shopping thoroughfares and had picnics in St. Stephen's Green. We went to galleries and bookshops and always visited at least two pubs to soak up the atmosphere. I remember the deep contentment that came over my father one lunch time because Seán O'Faoláin, a writer he admired, was having a drink in the same pub. He did not want to speak to O'Faoláin, just to breathe the same atmosphere. In the 1970s Dublin seemed a very shabby city, but it inspired passion, and of course it was liberating to escape the horrors of Belfast even for a day.

Twice I might have gone to university in Dublin, but both times I swerved at the last moment to go further afield, reckoning that I was bound to live in Dublin some day. It has not happened yet, but I am not altogether sorry that the city still retains for me the thrill of a holiday destination, even when I am there, as I am most often these days, to work in the much loved National Library of Ireland.

In common with most capital cities, Dublin has its fair share of fine architecture, statues and monuments, museums, galleries, parks and public spaces, and many of these are described in the pages that follow. But my own attraction to Dublin has always been based on its historical and cultural associations. I love to walk around the city and whenever I see a plaque commemorating a great life or an historic event I always want to know much more about it.

This is an outline history of life in the city that pauses to give close-up detailed descriptions of certain days in the past whose events illuminate some aspect of that history. I have selected days which seemed to me exemplary rather than attempted to give some comprehensive account of the majors events associated with Dublin. There are accounts of insurrection, repression, strikes, terror, executions, escapes and revolution; and there are events from the lives of scientists, artists, writers, musicians and sports people. Many years ago a friend brought me from Dublin a poster showing portraits of great Irish writers, and I was enraged that there was not a single woman to be seen. This book has plenty about women who deserve to be better known by Dubliners and visitors. I intended to write something about the wonderful Maeve Brennan, whose collection of stories, *The Springs of Affection*, set in a street in Ranelagh, is the book I would give anyone to read on her first visit to Dublin—but I ran out of time and space. My epilogue is an abecedary, a collection of scraps that is only apparently arbitrary: a homage to my jazz-playing, football-loving, whiskey-drinking, star-gazing Jewish husband, and to those days out in pubs, bookshops, galleries and teashops with mother and father.

As a visitor to Dublin over the years I owe a tremendous debt of gratitude to several hosts and guides: Aileen Douglas; Barry, Dolores, Laura and Luke Gibbons; Finnola Kilfeather; Bethan Kilfoil and John Downing; Bill McCormack; Anne Mitchell; and Oonagh Waurke. Most of my Dublin friends are blown-ins, seduced by the city and unable to leave. I have particularly enjoyed watching Barry Gibbons grow up in Dublin and enjoy the life I envied Dublin teenagers when I was young.

My thanks to my excellent publisher, James Ferguson, who gave me the idea for this book and then pestered me to finish it. Kevin Whelan was a most astute reader of the manuscript and saved me from many errors of fact and judgement—all remaining mistakes are entirely my own responsibility. Warm thanks to Terry Eagleton for so generously providing a preface. Robert Jones and Neil McKenna gave essential advice and support. Judy Coleridge helped me relax while I was writing—no easy task. John and Lynn Stockton made it possible for me to work by looking after Constance and Oscar; as did Richard Slowik, who also cooked, cleaned and brought wine and whiskey, those essential aids to writing. Peter Jameson is always at my side, helping out (especially with the index), and making me laugh.

I never visit Dublin without thinking of my father and mother, who loved it.

DEDICATION
To Gerard Kilfeather and Marie McColgan;
and in memory of Hugh, Matt, Patsy, Johnny and Alo Kilfeather.

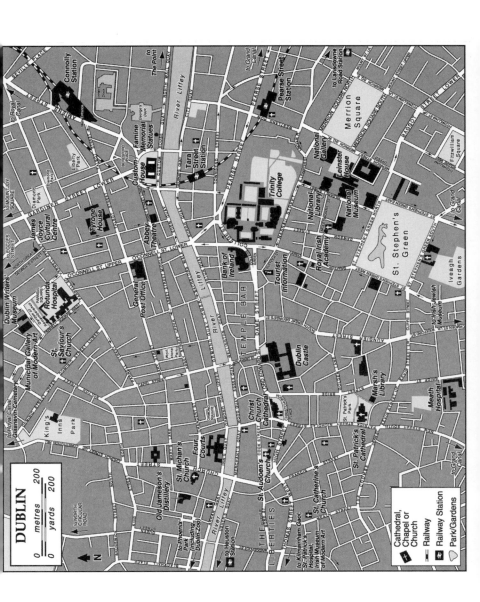

Introduction
THE DELIGHTS OF BRAY

"It is not generally known that two years in succession Chapman spent his summer holidays in Bray, Co. Wicklow. He was at that time a young man and had not yet met Keats, the poet with whom his name was fated ever to be linked. He spent most of his nights dancing and enjoying himself enormously. These holidays were such pleasant memories afterwards that he never tired of telling his friends about them and praising Bray. Indeed, on the occasion of his first meeting with Keats, he asked the poet whether he had ever visited this delightful Irish watering place. Keats said that he had.

'I am delighted to hear it,' Chapman said enthusiastically, 'I think Bray is wonderful. When I was there I went mad about dancing and spent the night in the Arcadia ballroom. I thought the floor was one of the best I had ever encountered and all the ladies I met there were expert dancers. I enjoyed myself immensely. Why, I practically lived there. Do you know the place yourself?'

'Et ego in Arcadia vixi,' Keats said wearily."

Myles na gCopaleen, *The Various Lives of Keats and Chapman*

People will tell you that Dublin isn't what it used to be. You may find some solace in the reflection that this is what people have been saying for over two hundred years, at least since the Act of Union in 1800. Dublin has sometimes been seen as a world capital of nostalgia. Preserving and memorializing the past has been one civic obsession, and yet anyone who visited Dublin for the first time in the late twentieth or early twenty-first century might have been more struck by the perpetual building works, the consequent destruction of historic buildings, the influx of a new population, the discussion of house prices and traffic, all of which seem to suggest a headlong gallop into a future predicated on voluntary change.

Dublin, like every capital city, is a set of paradoxes. Capital cities are required not only to house administration, and to host ceremonial state bodies and institutions, but also to exemplify the nation to the rest of the world; yet, at least since the romantic period, European nations have tended to imagine rural life as representing the quintessential national identity. In Ireland this fiction received expression in a radio broadcast by President Éamon de Valera on St. Patrick's Day, 1943:

> *That Ireland which we dreamed of would be the home of a people who valued material wealth only as the basis of right living, of a people who were satisfied with frugal comfort and devoted their leisure to the things of the spirit—a land whose countryside would be bright with cosy homesteads, whose fields and villages would be joyous with the sounds of industry, with the romping of sturdy children, the contests of athletic youths and the laughter of comely maidens, whose firesides would be forums for the wisdom of serene old age.*

This joyous vision of Ireland is given both a sentimental and parodic expression in John Ford's film, *The Quiet Man*, in which the hero, played by John Wayne, returns from dystopian scenes of industrial life in America to the peace and romance of the west of Ireland. When de Valera turns to imagining the role of the city in his ideal Ireland, he quotes the nineteenth-century founder of *The Nation* newspaper, Thomas Davis: "Our cities must be stately with sculpture, pictures and buildings, and our fields glorious with peaceful abundance."

The potential tension between urban and rural lives in the imagined identity of the nation is a feature of most European countries. One part of the history of civic Dublin is the history of an attempt to articulate the ambitions and self-imaginings of the citizenry in terms of public buildings and public spaces, particularly parks and gardens. The other side of the concern with public space has been the history of attempts to manage the impoverished underclasses, policing the spaces they inhabit and exiling them to various forms of ghetto. Dublin's history in this respect is much less marked than that of other European capitals, but Irish Travellers, Jews, Catholics and immigrants have all had periods when the city has adopted various structures to confine them or to limit their collective identities.

Dublin has another kind of history and identity analogous to that of many African, Middle Eastern and Latin American capital cities, for it was established and developed as a capital by colonizing powers, and for much of its history opposed as much as it represented native Irish culture and identity. As the locus of colonial administration, and the centre of greatest population density, it was both the engine room of foreign power and the site of indigenous resistance. To visit the great buildings of Dublin is to visit monuments to conflict and places of mourning. The public statues, the street names, the parks and museums, churches, universities and prisons have been sites of contention throughout the city's history.

It is possible to love Ireland and hate Dublin, as George Bernard Shaw claimed to do. "My sentimental regard for Ireland does not include the capital," he claimed in the preface to his first novel, but he left a third of his wealth to the city's National Gallery. Likewise, there are many Dubliners with no time at all for the rest of the country. For many Dubliners the country is the place they came from and to which they have no intention of returning, except for an annual holiday.

The culture of the city evolved in a number of ways in response to its contexts. There is no one story of Dublin partly because it has for centuries been inhabited by groups of mutually unintelligible peoples: Celts, Danes and Normans, Gaelic and Anglo-Irish, Jews, Travellers and immigrants. To walk the street may be to create a narrative, but as James Joyce's *Ulysses* demonstrates, it is another thing altogether to understand that narrative. In the city the clash of disparate elements produces multiple meanings rather than resolutions.

Since 1922 any proposed reading of Dublin has been aware of the shadow of *Ulysses*. The two most obvious narrative strategies for reading a city involve time and space. Some written companions to cities offer a history, others take a tour, and at first glance the tour seems closer to the way paved by Leopold Bloom. The rhythm of the interaction between time and space is felt in walking. As Bloom promenades along a street the traces of its history briefly glow like scraps of phosphorous in the narrative. What activates that glow of history, however, is a fusion of public and private memories, which pulse in point and counterpoint. A companion which attempts to take you down a street and activate historical memory, without that personal element, cannot but become a rather deadly litany: at no. 3 so-and-so was born; no. 23 used to be a sweetshop, &c. In three of the chapters that follow I take tours of some of the most-visited parts of Dublin, and I have not been altogether able to avoid a litany. I could not let go of my own love of catalogues and lists, but I have tried to thicken the descriptions of these familiar places with anecdotes and quotation. The exterior of a house is not always the best place from which to imagine the life lived within.

While I have been thinking so much about Dublin, I have returned many times to my admiration for Richard Cobb's writing on Paris. In *Promenades* he tells us that if the historian is

> *prepared to abandon the show-places—the voies triomphales, the successive pomposities of state architecture, the wide boulevards that statue-fy collective conformity in the frozen orthodoxy of official unanimity—to seek out the courtyards and workshops, the alleyways and closed passages, the semi-private, semi-secret cités or villas with iron gates to close them in at night, he must go about his search on foot, walking along abandoned railway lines, or little-used canals, behind breakers' yards and small chaotic workshops, and industrial waste, the borderlands of cities, the gasworks, the cemeteries, the marshalling yards, and bus depots, and bus cemeteries, two-decker trams converted into houses and covered with greenery.*

Every year, particularly on 16 June, a number of people set out from 7 Eccles Street or the Martello Tower at Sandycove and walk the city streets. Dublin is an eminently walkable city, but it is by throwing the maps—including the map of *Ulysses*—away, that one finds the semi-private, semi-secret world of the city.

There is less of the "frozen orthodoxy of official unanimity" in Dublin than in many European capitals, but there is another peril to be evaded and resisted here, and that is the management of heritage. Dublin has made a large and worthy commitment to public art, and much of the art around the city piously commemorates past lives. But it also exists as a part of the city's tourism. The desire to explain the city to tourists is not unworthy, but at times it seems to produce a "Disneyfication" of the past. Dubliners have cultivated the slightly cutesy habit of giving abusive rhyming nicknames to the city's sculptures—I have no intention of encouraging this sort of thing by repeating examples—which registers some scepticism about the ways in which civic space is managed.

The statue of Molly Malone opposite Trinity College Dublin is a striking example of the invention of tradition—a figure from a nineteenth-century Scottish comic song is given physical substance (a substance which in itself goes against the grain of the ballad since the very "fact" of Molly Malone is that her voice is meant to haunt the city long after her body has disappeared), and asked to stand in as a representative of the city's labouring classes. The statue resembles those poor souls who dress up as guides and parts of living history in theme parks around the world.

Molly Malone is the heroine of "In Dublin's Fair City" (or "Cockles and Mussels"), a late nineteenth-century comic song attributed to James Yorkston and arranged by Edmund Forman.

In Dublin's fair city,
Where girls are so pretty,
I first set my eyes on sweet Molly Malone,
As she pushed her wheelbarrow
Through streets broad and narrow,
Crying, "Cockles and mussels, alive, alive oh"!

Chorus:
Alive, alive oh! alive, alive oh!
Crying, "Cockles and mussels, alive, alive oh"!

Now she was a fishmonger,
And sure 'twas no wonder,
For so were her mother and father before,
And they each wheeled their barrow,
Through streets broad and narrow,
Crying, "Cockles and mussels, alive, alive oh"!
Chorus:

She died of a fever,
And no one could save her,
And that was the end of sweet Molly Malone.
Now her ghost wheels her barrow,
Through streets broad and narrow,
Crying, "Cockles and mussels, alive, alive oh"!
Chorus:

One cannot discount the possibility that this is based on an older folk song, but neither melody nor words bear any relationship to the Irish tradition of street ballads, which is not to say that "music hall" is any less authentic than other manifestations of popular culture. On the contrary, many of the songs, characters and jokes of nineteen-and twentieth-century music hall have entered into the popular imagination and had a long afterlife, recycled in subsequent shows, and through family anecdote and tradition. "Molly Malone" became popular in Dublin, naturally enough, and through its adoption by street performers and popularity with children it has become a sort of unofficial anthem for the city. In the 1970s it was taken up on Hill 16, the stand for the home Dubs supporters at Dublin County's Gaelic Athletic Association ground, Croke Park. Later it was adopted by rugby and football supporters at Lansdowne Road.

During the Dublin Millennium celebrations in 1988 it was decided to erect a statue to Molly Malone. A kind of myth had evolved that Molly was based on a genuine seventeenth-century fishmonger/sex worker who was alleged to have died either of typhus or of venereal disease. Since Mary, Molly and Malone are very common Irish names it was possible to find various birth, death and baptismal records for putative Molly Malones. One candidate endorsed by the Dublin Millennium Committee died on 13 June 1699, and it was decided to make 13 June "Molly Malone Day". The sculptor Jeanne Rynhart designed the statue as a pseudo-restoration figure, breasts partially revealed to suggest her evening activities. The location of the statue on the corner of Grafton Street and Suffolk Street alludes to one suggestion that the "real" Molly had been baptized in nearby St. Andrew's Church, now the tourist office, and to the idea that young men from Trinity College formed part of her clientele. The substitution of this nonsense for more considered historical commemorations may not appear to do any great harm, but it is part and parcel of the remaking of Dublin as one great Irish theme pub. Molly and other pieces of shamrock skulduggery are entertainingly exposed on Sean Murphy's website: http://homepage.eircom.net/~seanjmurphy/irhismys/molly.htm

Imagining Dublin
At least since the eighteenth century Dublin has been a city of projectors. It was never an Augustan city, in the sense that might be

claimed for Rome, London, Paris, Madrid or Berlin, because it was never required to articulate the power and prosperity proper to an imperial centre. The arts and government were never even briefly united in their interests. The nearest that Dublin came to having a sense of harmony between aesthetic achievement and political ambition was in the late eighteenth century, during the period of Henry Grattan's parliament, when patriotism found one of its expressions in civic pride. After the Act of Union the city's great projectors were not those with the power to execute their projects, but those like the Young Irelanders and later the women and men of the Revival who worked to imagine an alternative to the shabby, impoverished provincial metropolis in which they lived—a city of the imagination.

One of the most telling gestures of resistance to British rule in late nineteenth-century Dublin involved the occasion of Queen Victoria's Diamond Jubilee, when Maud Gonne arranged for the projection of magic lantern slides of rural evictions onto a building in Rutland Square. The projection of a thatched cottage onto a stately town house revealed their mutual dependence and exposed the symbiotic relationship that urban aesthetics sought to disguise. A town square is a different form of enclosure from a country field, but neither one is a natural arrangement of space and in an adversarial society both can provoke questions about public and private property, and the common good.

Photography might offer one useful way of imagining this city in which there is an intimate and co-dependent relationship between the positive and negative images. The superimposition of an alternative history and set of affiliations onto the city became possible in a different way after Irish independence, when victorious nationalists attempted to liberate their fantasy city from imperial Dublin by renaming so many streets and buildings. This gesture is now so commonplace that sometimes one simply has to arrest oneself to remember its magic—to think about the way that within a few years of their being criminalized and executed, the names of men like Pearse and Connolly were inscribed onto the map of the city.

One contemporary artist who has used photography to explore Dublin as a city of the imagination is Seán Hillen, some of whose photo-collages, in his *Irelantis* series, have combined Dublin scenes with exotic and transformative images. *The Oracle at O'Connell Street*

Bridge (1996) places the Delphi oracle on the bridge, and also creates a line of skyscrapers rising behind O'Connell Street, into the clouds.

The problems created by the use of public art as a mode of commemoration were brought into focus with a controversy over Rowan Gillespie's *Famine Monument* (1997), although they have also hovered around other examples of twentieth-century sculpture in the city. The more avant-garde and difficult the work of a writer like Joyce or Beckett, for example, the more ridiculous a straightforward representational statue of the writer is likely to seem. Public monuments to the victims of the Dublin and Monaghan bombings have also been contentious, since for survivors and relatives left unsatisfied by the justice system, no sculpture or plaque is going to help bring "closure".

The sesquicentenary of the Great Irish Famine produced several controversies which themselves revealed that even after 150 years the Famine was not a safe topic for politicians or commentators. The Famine is peculiar in terms of anniversaries, of course, since there is no absolute date on which it started and finished, and therefore even the primary decision by the Irish government as to *when* the anniversary would be marked, was problematic. The centenary, in the late 1940s, had been relatively little marked. Dublin already had one famine memorial, erected in 1967, a group of three human figures and a dog sculpted by Edward Delaney, and standing at the rear of Delaney's Wolfe Tone Memorial in St. Stephen's Green. In 1997 Gillespie's *Famine Monument* was erected on Custom House Quay, on the north bank of the River Liffey. It is a large piece, with seven life-size bronze figures, positioned as if they were walking slowly along the quayside. They carry small bundles of possessions. One carries the body of a child. A mangy dog harasses them from the rear. The sculpture was commissioned as an act of private philanthropy by businesswoman Norma Smurfit, who chose the site as the place from which so many emigrants departed during the Famine. Inevitably, the group calls attention to the changing city, asking spectators to imagine what it was then compared with present-day prosperity. Part of its drama is the background of the Custom House, symbol of eighteenth-century capitalism, and the backdrop of the Irish Financial Services Centre, representing contemporary global capitalism. The framing of the group against these institutions, and close to the river as it opens out to the sea, is very effective. Not everyone likes this kind of representational sculpture, but Gillespie's piece is a powerful example of its kind.

The controversy attached to this memorial had to do with the announcement by the Irish Famine Commemoration Fund website that individuals and corporations might have their names inscribed

around the Famine Memorial in return for donations of $1,000 for an individual and $5,000 for a corporation. The money raised was intended for projects to "aid the homeless, unemployed and disadvantaged youth" of Ireland, and the good intentions of such a scheme are apparent. The inscription of names is used to great effect on many memorials—almost every village war memorial lists the names of the dead—and it is also used increasingly to generate funds. Smurfit wrote of the symbolic resonance of a sea of names around the memorial, recalling those families who suffered and their descendants scattered about the globe. Some people were offended at the suggestion that we should specifically remember those whose families can now pay, and even more offended that corporations should be allowed to buy what is essentially advertising space on a famine memorial. This is a matter of sensibility. Clearly, a Famine Memorial should make people feel uncomfortable, and it is as well to be reminded that there are no safe and comfortable ways in which to harness symbols to represent traumatic events.

A Passion for Satire

Some of Ireland's most significant artists have been the people who have turned symbols of power against those who abused them. In 1736 Jonathan Swift looked at Edward Lovett Pearce's new building for the Irish parliament on College Green, and tore it apart:

As I strole the city, oft I
Spy a building large and lofty,
Not a Bow-shot from the College,
Half the Globe from Sense and Knowledge.
By the prudent architect
Plac'd against the Church direct;
Making good my Grandames jest,
Near the Church—*you know the rest.*

Tell us what this Pile contains?
Many a Head that holds no Brains.
These Demoniacs let me dub
With the name of Legion Club.
Such Assemblies, you might swear,
Meet when Butchers bait a Bear;
Such a Noise, and such haranguing,
When a Brother Thief is hanging.
Such a Rout and such a Rabble
Run to hear Jackpudding gabble;
Such a Croud their Ordure throws
On a far less Villain's Nose.

(from "A Character, Panegyric, and Description of the Legion Club")

If any one thing would seem to form a loose link in the history of the arts in Dublin, it is the passion for satire. Perhaps every Dublin artist is still coming to terms with the greatness of Swift, who saw the terror and the pity and the joy of the city, and more particularly heard its voices and made his work a conduit for Dublin's infatuation with language. There is a deep thread of scepticism about visual pleasure running through Dublin's history. Its architectural monuments, its statuary and its painting have been greeted with as much sardonic criticism as civic pride. One of the city's archetypal citizens and versifiers was the blind poet Zozimus (Michael Moran), who used to perform on the city's bridges, quays and thoroughfares.

Ah, kind Christian, do not grudge
The sixpence promised on the brudge.

Zozimus, like Swift, was attentive to the cries of Dublin, and Dublin remains a city in which conversation, banter and plain noise dominate the senses. Swift and his friends delighted in riddles and puns, and Swift was probably the author of the two following street cries, where he riffs on the sounds of Dublin:

Herrings
Be not sparing,
Leave off swearing
Buy my herring
Fresh from Malahide,
Better n'er was try'd.
Come eat 'em with pure fresh Butter and Mustard,
Their bellies are soft, and white as a Custard.
Come, six-pence a Dozen to get me some Bread,
Or, like my own Herrings, I soon shall be dead.

Asparagus
Ripe 'Sparagrass,
Fit for Lad or Lass,
To make the Water pass;
O, 'tis pretty Picking
With a tender Chicken.

One might also think of Austin Clarke's great grandfather, Henry Browne, the Watling Street tanner. Browne "used to compose satiric ballads about other merchants with whom he had quarrelled, have them printed as broadsheets, and sung by a ballad-maker outside their premises in Thomas Street and the neighbourhood."

Mindful of Dubliners' flair for speech I have been liberal in my use of quotation though this book. I tell a series of stories about Dublin, many of them using the events of a particular date to introduce a set of characters or an issue. I am not an historian and I have relied on the work of other people, with sources given in the Further Reading. Where I have recognized conflicting accounts of events I have tried to indicate the nature of the dispute. In the case of some of the events I describe, like Robert Emmet's speech from the dock or Sir Boyle Roche's Irish bulls, one is obliged to rely on partial, prejudiced historians. I have sometimes been reminded of one of Sigmund Freud's examples of an Irish joke, when a tourist asks his guide "Is this the place where the Duke of Wellington spoke those words?" and the guide answers, "Yes, it is the place; but he never spoke the words."

City of Sociability
Sometimes friends from overseas who are planning to visit Dublin ask me what they should see and do. I am happy enough to make suggestions until they ask the two questions I dread: Where should I go to hear live music, and which are the good pubs? Both these questions arise, I think, from the way that people choose to visit Dublin not to see anything in particular, but because they believe in its sociability. This, of course, is not a myth. Dublin is the most sociable of cities, although fifteen years ago one would have appended the caveats "unless you're black" and "unless you're gay". Happily, things have changed.

In the 1990s Dublin was marketed in Britain and Germany as a "stag night" and "office party" destination, with the new fast ferries (which cross from Holyhead in 100 minutes) and the cheap flights offered by Ryanair making it an easy place to spend a weekend. By the start of the twenty-first century the spread of low-budget airlines, adjustments in the exchange rates, European Union enlargement and changes in fashion saw a drop in that party tourism (which migrated to Prague and elsewhere). Aspects of the heavy drinking culture were unattractive to other kinds of tourists, and Temple Bar, for instance, now actively discourages the "stag night" trade. That increase in tourism from the young caused some public order problems, but also contributed to a relaxed attitude that appeals strongly to multi-cultural tourists.

But sociability is not a commodity that can be ordered with a pint of stout. A visitor might get a lot of pleasure from visiting pubs that are beautifully decorated and pubs that have interesting historical associations. Many a visitor enjoys a drink in the Palace Bar or McDaids in the knowledge that these are places where Patrick Kavanagh, Flann O'Brien and Brendan Behan might have been seen in the 1940s and 1950s. Fans of *Ulysses* will probably go into Davy Byrne's because that is where Leopold Bloom had his lunch. Neary's was traditionally a theatrical bar, and Doheny & Nesbitt's was always popular with politicians, journalists and lawyers. John Kehoe's, the pub closest to the National Library, has a great traditional decor and is very busy in the evenings, with customers spilling out into the streets. The Republic of Ireland has recently introduced a ban on smoking in public places, and this is felt most dramatically in the changed atmosphere in pubs. J. P. Donleavy's description of McDaid's in the 1940s is a reminder that it is people, not places, who make great pubs:

If a drink were needed in the pub as it invariably was following anyone's meeting one another for more than three minutes, folk would only have to descend the stairs, step out across the street and walk twenty yards to the corner, turn left by the exotic furs displayed in a window, and proceed past Tom Nisbet's painting gallery and into John MacDaid's pub. Which advertised "Where the drink is efficacious and the conversation effervescent". Slowly but surely this converted church at 3 Harry Street with its cold, barren, lofty interior, its grim downstairs lavatory and a back door out to a side lane, became an established meeting place for poets, painters, writers, and various chancers and con men, the latter who, poor souls, erroneously thought such people worth associating with. Although this public house had a bemused owner and an extremely pleasant and understanding bartender, the only one in Dublin ever to have bought yours truly a drink, nevertheless this big grim room to have become celebrated in any manner, was a mystery to all who went there.

Likewise you will find the music you are interested in by talking to people and by looking at the papers, but if you have never had the slightest interest in Irish music do not expect to be able to walk into some charming little pub and have the locals entertain you. There are a fair number of buskers, particularly around Grafton Street and St. Stephen's Green, and many pubs advertise live music and *craic, ceilidh* and *ceol.* Thirty years ago crack was a genuine slang term, applied to social occasions when conversation and drink flowed and people took real pleasure in one another's company. I have a feeling that it originated in the north and may have migrated to Dublin via students at Trinity College Dublin, which then had a large contingent of northerners. Some time in the 1990s, when Irish theme pubs swept across the world, it was gaelicized to *craic.* However sterling the crack, I do not think that any Irish person ever says that the *craic* is good, but there it is advertised all over the place. It is an odd promise to market.

A *ceilidh* is a social gathering which may—but need not—involve storytelling or music. When I was a child I always heard it used as a verb—"shall we go down the lane and *ceilidh* with Bridget Ellen?" *Ceol* is the Irish for music.

Big shows happen at The Point, which was built in 1878 as a train depot to service Dublin's docks. The decline in shipping to the North Wall Quay saw the depot close in the mid-1950s. In 1987 it was purchased by a local businessman, who transformed the disused building into a major music venue. It opened in 1988 and has presented many major acts, including David Bowie, James Brown, Bob Dylan, Van Morrison, Christy Moore, Nirvana, Oasis, Tom Petty and Frank Sinatra. Slattery's in Capel Street and O'Shea's Merchant are both pubs with long associations with Irish music. In 1967 Seán Corcoran and Mary McGannon started the Tradition Club at Slattery's, which was for over twenty years one of the best venues for traditional music in the city. Young people in Dublin are wild about music, and you might experience your most enjoyable gig if you simply listen for music from the street, and go into a bar or café to watch a teenage band play in public for the first time.

Your first day in Dublin is always your worst. So, with nice ambiguity, claimed John Berryman, the American poet who was sometimes drunk in Dublin. Give into it a bit, and Dublin gets better.

Chapter One

DUBH LINN/BAILE ÁTHA CLIATH

Dublin is a watery city, seated on the circumference of a semi-circular bay, divided by a river and a sea port; its focal points are quaysides and bridges. It is a place of wide limpid skies, grey clouds heaping up on equally grey horizons, of showers and rainbows, of wet shoes and ankles, of wind-battered umbrellas and buildings reflected in puddles. It rains so much that on a fine day the colours of a blue sky and green leaves or the orange lilies, red gladioli and purple Michaelmas daisies at the florist's stall on Grafton Street will shine with the jewel-like clarity of a painting by Pinturicchio. No Dubliner ever takes a fine day for granted, and if a fine summer lasted three months people would still stop one another every day to celebrate its loveliness.

A whole mythology has developed around the idea that Dubliners savour their world—it is the myth on which a lot of Guinness advertisements are based. When Dublin was poor and the people had very little else, they had time to enjoy a pint being poured or a conversation unfolding. In the 1950s and 1960s Ireland was often represented as having greater affinities with southern than northern Europe, and the inhabitants of Dublin were credited with a type of feckless charm (sometimes combined with petty criminality) for which time-wasting and idle conversation were major assets. The shabbiness of the city's old buildings, the poor repair of shops and pubs, the litter on the streets and a general atmosphere of scrounging cemented the image of a city that was being passed over by some aspects of modernity.

Today's Dublin, conversely, promotes itself as new, gleaming and fast-paced; the high, slender, polished steel needle in O'Connell Street, which represents nothing but pure aspiration, is its appropriate symbol. The chancer, the hero of the old Dublin mythology, is now more of a fly businessman than a scrounger or Lothario. The charm of the rich is very different from the charm of the poor, however, and there is now a harder edge to social encounters in the city. People seem to have less time for one another. Time was when there an interesting discrepancy between the Irish meaning of "cute"—a kind of sharp, low cunning—and the American usage of the word to refer to something attractive in a diminutive fashion. Now the Irish have been cute enough to have made Dublin cuter, with more heritage trails, revamped historic areas and themed bars and restaurants. The Irish are performing Irishness, both for foreign and for home consumption. *The Encyclopaedia of Ireland*, published in 2003, was marketed under the slogan "it's who we are", and the impulse to market "who we are" seems increasingly characteristic of Irish life in the twenty-first century.

Topography
Dublin was founded as a settlement and emerged as the Irish capital because of its geographic relationship to internal trade routes and because of its convenience as a point of entry for European invaders, and eventually for British traders. Topography is one of the narrative structures through which natives and visitors read and interpret the city. The relationship of centre to suburbs, of seashore to highlands, of streets to parks and gardens, of thoroughfares to squares and, above all, in Dublin (a city of two halves if ever there was one) of north side to south side, these relationships are a major element in the way that the city is imagined.

The Wicklow Mountains have been severely glaciated to form valleys, gorges and corrie lakes. The blanket peat over the mountains is covered with purple heather and yellow furze, and criss-crossed by paths. The area has many famous beauty spots: Lugnaquila Mountain, the Great Sugar Loaf, Glendalough, Glencree, Glenmalure, the Glen of Imaal, the Glen of the Downs, Baltinglass Abbey, the Sally Gap, the Vale of Avoca, and Powerscourt waterfall, among others. These are also names with powerful historical associations: in the seventh century St. Kevin is believed to have lived at Glendalough, and in the twelfth century St. Laurence O'Toole was abbot of a priory there; in 1580 the only significant military engagement of the Baltinglass rebellion was fought at Glenmalure; in the eighteenth century the Dublin gentry built villas throughout the area and the Royal Dublin Society awarded grants to landowners for the planting of native trees; from 1798 to 1803 Michael Dwyer led the remnants of the rebels in guerrilla warfare from his base in the Glen of Imaal; Charles Stewart Parnell emerged from the Wicklow gentry to lead the Irish Home Rule Movement in the nineteenth century; in 1972 the Glencree Centre for Reconciliation opened in response to the Northern troubles; in the late 1990s the woodlands of the Glen of the Downs were occupied by ecological activists protesting against a road-widening scheme and generating a debate about Ireland's attitude to the environment and landscape heritage.

The River Liffey rises on the slopes of Kippure, a short distance from the Sally Gap. Its eighty-mile course takes many turns, and feeds three reservoirs, before it flows into and through the city of Dublin, issuing in Dublin Bay. In the eighteenth century this semi-circular, sandy bay was often compared to the Bay of Naples. Today visitors arriving by ferry to Dún Laoghaire see its full sweep, and it is worth travelling from central Dublin to Bray and back on the DART (Dublin's overground rapid transport system) simply to enjoy the views. The construction of harbour walls in the eighteenth century caused North Bull Island to rise from the sea. The island's sand-dune and saltmarsh ecosystem make it an ideal home for many bird species, and in 1930 it became Ireland's first bird sanctuary. It is also home to two golf courses, and a small resident population. It is joined to Dollymount strand via a causeway. North of Dublin Bay is Howth Head, a large rocky projection of hard quartzites.

Ireland's Eye is a small island less than a mile from Howth harbour; there are remains of an early church and a Martello Tower. Martello Towers are circular stone or brick gun-batteries, erected around the

coast from 1804 as a defence
against an expected French
invasion during the Napoleonic
Wars. The most famous is at
Sandycove, and is now called the
James Joyce Tower because of its
association with *Ulysses*. Ireland's
Eye is home to seabird colonies:
shelduck, razorbills, guillemots,
auks, fulmars and shags all nest
there, while a large cormorant
colony inhabits the rocky outcrop
known as the Thulla.

To the south of Dublin Bay are the steep cliffs of Bray Head, a
similar projection. These two landmark features which once signalled a
kind of natural boundary to the city have come under increasing
pressure as the city's expanding population encroaches. For centuries
travel in and out of Ireland was via Howth, but bad weather caused
many delays to the mail boats and many accidents to shipping in
Dublin Bay. In the early nineteenth century Howth harbour was
constructed, with a lighthouse added to the end of the pier in 1818. In
the same period work began on an "asylum harbour" at Dún Laoghaire
(renamed Kingstown for a century after 1821). From 1826 the mail
packet ships transferred to Kingstown, and this increase in business was
further expanded by the opening of the Dublin-Kingstown suburban
railway in 1834. In the 1970s a car ferry terminal was built and Dún
Laoghaire continued to be the chief sea entry point for the city,
although ferries from Liverpool and the Isle of Man dock at Dublin
City Harbour.

If the mountains, the river and the bay are natural features around
which the story of the city has evolved, there are also major landscape
features constructed by people with projects for the city. I shall come to
buildings in due course, but thinking for the moment of how people
navigate the city leads me to the two great canals. Work on the Grand
Canal, linking Dublin to the River Shannon, began in 1756. Two rival
schemes had been presented to the Irish parliament, and that body
favoured the one which took the more southern route, through the Bog
of Allen. The first section, which went as far as Sallins, opened for

freight in 1779 and for passengers the following year. The final section, as far as Shannon harbour, opened in 1805; but the passenger service could not withstand competition from the railways and closed in 1852. The canal continued as a freight route for another hundred years. When the last freight services withdrew there were suggestions that the canal should be filled in to create a road, but it has been preserved by the heritage service, and in recent years it has been used more and more by pleasure craft.

Work on the Royal Canal, following the rival northern route, began in 1789, with the first section opening in 1798. It was never a great financial success and came under public management before its completion. It was taken over in 1845 by the Midland Great Western Railroad and the last passenger service was in 1849. It closed completely in 1960, but parts of it are now undergoing restoration. Patrick Kavanagh's (1904-67) two poems, "Lines Written on a Seat on the Grand Canal, Dublin, Erected to the Memory of Mrs Dermot O'Brien" and "Canal Bank Walk", both written when he was recovering from lung cancer, capture the tranquillity brought through the city on its waterways.

O commemorate me where there is water
Canal water preferably, so stilly
Greeny at the heart of summer
Commemorate me thus beautifully.

A visitor to Dublin today cannot fail to notice the crisis in road transport. The traffic is shocking. The M50 motorway ringroad to the west of the city has created a corridor which echoes the semicircle of Dublin Bay, but by no means contains a city rapidly expanding in every direction other than into the sea.

At the 2001/2002 census the population of Ireland was over 5,600,000, with the population of Dublin at around 1,000,000. Dublin experienced rapid growth in the 1990s, fuelled by the economic boom that earned Ireland the nickname of the Celtic Tiger, and this has put all kinds of pressure on the city's infrastructure but also created opportunities for development and conservation. Many of the city's service workers as well as many students are now people whose origin was overseas and who have come to reside temporarily or permanently in Ireland. While there is nothing like the ethnic diversity of Paris or London in Dublin, there is now a greater visible variety of religions, nationalities and cultures. There has also been a significant increase in tourism to the city in the last twenty years.

City of Bridges

When one walks about the city centre one is always conscious of the river. The Liffey is narrower than the Seine, the Thames, the Charles and the Tiber, and traffic and noise press in more to the quayside pavements, but to walk along the quays or cross the many bridges is to experience the sense of uplift and romance that one feels by the rivers of Paris and Rome. Until the eighteenth century Grattan Bridge, originally called Essex Bridge, between Capel and Parliament Streets, was the most easterly bridge, the river below that remaining as a wide estuary with no fixed crossings. After the building of the Custom House further down the river, new bridges were added and the river was closed in by the quays. Until the beginning of this century the last bridge was Butt Bridge (1879) at the Custom House, allowing ships access to the quays. In recent years the additions of the Millennium footbridge and the opening of the toll bridge in the docklands has helped close the river off to all but small river craft.

O'Connell Bridge was erected as Carlisle Bridge in 1794 and rebuilt in 1880. It was renamed after Daniel O'Connell, the nineteenth-century champion of Catholic Emancipation, and it feels like the centre of the city. It links O'Connell Street, the dominant boulevard on the north side, location of the General Post Office, with the smart south side roads leading up to Trinity College and the former Irish houses of parliament.

The elegant arched iron footbridge, now known as the Ha'penny Bridge from its history as a toll bridge, was erected in 1816 and named after the Duke of Wellington, a native Dubliner who led British forces to victory at the Battle of Waterloo in 1815. Pictures of the Ha'penny Bridge are among the most frequently used tourist images of the city.

Further upriver a series of bridges link north and south sides. The Grattan Bridge at Capel Street was originally called the Essex Bridge and renamed in honour of Henry Grattan, the eighteenth-century parliamentarian. O'Donovan Rossa Bridge at Winetavern Street has been through two other incarnations: when it was built in 1683 it was called Ormond Bridge after the then Lord Lieutenant, James Butler, Earl of Ormond; it was swept away in 1806 and the new bridge, opened in 1816, was first named after the Lord Lieutenant who commissioned it, Charles Lennox, 4th Duke of Richmond. The Father Mathew Bridge at Church Street is on the site of a medieval crossing, known as the Old Bridge and built by King John, c. 1210. The Queen Maeve Bridge (Queen's Street) is an eighteenth-century replacement of a seventeenth-century bridge, and was originally named Queen's Bridge in honour of Queen Charlotte, consort of George III. Rory O'More Bridge at Watling Street is on the site of the Bloody Bridge, a wooden structure given its suggestive name after an affray there in 1671. It was rebuilt in stone in 1704 and in iron in 1863, when it was opened by Queen Victoria and named after her. These re-namings are characteristic of the city's re-inscription after independence, when imperial and colonial associations were replaced with more Irish and nationalist designations.

Until the late eighteenth century many of the city's most fashionable streets, squares and great houses were erected north of the river. The south side was the home of the parliament, the cathedrals, the castle, the university and the park at St. Stephen's Green, while the city dissolved into satellite villages as it moved south towards Wicklow. When Swift was Dean of St. Patrick's some of the city's poorest inhabitants lived in the Liberties around the cathedral. Traditionally a Dub was someone born in the Liberties, within the sound of St. Patrick's bells. In the last quarter of the eighteenth century however, the rich and powerful began to relocate to the south side, around Merrion Square and St. Stephen's Green. Through the nineteenth century there were more middle-class developments in southern villages like Rathmines and Ranelagh and in the seaside settlements, from Sandymount south to Bray, which gradually became part of the city's suburbs. Some of the big houses on the north side degenerated into tenements, and over time "northside" became almost synonymous with working-class, while "southside" seemed to become more and more affluent.

The phrase "Dublin 4" is used to describe a particularly aspirational type of middle-class Dubliner. The postcode Dublin 4 includes the areas of Ballsbridge, Sandymount and Donnybrook, some of the city's most expensive residential areas and is also the home of

University College Dublin and of RTÉ, the national broadcaster. It is associated with a liberal intelligentsia, influential in the media. One of the curious ways in which Irish politicians, and particularly members of the ruling Fianna Fáil party, manage to cast themselves as "outsiders", even while they are in power, is to suggest that there is a privileged elite inhabiting Dublin 4, which is an enemy of "the plain people of Ireland", as Flann O'Brien used to describe that piously invoked population. Younger inhabitants of Dublin 4 are accused of communicating in "Dortspeak" (from their pronunciation of DART, the rapid transport system that carries them into the city centre), a transatlantic English in which the particularities of Hiberno-English are erased.

Early History
Dublin was established as a trading post on the banks of the River Liffey sometime in the tenth century by Norse invaders. An earlier village called Eblana appears on Ptolemy's map of Europe in AD 140, but Dubh Linn (Irish for the black pool) was a more permanent, ecclesiastical settlement, founded not later than the early seventh century. The black pool was a natural feature of the River Poddle, a small stream that merges with the Liffey from the south. Dubh Linn expanded to incorporate the nearby Irish settlement, Baile Átha Cliath (ford of the hurdles) on the north bank. The latter has survived as the Irish name for the city and is seen everywhere on signposts and on public transport. The position of the original man-made ford, crossable only at low tides, can be deduced from the alignments of prehistoric and medieval routeways. That hurdleford crossed at the east end of today's Usher's Island. The Vikings, then, did not found Dublin but the trading post established around 841 grew to incorporate the earlier settlements. There is limited archaeological evidence for this period, but at Essex Street West there are signs of late ninth-century habitation, and there are early burial sites along both banks of the Liffey. Dublin came under Irish control briefly during the period in the eleventh century when Brian Bóroimhe was High King of Ireland. Dublin celebrated its millennium in 1988, but 988 is a rough estimate rather than a sure date for the city's foundations.

In the early Norse period Dublin was a walled settlement, containing a tight cluster of houses, with no open spaces. The core streets of Castle Street, Christ Church Place, Fishamble Street and Werburgh Streets were established at this time. The assembly mound stood outside the walls. Most of the houses were clay and wattle, while stone building gradually appeared. Later the clay and wattle structures were replaced by wooden buildings. Apart from the local Danish ruler, the Jarl, and the Irish over-king, the King of Leinster, the most powerful residents of Dublin were the merchants, who traded with other settlements, with their homeland, and with Norse settlements along the western European coastline. Their ships imported silk, slaves, wine, salt and iron. Grain cattle, wool and hides were brought in from the countryside for export.

In the eleventh century the town expanded eastwards, and there is evidence of increasing affluence. As the Vikings became more entangled with local families and customs, the number of churches in and around Dublin increased. One of the most important dates in the history of Dublin is the arrival of the Anglo-Normans in 1169/70. Recent archaeological discoveries have indicated, however, that there were significant Norman commercial interests developing in Dublin through the twelfth century.

Nevertheless the arrival of an invading army produced a sharp change and acceleration in that process. Diarmuid MacMurchadha, King of Leinster and holding the allegiance of the Dublin foreigners (Danes) was exiled by Ruaidhrí O'Conchobhair, High King of Ireland. MacMurchadha went to England and secured the help of King Henry II for an Irish conquest. With the help of fighters mainly recruited from the Welsh marches, MacMurchadha returned to Ireland with a new ally, Richard Fitz Gilbert, Earl of Pembroke, also known as "Strongbow" and as Richard De Clare, and they began the process of Norman colonization. When Fitz Gilbert landed at Waterford in 1170 he was immediately married to MacMurchadha's daughter, Aoife. A magnificent nineteenth-century painting of *The Marriage of Strongbow and Aoife* (1854) by Daniel Maclise hangs in the National Gallery of Ireland. In Maclise's painting the marriage is solemnised amidst battlefield scenes of death and mourning. Hugh de Lacy, a Norman lord who accompanied Henry II to Ireland, was granted custody of Dublin. Henry came to regret this decision as de Lacy became stronger and less biddable, particularly after his second marriage, to a daughter of Ruaidhrí O'Conchobhair. Henry was reported to be delighted at news of de Lacy's murder in 1186. Wars between the Irish and the colony, which continued to draw support from England, lasted several hundred years, during which time their respective fortunes fluctuated.

Beyond the Pale

Dublin was the centre of the colonial project and the place where a parliament was established, but confirmation of this status only came in 1204 when King John decided to build a royal stronghold on the site of the old Norse fortification beside the River Poddle. At many points the only firm arena of colonial control was within the English Pale, the small area of Leinster surrounding Dublin in a twenty-by-thirty-mile strip. A parliamentary statute of 1495 stated that this area was to be surrounded by a double ditch, six feet high. The Irish "beyond the pale" turned for help to England's foreign enemies, and this in turn gave the English an interest in continuing to support the colony. The English King Richard II made two expeditions to Ireland in an attempt finally to subdue the Irish; the second of these in 1399 probably cost him his throne. A recurrent source of anxiety in England was the way in which the Anglo-Norman colonizers were inter-marrying with the indigenous Irish and adopting Irish language and customs, becoming *Hibernis ipsis hiberniores*, more Irish than the Irish themselves.

Inside the Pale, English common law was applied. The language of the ruling class was at first Norman-French, and later English, but since Irish people came into Dublin to live and work, Irish was also widely spoken. Medieval Dubliners ate bread, meat and fish, and drank wine and beer. An aqueduct brought water from outside the city into a central cistern from which it was piped to outlets in the city walls. Like most medieval urban dwellers, Dubliners worried about hygiene, disease and fire. In 1348-9 Dublin and the colony on the east coast suffered huge losses during the Black Death. City ordinances made citizens responsible for fire protection, and for defence of the city, which came under repeated harassment from the Irish outside.

The first coinage in Ireland appeared in Dublin in the early eleventh century. Guilds protected the interests of tradesmen such as blacksmiths, cooks, chandlers, weavers, carpenters and other urban workers. The guilds were also centres of social and religious customary practices. Each guild had a patron saint, and the guilds presented lavish entertainments such as mystery plays and festivals. The Church in the colony was administered by English bishops rather than by those of the Irish Church, whose primary see was at Armagh. By the sixteenth century there were schools of law and medicine, but no university, so that the colony's ruling class was largely Oxford-educated.

Medieval Government

In 1229 the English King granted the citizens of Dublin the right to elect their own mayor. In the town the wealthiest members of the community enjoyed full rights of citizenship and their privileges were embodied in charters. In 1171-2 Henry II gave Dublin to the citizens of Bristol, which meant that Bristol merchants were entrusted with the process of colonization. In 1192 a charter of liberties granted by King John asserted the rights of the Dublin citizen merchants over any foreign traders attempting to do business in the city. At the beginning of the 1192 charter the city's "liberty", or area of jurisdiction, is described. The royal provost and later the mayor presided over the court. A city prison was established in the dungeons of Newgate, and there were gallows about the city for the punishment of serious crimes. Much of the land within the Dublin boundary was owned by great churchmen, who could try and punish people in ecclesiastical courts. Most of the private liberties were located in the area around St. Patrick's Cathedral, which is still known as "the liberties". The citizens of Dublin formulated their own laws and customs, many of which concentrated on trade regulation, particularly regarding food suppliers.

Of medieval architecture what survives today, unsurprisingly, are chiefly a few buildings of great size and prestige. Ireland's earliest churches were built from wood but none of these survives. Some stone churches began to appear in the ninth and tenth centuries, but these were still exceptional. In the late twelfth century Christ Church Cathedral was built in a style that suggests that English masons came over to assist in the construction. It was clearly established as the principal church of the colony by the time Strongbow was buried there in 1176. What has become known as Strongbow's tomb in the cathedral has an impressive figure of a recumbent knight, but the actual tomb is more probably the smaller, older monument by its side. Most of the present structure of Christ Church dates from the substantial restoration in the 1870s, but there is twelfth-century fabric in the crypt and transept.

The nearby St. Patrick's Cathedral was built by Archbishop John Comyn as a collegiate church, and dedicated in 1192. In 1213 the archbishop of Dublin, Henry Blund, also known as Henry de Londres, after an argument with the Dean and chapter at Christ Church, advanced St. Patrick's to cathedral status, and began to rebuild it on a larger scale. The oldest surviving parts of the fabric of St Patrick's date from the thirteenth and fourteenth centuries, and include the marvellous choir, with its gothic windows and arcades. Like Christ Church, St. Patrick's underwent extensive restoration and transformation in the nineteenth century. Both these great cathedrals became buildings of the established Church of Ireland, when that part of the Anglican dominion separated from the Roman Catholic Church under the authority of the Irish parliament in 1534-7. Today St. Patrick's is the national cathedral of the Church of Ireland and Christ Church is the cathedral church of the Church of Ireland diocese of Dublin and Glendalough.

The Roman Catholic Church has no place of worship of such antique historical or architectural distinction in the city, although the neo-classical Pro-Cathedral on Marlborough Street is a significant building, and there are some good examples of gothic revival churches, my own favourite being J. J. MacCarthy's St. Saviour's in Dominick Street (1861). In the middle of the twentieth century the Catholic Church formulated various plans to build a great cathedral in the park at the centre of Merrion Square, which was owned by the Church. It was eventually realized that the loss of the square would not be tolerated, and the Church donated it to the Corporation as a public park.

The third great medieval building in Dublin is the Castle, begun c. 1204 on the order of the English King John, and under direction from Henry Blund. This replaced an earlier castle and was built both to withstand attack and to symbolize Archbishop Henry's power as governor of Ireland. Today visitors tend to enter the Castle from Palace Street, passing a carefully restored eighteenth-century house, the former location of the Sick and Indigent Roomkeepers' Society (founded 1790), Dublin's oldest charity. Lower Castle Yard is home to several government offices, housed in a modern block. The yard itself is dominated by the Chapel Royal, built in neo-gothic style in 1807. The chapel crypt is now used as a performance space. Within the Castle precincts one can trace the bed of the former moat, and the Castle itself runs over the River Poddle, which once formed part of the moat. Disparate administrative activities, from Civic Guards' quarters to the Carriage Office for Dublin Taxis, are located within the Castle walls. Its medieval origins are most apparent in the Record Tower and the Bermingham Tower, once strongholds and prisons.

The Castle's state rooms are surprisingly small, and although there are fine pieces of individual craftsmanship the overall effect is of vulgarity and pomposity. The Castle is still used for state functions, and there are attractive views from some of the balconies in the reception rooms. A stronger sense of the history of the Castle is felt from the exterior than the interiors. Among recent additional attractions to the site has been the opening of a new home for the Chester Beatty Library of oriental art and manuscripts. New exhibition galleries were built adjacent to the eighteenth-century clock tower, and the atrium and roof garden are popular venues for private entertainments.

Other architectural traces of medieval Dublin are to be found in the surviving parts of the city walls, for example at Lamb Alley, at Wood Quay and in Cook Street, where the only surviving city gateway, St. Audoen's Arch, stands. In the basement of a restaurant in Cecilia Street it is possible to see part of the precinct wall of Holy Trinity Friary, an Augustinian monastery excavated during the renovation of the Temple Bar area. Isolde, or Izod's Tower, was a circular fortification that was part of the city wall. It was demolished in 1675. In 1993, in an act of vandalism characteristic of late-twentieth-century redevelopment in Dublin, a group called Temple Bar Properties demolished buildings in the Essex Quay area. The site of the houses was excavated before the building of new apartment blocks, revealing the base of Izod's Tower, which can now be seen beneath the apartments in Lower Exchange Street.

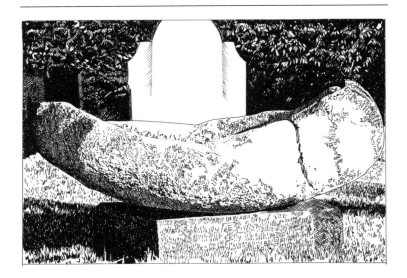

One also finds relics of the Middle Ages in the suburbs. Goat Castle was one of seven watchtowers built in Dalkey in the fifteenth century, and is now the site of the Dalkey Heritage Centre. St. Máel Ruáin (d. 792) was founder of a monastery at Tallaght and involved in the anchoritic reform movement of the *céilí dé* centred on his church. A lovely medieval stone baptismal font can be seen at St. Maelruain's church.

St. Audoen's

Perhaps the best place in which to get a feel for the way in which the medieval past lives on in the present as a set of fragmented ruins is to be found in the atmospheric St. Audoen's Church, off Cornmarket, the only medieval parish church to survive today. St. Audoen was Bishop of Rouen and patron saint of Normandy, so he is an apt patron of the Norman conquest. St. Audoen's was once a guild chapel, being located in the vicinity of a number of guildhalls, of which the only one that survives is the Tailor's Hall (1710) in High Street. It has been suggested that St. Audoen's replaced an earlier church, since a ninth-century decorated grave slab was found on the site. Known as the "Lucky Stone", this slab is now mounted in the church porch.

St. Audoen's is divided into four sections. One quarter of it is the Norman church and nave, and this is still occupied by the Church of Ireland, so that St. Audoen's can claim to have been a functioning place of worship for over eight hundred years. On Sunday morning one can hear the peal of bells, three of which were cast in 1423. There are seventeenth- and eighteenth-century wall tombs on the north wall of the church and these have been recently restored. Part of the church floor is paved with medieval grave slabs. Bishops, lord mayors and aldermen are interred here.

St. Anne's Chapel is to the south of the nave. It was roofless from the early nineteenth century until a re-roofing and restoration by Dúchas, the now abolished national heritage service, turned it into a visitor's centre and heritage site. The Porlester Chapel was unroofed in 1773, and in 1887 the tombstones were laid on the ground. Some of the older dates still visible are from the seventeenth century. There is a memorial to William Molyneux (1656-1698), the Dublin philosopher, scientist, and member of parliament for Trinity College. Molyneux is best-known for his natural rights defence of Irish legislative independence, *The Case of Ireland Being Bound by Acts of Parliament in England Stated* (1698). This work was condemned as seditious by the English parliament. Molyneux was a founder member of the Dublin Philosophical Society (1684), and his major contribution to philosophical thinking is "the Molyneux problem", directed as a problem to his friend and mentor John Locke. If a man blind from birth were able to distinguish two shapes by touch, and if such a man suddenly gained sight, would he be able to distinguish the objects by sight alone? Locke and Molyneux answered that sight alone would not be enough.

The Arts of the Middle Ages

Ireland has a remarkable medieval literature, but relatively little of it was produced in Dublin. The earliest literature associated with Dublin is in Middle English, although Norman Ireland also produced literature in Norman-French and in Latin, while a written literary tradition in Irish had existed since the sixth century. A manuscript from around 1330 offers "A Satire on the People of Dublin", with a mock salutation to the habits of various tradesmen:

Hail be ye skinners with yure drench kive!
Who so smilith thereto, wo is him alive,
Whan that hit thonnerith, ye mote ther in schite.
Datheit yur curtesie, ye stinketh al the strete,
Worth hit wer, that he wer king
That ditid this trie thing.

[Hail be ye skinners with your drenching-vat!
Whoever sniffs in it, woe is him as he goes about his daily business.
When it thunders, ye might shit yourself during it.
Woe to your courtesy, ye stink all the street.
It would be a worthy thing if he were a king
Who prepared this choice piece.]

The majority of the population was non-literate, but it was familiar with a rich oral culture which included stories, recitations, music and performance. The *fili* were early medieval professional poets, who often had ecclesiastical ties, and who served as historians and genealogists as well as storytellers and entertainers. After the Anglo-Norman invasion the *fili* became more secularized. They were distrusted by the invaders and attempts were made to suppress their activities. In early Dublin people would also have heard religious texts, such as saints' lives and sermons, read aloud.

Dublin's most famous medieval manuscript, *The Book of Kells*, on public display in the library at Trinity College Dublin, dates from around 800. It is thought to have been created on Iona, the small Scottish island in the inner Hebrides, where Colm Cille, the sixth-century Irish missionary, founded a monastery. *The Book of Kells* is an illuminated manuscript of the Latin text of the four gospels. It was in Kells, a market town 31 miles north-west of Dublin, whose monastery replaced Iona as the head of the Columban foundations in Ireland, by the eleventh century and removed from there to Dublin in the 1660s.

Other medieval decorative arts include wall painting, of which few examples survive in Ireland. A painting of the Trinity at St. Audoen's completely deteriorated. Pottery from the excavations at Wood Quay and Winetavern Street can be seen in the National Museum of Ireland, where there are also many examples of medieval metalwork, book shrines, and jewellery.

In 1183 and 1185 Giraldus Cambrensis visited Ireland as a member of one of the leading families involved in the Norman invasion. He wrote a topography and an account of the conquest. He had very little good to say about the Irish ("This people is, then, a barbarous people, literally barbarous") but he did praise their musical skills:

It is only in the case of musical instruments that I can find any commendable diligence in the people. They seem to me to be incomparably more skilled in these than any other people I have seen.

The music is not, as in the British instrument to which we are accustomed, slow and easy, but rather quick and lively, while at the same time the melody is sweet and pleasant. It is remarkable how, in spite of the great speed of the fingers, the music proportion is maintained. The melody is kept perfect and full with unimpaired art through everything—through quivering measures and the involved use of several instruments—with a rapidity that charms, a rhythmic pattern that is varied, and a concord achieved through elements discordant... They glide so subtly from one mode to another, and the grace notes so freely sport with such abandon and bewitching charm around the steady tone of the heavier sound, that the perfection of their art seems to lie in their concealing it, as if "it were the better for being hidden. An art revealed brings shame."

Dublinia

Since 1993 an exhibition called "Dublinia", located in the former Synod Hall adjoining Christ Church Cathedral, has provided an introduction to medieval Dublin. The building occupied by Dublinia served as the Synod Hall of the Church of Ireland from 1875 to 1983, a bridge linking it to the cathedral. The Synod Hall and bridge were built in the 1870s as part of major restoration work being carried out on Christ Church Cathedral, funded by Henry Roe, the distiller. The Synod Hall is built in the gothic revival style with pointed arches, doorways and windows. It stands on the site of the twelfth-century Church of St. Michael, the original tower of which is incorporated into the building.

Dublinia has offered a space to present to the public some of the material excavated by archaeologists. The choice of the name Dublinia comes from the fact that after the Anglo-Norman invasion of 1170, several Latin versions of the place name are recorded, among which Dublinia is one of the commonest. Dublinia was founded and is managed by The Medieval Trust, a charitable company established with the aim of restoring and preserving the Synod Hall and fostering the accurate portrayal of life in Dublin during the period 1170-1540.

The Decline

The thirteenth-century boom that saw the building of Dublin Castle, the development of the cathedrals and the expression of the city's identity in its charters was followed in the fourteenth century by a series of crises that once again reduced Dublin to a port of hardly more importance than any other in Ireland. There was a series of famines in the early part of the century, and the city was several times badly damaged by fire. In 1315 Edward Bruce led an invasion of Ireland from Scotland. He established a stronghold in the north and was joined by some of the Irish. In 1317 Bruce's forces approached Dublin, but the citizens re-fortified the walls and burned outer areas of the city. Bruce decided not to engage in a siege and he was eventually defeated and killed at the Battle of Faughart, but his adventure had exposed the vulnerability of the Anglo-Norman colony.

The Black Death of 1348 took a heavy toll of the population. A chronicle by John Clyn, written at the friary in Kilkenny, describes the devastation, noting that there was hardly any family where only one person had died, and describing how thousands of people went on pilgrimages to pray for respite. Since plague spread more quickly in densely populated areas it had much greater devastation in the colonist population than amongst the Irish, and it has been estimated that up to half the colonists died. The archbishop of Armagh, preaching before the pope in 1349, claimed that two-thirds of the English population had died, but that the Irish and Scots had not been so badly affected.

The Seventeenth Century

The dissolution of the Dublin monasteries in the 1540s enriched many of the city's merchant families and began a period of regeneration for the city. There were tensions between the citizens and the Castle over religion, with the citizens less willing to embrace Reformation changes, but the story of seventeenth-century Dublin is a story of economic growth and new prosperity. The population grew from around 10,000 in 1600 to over 50,000 in 1700, and this in spite of another plague epidemic in 1649-51. During the Confederate War of 1641-53 there was a period of stagnation, but the overarching story is of a city attracting new immigrants and new projects. From 1651 Protestant strangers who came to the city were offered citizenship, and this drew in some French and Dutch as well as English and Scottish influences. There was a brief revival in the influence of Old English families in the period 1685-90, when the corporation was Jacobite, but the dominant interests jostling for power in the city were predominantly Protestant. When the Duke of Ormond became Lord Lieutenant at the Restoration he sponsored a number of building projects that began to create a sense of civic grandeur.

Luke Gernon came to Ireland as a judge in 1619 and composed *A Discourse of Ireland Anno 1620*, in which he describes Dublin as follows:

> *Dublin is the most frequented, more for convenience than for majesty. There reside the Deputy and the Council; there she receives intelligences, advertisements, instructions. The buildings are of timber, and of the English form, and it is resembled to Bristol, but falleth short. The circuit of the castle is a huge and mighty wall, foursquare and of incredible thickness, built by King John. Within it are many fair buildings, and there the deputy keeps his court. There are two cathedrals under one archbishop, St. Patrick's and Christ Church. St. Patrick's is more vast, and ancient, the other is in better repair. The courts of justice (the same as in England) are kept in a large stone building of Christchurch, which is built in form of a cross; at the four ends are the four courts well adorned, the middle is to walk in. There is a house of court where the judges and other lawyers have chambers, and a common hall to dine in, and it is called the Inns. The judges and the King's Council make the bench, in which number I am. The rest are barristers and attorneys. Further there is a college which is also a university. You will expect to know the state of our state. It is not very magnificent, nor to be disregarded.*

The sense of security and prosperity experienced in Dublin from the 1690s onwards has to be explained in terms of the changes that had been happening in the rest of Ireland during the seventeenth century. In the 1640s Irish Catholics had supported the monarchy during the

English Civil War. Oliver Cromwell came to Ireland as Lord Lieutenant in 1649 and over the following year his military campaign routed Catholic forces and destroyed many pockets of resistance. The massacres which accompanied some of his victories made him reviled. Following his victories there were wholesale confiscations of Catholic land, and the execution, transportation or imprisonment of numbers of Catholic clergy. The Cromwellian land settlement of 1652 identified rebel landowners and cleared them from their lands, sometimes by execution or transportation, and in some cases through internal banishment to Connacht. The government then denominated ten Irish counties for division between soldiers and adventurers, with many portions of land distributed by lot. This redistribution of land and destruction of the Catholic elite (though the details are of course more complicated than can be indicated in a brief overview) made it possible for the Protestant parliament in Dublin, after the Battle of the Boyne (1690) seemed finally to settle the succession of the English monarchy, to claim that it represented not a colony nor a small Protestant interest, but a Protestant nation.

A cautionary note is, however, struck by one visitor to the city at the end of the seventeenth century. Like many other great European cities, life in Dublin was to be characterized by the striking contrast between the lives of rich and poor. John Dunton, an English journalist, came to Dublin in 1698 and gave the following description of the Dublin poor:

> *You may suppose, perhaps, Madam, there are no beggars in Dublin, since I have all this while been so silent, and said nothing of alms-giving: but assure yourself, Madam, to the contrary; for, to the best of my knowledge, I never saw them so thick anywhere else in the whole course of my life; and how to carry myself in respect to these wretches has been a matter which often disturbed me. To give unto all, is impossible; for a man then must be richer than Croesus; and not to give at all, is unchristian: but the main difficulty lies in the right distribution, and to relieve those who are most necessitous. But who can know this?*

This problem was common to many cities but in Dublin the rich and poor came increasingly to feel themselves on opposite sides of a religious and political as well as social divide so that it was never possible to subsume their differences in common interests or civic ideals.

The Coronation of Lambert Simnel
Saturday 24 May 1487

> "*Pretenders: live their lives. The Bruce's brother, Thomas Fitzgerald, Silken knight, Perkin Warbeck, York's false scion, in breeches of silk of whiterose ivory, wonder of a day, and Lambert Simnel, with a tail of nans and sutlers, a scullion crowned. All kings' sons. Paradise of pretenders, then and now.*"
> James Joyce, *Ulysses*

> "*In all haste they assembled at Dublin and there in Christs Church they crowned this idol, honoring him with titles imperial, feasting and triumphing; raising mighty shouts and cries, carrying him thence to the castle on tall men's shoulders that he might be seen and noted, as he was surely an honourable child to look upon.*"
> Holinshed's *Chronicles*

In 1487 Sir Richard Simon, a Yorkist priest, brought to Gearóid Mór, Gerald, Earl of Kildare and Governor of Ireland (1456-1513), a boy aged about twelve, who was, claimed Simon, Edward Plantagenet, Earl of Warwick, pretender to the English throne. The boy was Lambert Simnel, born in Oxford, who had been trained by Margaret Duchess of Burgundy, sister to the late Kings Edward IV and Richard III, to impersonate her imprisoned nephew, Warwick. Whether or not Gearóid Mór believed in the pretender, he embraced the boy's cause and had him crowned King Edward VI of England, Ireland and France. Some 2,000 German mercenaries arrived in Ireland, sent by Margaret and by the Holy Roman Emperor, to join 4,000 Irish troops and help the young king's invasion of England.

Although some English Yorkist soldiers joined the pretender, on 16 June his forces were defeated at Stoke, near Newark. Simnel was captured and Gearóid Mór's brother died at the battle. Henry VII, who had already produced the real Warwick from the Tower of London, pardoned Simnel and made him a servant in the royal kitchens, where he lived for almost forty years.

Red Hugh O'Donnell Escapes from Dublin Castle
Monday 6 January 1592

"Anocht is uaigneach Éire,
do-bheir fógra a fírfhréimhe
gruaidhe a fear 's a fionnbhan fliuch,
treabh is iongnadh go huaigneach. "

[Tonight Ireland is lonely. The banishment of her true race causes
the cheeks of her men and her fair women to be wet—it is strange that
this tribe should be lonely…]
     Aindrias Mac Marcais, from *The Deserted Land,* translated by
     Alan Harrison

Red Hugh O'Donnell (c. 1571-1602), a scion of the Donegal
O'Donnells, was kidnapped in 1587 under the orders of the Lord
Deputy, Sir John Perrot, who wished to use him as a hostage in the
English struggle to control the great Gaelic families of the north of
Ireland. Perrot had been alerted by rumours of O'Donnell's betrothal
to a daughter of Hugh O'Neill, and was concerned about the
strengthening of alliances between Gaelic families in the north. The
young O'Donnell was lured on board a ship to drink at Rathmullen,
on Lough Swilly, and was brought to Dublin, where he was
incarcerated in the Castle for more than three years. In 1591 he made
an unsuccessful escape attempt. He was imprisoned in the Record
Tower, guarded by a group of English soldiers. One of the guards was
bribed to help him, and he descended one night by rope from his
window with some companions. They locked in the pursuers and fled
through the streets, with some of their supporters, eventually making
their way to the Wicklow Mountains. O'Donnell asked for shelter
from a kinsman, who betrayed him to the English and he was taken
back to the Castle.

     On 12 January 1592 he succeeded in a dramatic break-out from
Bermingham Tower. He was aided from outside the prison by the
influence of Hugh O'Neill, Earl of Tyrone (1550-1616). He and a
fellow prisoner from the O'Neill clan overcame their guards on their
way to eat in the refectory and once again used a rope to lower
themselves, this time from a privy into the moat around the Castle

walls. They were met by a guide who took them through the city, where they discreetly mingled with people in the streets. Once beyond the city gates, they once again fled towards the Wicklow Mountains. In the snowy blizzards Art O'Neill, older than O'Donnell and unfit after his long period in prison, weakened quickly, and had to be supported by O'Donnell and a servant. When they had made the strenuous journey across the Red Mountain they sent on a plea for help to their allies in Glenmalure. When that help finally arrived, the escapees were in poor condition, their thin prison clothes frozen to their bodies, and half buried in in snow and hail. Their rescuers attempted to revive them, but Art O'Neill died. Red Hugh O'Donnell suffered so badly from frostbite that he later had to have toes amputated.

O'Donnell returned to his base in the north, where he became a military leader against the English in the Nine Years' War (1594-1603). The rebels, led by O'Donnell and Hugh O'Neill, had significant successes against the English and in 1601 Spanish soldiers arrived to support the Irish, landing at Kinsale in County Cork. Rebel troops marched all the way down from the north of Ireland to meet them, and suffered a decisive defeat at the Battle of Kinsale (1601). Nevertheless, rebel troops held out for a further sixteen months, securing for O'Neill the relatively favourable terms of the Treaty of Mellifont (1603), which brought the war to an end. During the period between the defeat at Kinsale and the Treaty of Mellifont Red Hugh O'Donnell travelled to Spain in an attempt to rally further Spanish assistance. He died at Simancas near Valladolid, and there were rumours that he had been poisoned by an assassin.

Red Hugh was the subject of one of the great prose texts of seventeenth-century Ireland, Lughaidh Ó Cléirigh's *Beatha Aodha Ruaidh Uí Dhomhnaill* (Life of Red Hugh O'Donnell).

On 4 September 1607 Hugh O'Neill, Earl of Tyrone, Rory O'Donnell, Earl of Tyrconnel, and Cúchonnacht Maguire, Lord of Fermanagh, with numbers of their followers, left Rathmullen on a ship bound for Spain. The government of Ireland declared their flight to be treasonous and confiscated their lands to make way for the Ulster plantation. The Flight of the Earls has been identified as a significant moment in the decline of Gaelic power and culture in seventeenth-century Ireland.

The Battle of Rathmines
Monday 2 August 1649

*"This is an astonishing mercy, so great and seasonable as indeed we
are like them that dreamed. What can we say! The Lord fill our souls
with thankfulness, that our mouths may be full of His praise."*
Oliver Cromwell.

The background to the Battle of Rathmines involves the Irish
Confederate war, waged on and off between 1641 and 1653.

In the course of 1641, during the crisis engulfing the British
monarchy of Charles I, several plots against the government were
hatched in Ireland. Rory O'More, an army officer with links to both
Gaelic and Old English interests, planned with Conor Maguire to
capture Dublin Castle. The plan was discovered, but Rory escaped and
went on to lead a force in the Confederate War. Later in the year officers
disbanded from Wentworth's army were also plotting insurrection.
These rebellious strands came together in support of a plot by Sir
Phelim O'Neill, MP for Dungannon, who had become disenchanted
with the parliamentary means of resisting the oppressions suffered by
the Catholic population. For the leaders of the rising this had as much
to do with securing their own property rights and preserving religious
freedoms, as attacking the Ulster settlements, *per se*. Nevertheless, the
capture by O'Neill of Charlemont Fort on 22 October led to a series of
sectarian massacres, in which some 4,000 settlers were killed, and to
reprisal massacres against the Irish population. The Ulster Irish and the
Old English of the Pale formed an alliance and the insurrection spread
nationwide. The insurgents formed themselves into a group called the
Confederate Catholics of Ireland, based at Kilkenny. The commander
of the Royalist forces was James Butler, 12th Earl of Ormond. In 1643
Sir Phelim O'Neill was replaced as Confederate leader by Eoghan Rua
Ó Néill, who had gained significant military experience in exile as a
Spanish general, and Thomas Preston, who had similar continental
experience.

In 1643 the English Civil War forced the king to conciliate the
Confederates, and Ormond negotiated a cease-fire. In 1644 Ormond
became the first Irish Lord Lieutenant in over a century. By 1646 the
tide had turned against King Charles. Dublin was virtually besieged by

the confederacy in the surrounding countryside and the parliamentary forces at sea. Ormond knew that he must settle with one side or the other and he decided to uphold the Protestant interest. On 7 June 1647 Ormond surrendered to Michael Jones, who arrived in the city as commander of the parliamentary forces, and Dublin became a Roundhead stronghold.

To some extent, the war became regional and factionalized. The Royalists who supported the Protestant interest in Ireland had to reposition themselves when King Charles was captured in England and sentenced to death. The Confederacy found it difficult to hold together the competing interests within the umbrella group. A truce between one part of the alliance and the Protestant Inchiquin caused O'Neill to leave the Confederacy. All sides were put under pressure by the economic hardships of the decade, when trade often almost came to a standstill. At times the confederacy was buoyed by financial help from Rome. At other times Confederate pirates blocked access to Ireland via the Irish Sea, but as parliamentary forces gained military strength they were also able to mount effective blockades. In 1648 the country was ravaged by famine, and in 1649 plague followed famine.

Life in Dublin was grim. The citizens were forced to bear the financial burden of maintaining a garrison at a point when trade was frozen by the blockades. Soldiers were billeted with and fed by the population. Houses had been levelled to build up fortifications. Morale was low, with people suspecting one another's allegiances. At one point, Jones' troops mutinied and there was a battle in the city to suppress them. Large numbers of Catholics were expelled from the city and made their way to the neighbouring villages and countryside. Hunger and disease were everywhere.

After Ormond's surrender of Dublin he went into exile in France, but when Charles I was executed on 29 January 1649, Ormond was moved to support the exiled heir to the throne, who assumed the title of Charles II and appointed Ormond Viceroy of Ireland. Ormond returned to Ireland with his sights set on regaining Dublin for the Royalists. He found himself entering into an alliance with a mixture of former enemies. Murrough O'Brien, Earl of Inchiquin, had started the war on the parliamentarian side, and was responsible for some heavy Confederate defeats, but he switched to the Royalist camp and forced a truce with the Confederate Catholics. Ormond sealed this peace treaty in January 1649.

At the end of May 1649 Ormond left Kilkenny accompanied by Inchiquin and Preston, advancing slowly towards Dublin. On 19 June he arrived at Finglas with 1,500 cavalry and 5,000 infantry. More troops gathered around him, but given their divergent backgrounds and recent enmities it was hard to forge morale and unity in his army.

One of the mysteries of Ormond's leadership is that he lingered for over a month at Finglas, while Inchiquin took part of the army to the north, returning in late July with 4,000 troops. In the early stages of the campaign Dublin was poorly fortified and supplied, but Ormond's delay gave the parliamentarians time to build resources and plan a strategy. In late July Ormond moved his forces to the south of the city between present-day Palmerston Park and Ranelagh. Meanwhile, Roundhead ships were arriving in the city with heavy reinforcements. Ormond had planned to construct a battery at Ringsend to prevent such reinforcements, but he was too late. News of the reinforcements demoralized Ormond's troops, and some of them departed with Inchiquin to meet Oliver Cromwell's anticipated invasion of Munster.

Ormond's camp at Rathmines was well outside the walled city. His soldiers had a view of Dublin Castle across the open countryside. He controlled major access routes to the city. In the days leading up to the battle Ormond moved to strengthen his own position and weaken that of his enemies. He took over Rathfarnham Castle. He cut off water supplies to the city. He attempted to drive away from their grazing grounds between Trinity College and Ringsend the horses and cattle belonging to the parliamentarians, but his force was repelled.

Ormond and his generals then made plans to seize and fortify Baggotrath Castle, which would, they believed, give them a strategic advantage from which to launch and support their attack on the city. The exact location is not established with certainty, but 12 Pembroke Road and 44-46 Upper Baggot Street have been advanced as probable.

After dark on the Sunday evening, 1 August, a party of 1,200 foot soldiers and 500 horses set out from Palmerstown Park to Baggotrath Castle. The distance was one mile. The night was dark, and the moon came up after 11pm. They were led by Major General Purcell. It has been suggested that their guides betrayed them. Even so, it remains mysterious how they can have taken so long to cover such a short distance. They arrived before daybreak and occupied the castle, but little was done to fortify it and soon after dawn their position was obvious to Jones and the loyalist forces.

The parliamentarians were lined up behind burned houses at Lowsey Hill. They advanced in extended formation, taking cover where they could find it. Ormond inspected the situation at Baggotrath but does not seem to have grasped the danger. He went back to Rathmines, but was soon forced to return by the noise from Jones' onslaught. The parliamentary forces attacked the Royalists, took the castle, and pursued the retreating soldiers along the Dodder, and advanced through Ranelagh towards the Royalist camp. Ormond's troops, many of them English, disintegrated under the assault and a number defected to Jones. The battle lasted two hours and was a complete Roundhead victory. Jones claimed to have killed 4,000, while Ormond suggested that 600 of his men had died in battle and a further 300 had been executed.

The place where they fell became known as The Bloody Fields.

Ormond survived the day, and returned to exile. At the Restoration he returned to Ireland as first Duke of Ormond, and was also rewarded by Charles II with the position of Lord Lieutenant. During his tenure he sponsored many projects in Dublin, including the building of the Liffey Quays and the Royal Hospital at Kilmainham.

Chapter Two
From the Glorious Revolution
to the Act of Union

"What if the glory of escutcheoned doors,
And buildings that a haughtier age designed,
The pacing to and fro on polished floors
Amid great chambers and long galleries, lined
With famous portraits of our ancestors;
What if those things the greatest of mankind
Consider most to magnify, or to bless,
But take our greatness with our bitterness?"
W. B. Yeats, from "Meditations in Time of Civil War"

Penal Laws

Walking around Dublin, one might gain the impression that in the eighteenth century there reigned in Ireland a particular harmony and prosperity that gave rise to some of the city's greatest civic achievements. This is not how it would have struck Roman Catholics living under the Penal Laws, a series of discriminatory laws passed by the Irish parliament following the Williamite victory of 1691. When James II was deposed from the British throne by his daughter and son-in-law, Mary and William of Orange, his forces retreated to Ireland, where the last stage of the war for the crown was fought. William was present at his forces' victory at the Battle of the Boyne in 1690, and the Jacobites were finally defeated a year later at Aughrim, when 7,000 of their supporters were killed in the bloodiest battle in Irish history. The subsequent Williamite settlement was crushing for the Catholic supporters of the Jacobite cause. The Penal Laws were initially presented as a countermeasure to the pro-Catholic measures passed by the Jacobite Patriot parliament of 1689.

The principal Penal Laws were as follows. An act in 1692 encouraged Protestant settlement in Ireland. An act in 1695 prevented Catholics sending their children abroad to be educated. A further act in 1697 aimed to banish all Catholic clergy. The same year, marriages between Protestants and Catholics were prohibited. The Act to Prevent the Further Growth of Popery (1704) prohibited Irish Catholics from buying land or obtaining a lease for longer than 31 years, and decreed that Catholic estates be divided among all sons, unless the eldest joined the Established Church. It also introduced a sacramental test, requiring anyone assuming public office to take communion under the auspices of the Church of Ireland—a rule intended principally to discriminate against Protestant dissenters. The Registration Act (1704) required all Catholic priests in Ireland to register in court, to furnish two £50 bonds for good behaviour, and not to leave the county in which they were registered. A General Sessions of the Peace sat in the Tholsel, Dublin, in 1704 to discuss the registration of "Popish Priests in the City of Dublin". All registered Catholic priests in Ireland were required to renounce the claims of the Stuarts to the thrones of England and Ireland; only 33 out of 1,089 complied.

The Penal Laws produced some conversions to the Established Church among Catholic landowners, and partible inheritance reduced the power of those who did not convert. It has been argued that the laws were not vigorously prosecuted, but the cultural effects of such systematic discrimination were profound. The Jacobite risings of 1715 and 1745 inevitably created anxiety in the Irish Protestant establishment, but the death of the Old Pretender in 1766 and the formal recognition of the Hanoverian monarchy by the Papacy removed some of the excuse for this legislation. Catholic relief began to be a cause of interest to liberal Protestants and during the heyday of Patriot politics, from the late 1770s to the Act of Union, a series of relief measures removed many of the Penal Laws.

"Patriots" was the name given to the minority of Irish Protestants in the late eighteenth century who espoused principles of civic humanism and political virtue. The Patriots were sympathetic to liberal Enlightenment principles. They responded to the American revolution with sympathy for the colonists, and believed that the interests of Catholics, Protestants and Dissenters in Ireland would all be best served by an independent Protestant parliament. They took much of their inspiration from William Molyneux and Jonathan Swift.

Jonathan Swift

Swift (1667-1745) was born in Dublin
and educated at Kilkenny College
and at Trinity. He went to
England in 1689 and in 1691
became secretary to Sir
William Temple at Moor
Park, Surrey. While he was
there the 23-year-old Swift
befriended a ten-year-old
child called Esther Johnson,
daughter of Temple's
housekeeper (and possibly of
Temple himself). Swift
became her mentor, and gave
her the pet name "Stella".
When she grew up she moved to
Dublin to be near him, and she
remained his closest friend for life. It
has sometimes been speculated that they
were secretly married. Swift was ordained in
the Church of Ireland in 1695 and appointed as a curate in County
Antrim. His first major work, *A Tale of a Tub* (1704) was a satire on
corruption in learning and in religion. He spent much of the first
decade of the eighteenth century in London, where he became intimate
in powerful political and literary circles, moving from Whig to Tory
allegiance when Harley and Bolingbroke came into power. From
London he wrote his *Journal to Stella*, an intimate daily record of his
conversations and activities. At this time Swift believed that his loyalty
should have earned him an English bishopric. Instead he was sent back
to Dublin and installed as Dean of St. Patrick's Cathedral in 1713.

Cometh the hour, cometh the man. Swift was not a clergyman
completely by vocation, but he took his role very seriously, and as he
began to observe the poverty and injustices under which the Irish
laboured he was roused to write in their defence. His *Proposal for the
Universal Use of Irish Manufacture* (1720) urged the Irish to boycott
English goods. *The Drapier's Letters* (1724-5) protested against the
scheme to foist on them devalued new coinage (Wood's halfpence). His

most celebrated pamphlet is *A Modest Proposal for Preventing the Children of Poor People in Ireland, From Being a Burden to Their Parents or Country; and for Making Them Beneficial to the Publick* (1729) in which a projector suggests a scheme to nurture Irish children for human consumption. The economy and ferocity of the satire make it one of the most brilliant pieces of short prose in English. With remarkable prescience Swift imagined famine as the spectre haunting Ireland. His daily acts of charity and negotiations with the beggars of the liberties around St. Patrick's Cathedral inspired his sense that Ireland was in the grip of a critical economic malaise. Swift received the freedom of the city of Dublin in 1729 for his defence of Irish rights.

Gulliver's Travels (1726) represents the terrible mistakes and misunderstandings that arise in colonial encounters. There is no critical consensus on whether Swift expresses more pity or contempt for the degraded Yahoos who so much resemble English stereotypes of the Wild Irish. In *Gulliver's Travels*, as in *A Modest Proposal*, it is the mixture of rage and contempt with kindness and compassion that produce one's sense of a generous imagination deeply engaged with the world around him. The narrator, Lemuel Gulliver, travels to four lands. In Lilliput the people are very small, in Brobdignag they are giants, and in Balnibarbi they are consumed with projects but lack common sense. In Houyhnhnmland Gulliver cannot discover which "people" are equivalent to humanity. He identifies himself with the rational and civilized horses who rule that land, but disconcertingly they regard him as one of the ugly, brutish Yahoo slaves. Gulliver not only discovers that size matters but that the urge to assimilate is a quintessential human characteristic and can draw apparently decent people into the perpetuation of atrocities. How was it possible for men who believed in virtue to invent and perpetuate an abusive system like the Penal Laws? One might ask Lemuel Gulliver.

Everything we know about Swift is provocative and interesting. His friendships, his love affairs with Esther Johnson and Hester Van Homrigh (Vanessa), who also followed him to Dublin (if they can be described as love affairs), the help and encouragement he gave to other writers, his jealousies and depression, his support for the Anglican Church and his apparent dislike of music are all translated into a set of writings—across the genres of essay, letters, pamphlets, novel and poetry—whose intelligence has never been equalled.

All through his work one can see and hear the influence of Dublin, but I want to single out three areas in which he drew on life in the city to develop themes that remained current in Irish writing for centuries to follow. One is in the area of language, where he picked up on the anti-Irish jokes about linguistic incompetence and, in collaboration with his friend Thomas Sheridan, and perhaps influenced by whatever he knew of the Irish language, demonstrated that the Irish had a particular gift for punning and verbal wit. Secondly, Swift produced a remarkable set of writings about the experience of living in the body, and feeling hunger, illness, pain and desire. Some people find poems like "A Beautiful Young Nymph Going to Bed", which describes how a prostitute removes her prosthetics in a dingy hovel, and "The Lady's Dressing Room", which ends with mock horror at the discovery "Oh, Celia, Celia, Celia shits!" to be distasteful and misogynistic. These poems are discomforting, for they make each reader confront her/his own forms of disgust, compassion and fear of mortality. Swift's interest in the body in transformation also informs great comic poems like "Baucis and Philomen" where an elderly couple receive the dubious blessing of being metamorphosed into trees.

Towards the end of his life Swift amused himself compiling his *Directions to Servants*, which is a guidebook to domestic resistance, bordering on warfare. It is an extraordinary anatomy of the mutually corrupting relationship of dependency between the classes, and like Maria Edgeworth's *Castle Rackrent* it exuberantly describes the strategies of surveillance and insubordination central to domestic space. Like Edgeworth, Swift succeeds in making deeply strange what most people of his class took for granted, that other people should labour for their bodily comforts.

Mary Barber and Constantia Grierson

Among the writers assisted by Swift were a group of Dublin women poets, all known to one another. Mary Barber was the wife of a woollen draper in Capel Street, Constantia Grierson and her husband George were printers, and Laetitia Pilkington was the daughter of a male midwife and the wife of a young clergyman, until she became in Swift's (unjust) phrase, the "most profligate whore in either kingdom". Pilkington's memorial is in St. Anne's Church in Dawson Street: "In the Crypt of this Church, near the Body of her honoured Father, John

Van Lewen M.D. lies the Mortal Part of Mrs LAETITIA PILKINGTON Whose Spirit hopes for that Peace, thro' the infinite Merit of Christ, which a cruel & merciless world never afforded her. Died July 29th 1750."

Barber and Grierson are particularly interesting as some of the first Irish writers in English to represent and discuss children and education. Barber ventriloquizes her children in several poems where she has them make sharp comments to teachers and friends on topics such as learning Latin, wearing trousers, fine clothes, domestic life and patriotism.

> *Our Master, in a fatal Hour,*
> *brought in this Rod, to shew his Pow'r.*
> *O Dreadful Birch! O baleful Tree!*
> *Thou instrument of Tyranny!*
> *Thou deadly Damp to youthful joys;*
> *the Sight of thee our Peace destroys.*
> *Not DAMOCLES, with greater Dread,*
> *Beheld the Weapon o'er his Head.*
>   (from "Written for my Son, and Spoken by him in School,
>   upon his Master's first bringing in a Rod")

Swift helped Barber to have her volume of poems published by subscription in 1734 and he also helped with the publication of *Polite Conversation*, from the proceeds of which she was able to live out her life in some comfort. Most of the poems of advice to her son are addressed to Con, but it was the younger son, Rupert (1736-1772), who went on to become an artist. The Barber tomb is at St. Mobhi's in Glasnevin, near Delville where Dr. Patrick Delany lived with his wife Mary. Mary Delany was a patron to Rupert Barber and gave him a house at the bottom of her garden. He painted portraits of her and of Swift.

Seán Ó Neachtain and His Circle

Jonathan Swift is properly commemorated in many places and many ways in Dublin today. Before the advent of the Euro he even figured on the Irish ten-pound note, an ironic homage to the man who condemned "Wood's dross". Irish-language literary culture in Swift's Dublin is much less visible in public monuments. Near St. Patrick's

Cathedral, in Pimlico, lived Seán Ó Neachtain (c.1650-1729), a Roscommon school teacher, and a poet and scribe. The Ó Neachtain family was at the centre of a circle of scholars and writers, mainly Jacobites, teaching and working in Dublin. There were priests, who fell foul of the Penal Laws, and there were some of the first identifiable Irish women writers, Úna Ní Bhroin (d. 1706/7) and Máire Ní Reachtagáin (d. 1733), wives respectively of Seán and Tadgh Ó Neachtain.

Seán Ó Neachtain composed a number of tales, the best-known of which, *Stair Éamuinn Uí Chléire*, a burlesque story of a man's relationship with drink, combines English and Irish in interesting and revealing ways. He was also a poet. In the Ó Neachtain circle were his son Tadgh Ó Neachtain; Aodh Buí Mac Cruitín, who published the first grammar of the Irish language in English (Louvain, 1728); and Diarmaid Ó Conchobhair, who was author of the first printed English translation of Seathrún Céitinn's *Foras feasa ar Éirinn*.

It has long been a matter of speculation whether Swift knew much about this circle of writers and scholars, but he certainly knew enough to write a poem, "The Description of an Irish Feast, Translated Almost Literally out of the Original Irish", which was based on the poem "Pléaráca na Ruarcach" by Aodh Mac Gabhráin (fl. 1720), who may have given Swift a crib from which to translate.

The Sheridan Family

The Patriot politics inspired by Swift and Molyneux developed in the second half of the eighteenth century. No single figure dominated literary and intellectual life in the late century as Swift had done in the early period, but the Sheridan family included a number of very talented writers who excelled in a variety of genres. Swift's friend, Dr. Thomas Sheridan, the punster, ran a distinguished school for boys in Capel Street. He also had a home at Quilca, County Cavan, to which Swift frequently retreated.

His son, Thomas Sheridan (1719-88) was an actor, theatre manager and elocution teacher, who became manager of the Smock Alley Theatre in 1745. In 1747 rioting broke out in the theatre and on the streets outside when Sheridan had a row from the stage with a Trinity student who attempted a drunken sexual assault on one of the women actors in the company. What caused the disturbance to spread beyond the immediate drunken brawl was Sheridan announcing to

Kelly (the student) from the stage: "I am as good a gentleman as you are." The claim that an artist (or indeed a doctor or lawyer) could be a gentleman was quite contentious in the mid-eighteenth century and one can trace in the careers of many of Sheridan's English contemporaries, including Charles Burney, Thomas Gainsborough, David Garrick and Samuel Johnson, deep social anxieties. A male actor might possibly rise to a position where he could present himself as a gentleman, but a female actor could never be a lady. Sheridan's granddaughter commented on his working friendship with the Irish actress Margaret Woffington, that he could never introduce her to his wife.

Thomas Sheridan became a victim of Patriot politics in 1754, when a riot broke out during a performance of Voltaire's *Mahomet*. Sheridan was a friend, or at least client, of the Lord Lieutenant, the Duke of Dorset, who was a keen theatre-goer. They were both members of a private dining club called the Beefsteak Club, which held weekly dinners presided over by the Smock Alley Theatre's star performer, Peg Woffington. In December 1753/January 1754 a crisis developed in the Irish parliament over the progress of the Money Bill. On 5 February Dorset prorogued the Irish parliament. Three days earlier he had been at a production of *Mahomet* at Smock Alley, and the newspapers recalled his applause for the line, spoken by Alcanor: "Power is a curse when in a Tyrant's hands." The play instantly took on a significance that Sheridan could hardly have anticipated. It was his custom to perform plays according to public request, and Patriots flooded his box office with requests for another performance of *Mahomet*. It was customary at eighteenth-century performances for audiences to applaud enthusiastically any speech they particularly liked and to request an immediate encore. When West Digges, the actor playing Alcanor arrived at the following speech in Act One, that is just what the audience did:

> *If, ye Powers Divine!*
> *Ye mark'd the Movements of this Nether World,*
> *And bring them to account, crush, crush those Vipers,*
> *Who, singled out by a Community*
> *To guard their Rights, shall for a Grasp of Ore,*
> *Or paltry Office, sell 'em to the Foe.*

Digges looked startled at the wild applause, and eventually called for silence. "It would give him the Highest Pleasure imaginable to comply with the Request of the Audience; but he had his private Reasons for begging that they would be so good as to excuse him, as his Compliance would be deeply injurious to him." From this the audience inferred that Sheridan had threatened him before the performance. So they began to call for the manager. At this point Sheridan, who was in the wings, began to lose his temper, claiming that the audience had no right to call for him. He then called a sedan chair and went home to Dorset Street.

Meanwhile back in the theatre various actors, including Peg Woffington, came on stage to plead with the audience to be quiet. They would not, and when they were offered refunds of their ticket money, they began to throw oranges, bottles and stones. The ladies and gentlemen in the boxes quickly departed and eventually the occupants of the pit began to tear down the fabric of the theatre, slashing curtains and smashing benches. Candles were pulled from the walls and a number of small fires were started. Rioting went on into the early hours of the morning, causing extensive damage. A few days later, Sheridan published the announcement that he was quitting Dublin and the theatre.

An earlier theatrical controversy—a dispute with fellow-actor Theophilus Cibber—had brought Sheridan a particular piece of good luck, since it was the occasion of his meeting his future wife. Frances Chamberlaine (1724-66) was the daughter of a clergyman who had such a strong prejudice against women's education that she was only taught to read and write in secret by her brother. Her father's illness had permitted Frances to venture for the first time to the theatre, "Dr. Chamberlaine's objection to the drama being equal to his prejudices against female literature." There she had seen Thomas Sheridan perform, but apparently had not made his acquaintance before he became embroiled in a public dispute with fellow actor Theophilus Cibber in 1743, an event which became a cause of public partisanship, including letters to the press and pamphlets in favour of each of the contenders. Frances Chamberlaine entered the fray with an anonymous poetic fable, entitled "The Owls", which was "Addressed to Mr. Sheridan, on his late affair in the theatre". In this fable she enthusiastically compares Sheridan to Phoebus, while the owls are envious spirits of night who cannot bear his brightness. These sentiments seem to have adequately flattered the actor. She followed the poem with a pamphlet (also anonymous), and both pieces defended his cause so eloquently that Thomas Sheridan only awaited the resolution of his difficulties to seek out their author. The discovery led to a courtship, and eventually to marriage, probably in 1747.

Frances Sheridan herself became a novelist and dramatist. Her plays were encouraged by Garrick and her novels by Samuel Johnson and Samuel Richardson. The Irish actor John O'Keeffe recorded in his *Recollections* that "Mrs Sheridan's 'Sidney Biddulph' was more read and admired in Ireland than any novel I ever heard of." Equalled in her own generation only by Oliver Goldsmith, Frances Sheridan is certainly the most significant Irish novelist between Swift and Maria Edgeworth.

When the Sheridans departed Dublin for London in 1754 they left their sons as pupils at Samuel Whyte's academy on Grafton Street. One of the boys, Charles, became a Dublin MP. The other, Richard Brinsley Sheridan (1751-1816) grew up to be one of the most famous dramatists and political orators of his day. R. B. Sheridan left Ireland at the age of eight, to be educated at Harrow. As a young man he had great success as a dramatist with *The Rivals* (1775) and *The School for Scandal* (1777). He made a celebrated romantic marriage with the singer, Elizabeth Linley (with whom he had eloped) but it was not a happy-for-ever-after marriage and she became the lover of Lord Edward Fitzgerald before her early death. In 1780 Sheridan was elected Member of Parliament for Stafford. He distinguished himself as an orator during the hearings for the impeachment of Warren Hastings for corruption in India. He lived a very extravagant life, and died in poverty in 1816. His reputation as an Irish writer was confirmed in Thomas Moore's biography, *Memoirs of the Life of the Right Honourable Richard Brinsley Sheridan* (1825).

The Wide Streets Commission

Dublin before the Act of Union grew in size and prestige because of a number of factors. One was the presence of the vice-regal court and the parliament. Nearly all the great buildings of eighteenth-century Dublin were commissioned by active politicians. In the seventeenth century it had established itself as the leading port and the centre for the distribution of goods throughout the country. It was also the nation's financial centre. It had a monopoly of professional services, including higher education and the higher courts of law. As in London, the sittings of parliament became linked to a social season. The landed classes built houses in Dublin and came to spend the winter months in social relations that were productive of employment in the city: domestic service, sex work, tailoring, building, interior decoration, and supplying luxury food and drink.

In the eighteenth century the Corporation began to think about developing the city in a way that was fitting to its role as capital. From 1757 the Wide Streets Commissioners were given extensive powers to control the planning of the city and solve the problems of congestion that had been troubling Dublin for over a century. The Commissioners for Making Wide and Convenient Ways, Streets and Passages were appointed by parliament and controlled the planning of Dublin until 1851. They aimed to provide the city with wide straight streets, hoping both to alleviate traffic congestion and also to enhance the city's built environment in a manner appropriate to its status as a capital city. The commissioners had powers of compulsory purchase and significant control over architectural planning. They also liaised with the many private individuals who were contributing to the architectural dignity of the city in the later eighteenth century.

Among the many powerful individuals and families who were involved in this process were the Dukes of Leinster, Lord Charlemont, and Luke Gardiner (1745-98), Lord Mountjoy. Gardiner's grandfather (also Luke Gardiner) was a banker and property developer who owned and developed important sites on the north side of the city. The second Luke Gardiner built eastwards from Marlborough Street, along Gloucester Street. Mountjoy Square was his last great project.

Developed by three generations of the family between 1720 and 1820, the Gardiner estate was made up of holdings bought in individual segments leaving it interrupted by other holdings. Several eighteenth-century schemes to link these segments came to nothing. Mountjoy Square is one of Dublin's largest squares, and the grandest in design and execution on the north side of the city. The façades are particularly uniform, and the dark, almost bluish tinge to the brickwork gives the buildings a certain austerity. Originally there was a plan to place a church in the centre of the square, but this proved too expensive, and instead there are gardens, now including a fine children's playground, popular with many recent immigrants to the city. There are also tennis and soccer facilities and basketball courts.

Original schemes for the design of Mountjoy Square show symmetrical terraces with domed pavilions at each end, and carefully placed entrances to maintain the symmetry. The original vista looked down Gardiner Street to the back of the Custom House, a view destroyed when the loop railway was constructed.

Luke Gardiner was killed leading the County of Dublin Militia at the battle of New Ross in 1798. With the third generation of Gardiners, the estate started a descent into bankruptcy, finally collapsing in the mid-1840s. Its decline was a serious blow to the northside of Dublin. The fine houses decayed into slums until the 1950s, when demolition and redevelopment led to significant destruction of interiors and exteriors. The area is undergoing gentrification, but its recent impoverished history is still evident both in the square itself and in the surrounding streets. The Society of St. Vincent De Paul runs Ozanam House, a community centre for the local community. Part of the campus of the Dublin Institute of Technology is housed in the square, and many tourists will have made their first ever visits to Mountjoy Square while staying at the nearby youth hostel in Mountjoy Street.

James Gandon and Francis Grose

The architect most closely associated with late eighteenth-century Dublin is James Gandon (1742-1823), the English Huguenot who arrived in Ireland on 26 April 1781 to begin work on the Custom House. Gandon trained with William Chambers and would have seen the design for Lord Charlemont's Casino at Marino while it was being drawn up at the office (its influence is detectable on Gandon's Custom House). Gandon set up his own practice, and in 1768 he came second in a competition to design the Royal Exchange in Dublin.

It was the Rt. Hon. John Beresford (1738-1805), the unpopular Chief Commissioner of Public Works, who persuaded Gandon to come to Dublin in 1781 to build the Custom House, sited on the North Quay of the River Liffey. The old Custom House, built on Wellington Quay in 1707, was unsatisfactory because large vessels coming up the river to discharge their cargoes were liable to strike "Standfast Dick", a large reef, and because the city had grown eastward. Many Dublin merchants were eager to keep the ships coming all the way into the commercial heart of the city and opposed the new Custom House, fearing that its move down river would lessen the value of their properties while making property owners to the east wealthier.

The project was opposed by Dublin's more radical politicians, including Henry Grattan and Napper Tandy, and there was a politically motivated strike during the construction. Gandon himself received threatening letters and found it advisable to carry a sword when he visited the building site. The building was built on slob land reclaimed from the estuary of the Liffey when the Wide Streets Commissioners constructed the Quays. Beresford wanted all the available space for the building of Beresford Place, a development which he intended to have occupied by merchants and traders. In the event of the Act of Union, Beresford Place never materialized as the planned mercantile centre of the city. The Custom House is one of the most striking buildings in the cityscape, with its wonderfully clean lines and neo-classical form, accompanied by fine sculptural detail. It was destroyed in a fire started by the IRA in 1919 to destroy the records housed within. It was restored in 1932 and again in 1999.

Five years after he started the Custom House, Gandon began work on the shallow-domed building of the Four Courts, the centrepiece building for Dublin's judicial system, which also has a wonderful setting on the river front and effortlessly incorporates an earlier building by

Thomas Cooley. The Four Courts was severely damaged during the Civil War and restored in the early 1930s. Gandon went on to add a portico to the Irish parliament building at College Green, and he also designed Carlisle (O'Connell) Bridge. The Four Courts was severely damaged during the Civil War, and the archives of the Public Record Office housed in the building were completely burnt; it was restored in the early 1930s

The Loop Line Railway Bridge, built in 1891 to connect the station in Westland Row on the south side and Amiens Street on the north, brutally interrupts views of the Custom House and Beresford Place from the west. To the rear of the Custom House is Busáras, the Central Bus Station, designed in 1953 by Michael Scott and one of the first major buildings in Dublin in the modern style.

Gandon's wife died during the period when the Custom House was being built and Gandon later forged a close friendship with Francis Grose, but Grose died suddenly in 1791. Grose was an Englishman who in his youth joined the militia, but found it did not suit his temperament. He travelled through Britain sketching and studying antiquities. In Scotland he became a friend of the poet Robert Burns. He eventually settled in Dublin, where he was at work on a history of Irish antiquities at the time of his death. He was buried in Drumcondra churchyard, known as God's Little Acre. James Gandon spent the rest of his life in Dublin, living first at 7 Mecklenburgh Street and later at Lucan, working on domestic architecture as well as on the great civic projects for which he is famous.

When Gandon died, over thirty years after Grose, he asked to be buried with his friend. The day of the funeral was wet. The gravediggers removed the heavy slab covering Grose's grave and set it on some damp clay to the side of the grave. As they bustled about preparing the open grave, the slab slipped from the clay and fell into the grave, crashing through Grose's coffin and smashing the skull. On the large stone slab is the inscription:

> *To the Memory of Captain Francis Grose, Who while in cheerful conversation With his friends, Expired in their Arms Without a sigh, 18th of May 1791 Aged 60 Also his friend James Gandon Architect Born 1742 - Died 1824 Captain Grose was a Friend of Robert Burns and the Inspirer of Tam O' Shanter.*

Grattan's Parliament and the United Irishmen

The period 1782-1800 was the heyday of the Irish parliament, an arena dominated by the Patriot politicians Henry Flood and Henry Grattan. The last decade of the eighteenth century saw the rise of the United Irishmen. Inspired by the revolutionary movements in America and France, the United Irishmen were in favour of a reform of the Irish constitution and an extension of the franchise to Catholics and Dissenters. Founded in Belfast in 1791, banned in 1794, the United Irishmen became a secret society increasingly tempted by alliance with revolutionary France, and with some members attracted to republicanism. Prominent amongst the Dublin leaders was Theobald Wolfe Tone (1763-1798), the son of a coach-maker and educated at Trinity College, where his brilliance seemed to promise a distinguished legal career (he did become a barrister in 1789). In the early 1790s he became secretary to the Catholic Committee and published *An Address on Behalf of the Catholics of Ireland* (1791). When the United Irishmen were banned he went first to America and then to France where he worked to secure French assistance for an Irish republican revolution. During the 1798 rebellion organized by the United Irishmen—the first attempt to establish an independent Irish republic—Tone was captured on a French boat in Lough Swilly and he committed suicide in prison in November 1798.

The arrest of several leaders of the United Irishmen in the days before the outbreak of the rebellion deprived the movement of leadership at a crucial moment. Some 30,000 people lost their lives as British troops put down the rebellion in the three areas where rebel forces achieved significant mobilization. Following the 1798 rebellion the British government became convinced that it was necessary to abolish the Irish parliament. Through a combination of patronage, bribery and intimidation the Act of Union was pushed through the Irish parliament at the second attempt in 1800, and came into effect on 1 January 1801. George III refused to fulfil his government's promises of Catholic emancipation to accompany the Union, provoking the resignation of his Prime Minister, William Pitt.

The removal of the parliament from Dublin sent the city into a significant economic and social decline. The Irish landed gentry, whose social season had included an annual period in Dublin during the sitting of parliament, had less reason to maintain town houses and to host great social gatherings in the city. Many of them migrated to England, while others scaled down their engagement with Dublin. The jobs generated by the parliament and by this social scene disappeared. Other industries badly hit immediately after the Act of Union included Dublin's publishing and book selling business, which was brought under the regulation of British copyright laws. The inner city became associated with poverty and disease. The more prosperous professional middle class, which grew in numbers through the nineteenth century, tended to settle in the then independent suburban townships and did not exercise much beneficial influence on the governance of Dublin itself.

The rest of this chapter describes the events of four days in eighteenth-century Dublin, when various significant political, cultural and scientific events occurred.

Handel's *Messiah* in Neal's Musick Hall
Friday 13 April 1742

> *"In the year 1740 [sic], the sublime genius of Handel roused our feelings from the lethargy into which they had fallen. Banished from London by the spirit of party, he sought protection in Dublin. Here he was kindly received, and due regard was paid to his extraordinary merit. Soon after his arrival, he performed that matchless Oratorio, The MESSIAH, for the benefit of the City Prison. This was a master-stroke; for by means of it he conciliated the affections of the People, and established his Fame on a permanent foundation."*
> Joseph Walker, *Historical Memoirs of the Irish Bards*

George Frederic Handel arrived in Dublin on 18 November 1741 at the invitation of the Lord Lieutenant, the Duke of Devonshire. He lodged in the city until the following August, staying in Abbey Street. He was invited to play the organ at a concert largely comprised of his own music at St. Andrew's Round Church, for the support of the Mercer's Hospital, on 10 December. A subscription series of six musical entertainments began on 23 December at the New Musick Hall, Fishamble Street. There were two performances each of *L'Allegro, Il Penserosos ed Il Moderato*, the masque *Acis and Galatea*, and *Esther*. A second subscription series began on 17 February 1742. On 3 April public rehearsals for *The Messiah* were announced in *Faulkner's Dublin Journal*. It was planned as a benefit performance for "the relief of prisoners in several gaols, and for the support of Mercer's Hospital in Stephen's Street, and of the charitable infirmaries on the Inns Quay".

The Messiah was publicly rehearsed on 9 April and performed on 13 April in the New Musick Hall, with members of the choirs of St. Patrick's and Christ Church Cathedrals taking part.

The report in *Faulkner's Dublin Journal* was enthusiastic: "The Sublime, the Grand, and the Tender, adapted to the most elevated, majestick and moving words, conspired to transport and charm the ravished Heart and Ear."

Handel is often presented as an exception to the rule that eighteenth-century citizens of property in Dublin were not much interested in European music, in spite of the presence of several notable musicians who visited the city and settled there intermittently during the period. Instead, there seems to have been a strong preference for ballad opera. Swift claimed to have given Gay the idea for *The Beggar's Opera*, which was a huge success in Dublin, spawning many productions and many imitations.

Nevertheless, it is clear that Dubliners knew that they had been the audience for a remarkable musical event, unlike the Londoners who in the following few years were cool in their reception of *The Messiah*. Laurence Whyte, the poet *par excellence* of the Dublin musical scene, wrote a poem on *The Messiah* and it is mentioned repeatedly in other works. Whyte, like Walker, is interested in the clash of sensibilities between the world of European music and that of an indigenous Irish tradition. *The Messiah* became one of the sounds of Dublin, part of the cacophony, noise and babble of Dublin life, where the city was contested in terms of language, culture and mores. The privileged eighteenth-century Anglo-Irish audience was not notable for its discerning musical judgements, but it proved alert to the resonance between Handel's music and philosophical philanthropy. When Dubliners turned out to listen to serious music it was often in the context of charitable events. The majority of the non-theatrical audience for music in the city was to be found at concerts promoted by the boards of hospitals or charitable societies. The Charitable Musical Society for the Relief of Imprisoned Debtors, the Musical Academy in Crow Street, the Charitable Society for the Support of the Hospital for

Incurables and the Earl of Mornington's Musical Academy were the organizations most associated with public musical events. So central was this activity to the ways that charities operated that the construction of venues for music became part of the philanthropic provision. The Board of the Lying-In Hospital famously built the Dublin Rotunda, associating music and pleasure gardens with the maternity hospital.

In 1741 the New Musick Hall in Fishamble Street was built by the Charitable Music Society. It could accommodate 600 people and was elaborately decorated throughout:

> *The interior of the house formed an ellipse, and was divided into three compartments—pit, boxes, and lattices which were without division, the seats were covered with rich scarlet, and fringed to match, while a stuffed handrail carried round gave them the form of couches, and rendered them particularly agreeable for any attitude of repose or attention. The pilasters which supported the front of the boxes were cased with mirror, and displayed various figures on a white ground, relieved with gold. The festoons were fringed with gold, and drawn up with golden cords and tassels. The ceiling was exquisitely painted. In the front was a drop curtain on which was painted an azure sky with fleeting clouds from the centre of which was Apollo's lyre emerging in vivid glory.*

Since 1989 Our Lady's Choral Society has performed excerpts from *The Messiah* every year on 13 April at the site of the New Musick Hall where it had its first performance.

The Volunteers on College Green
Thursday 4 November 1779

> *"You contrived mighty ill to leave town to-day, for by doing so you lost a most glorious sight; a large body of our Volunteers assembled, to honour the memory of King William, who made a very fine appearance, and fired several vollies, even better than the Regulars, who performed the same task an hour or two after. Every one looked delighted, except some few, who want to be thought friends to Government, but for me who am an enthusiast in the cause of*

Liberty and my country, I was wonderfully delighted to see our men of the first rank and property, as well as our most eminent citizens, voluntarily arming in defence of both: I think it warms one's heart, and I really pity your lukewarm souls, who can see such a sight without emotion."

Anon, *The Triumph of Prudence Over Passion (1781)*

In the National Gallery of Ireland is a painting by Francis Wheatley (1747-1801), a London painter who spent four years in Dublin avoiding his creditors, of *A View of College Green with the Meeting of the Volunteers on the 4th November, 1779, to Commemorate the Birthday of King William*. The painting was first shown publicly at the Society of Artists' exhibition in Dublin, in the spring of 1780, just six months after the events depicted. Its topicality made the painting celebrated as soon as it went on show in an exhibition otherwise dominated by conventional portraiture and landscape. Wheatley was instead offering a new form of history painting, which combined elements such as the topographical picture (his background carefully depicts the buildings on College Green, including the parliament and the facade of Trinity College, along with the equestrian statue of William); the group portrait (there are many recognizable figures in the painting including the Duke of Leinster and James Napper Tandy); and an element of the dramatic, which is evoked with the smoke of the guns and cannon.

During the American Revolution, through the period of military engagements between Britain and the colonists from 1775 to1873, regular forces were redeployed from Ireland to fight in the colonies. Fearing that either France or Spain might take advantage of this depletion of defences to invade Ireland with Catholic help, the Protestant establishment raised local volunteers to defend their interests in 1778-9. Volunteer companies were independent, supplying their own equipment and holding no official posts or commissions. Numbers rose from 12,000 in spring 1779 to 40,000 by the following September, and to a peak of around 80,000 in the early 1780s. The activities of the Volunteers developed a political dimension through their involvement with Patriot politics. Henry Grattan (1746-1820) the Dublin Patriot MP, the Duke of Leinster, the Earl of Charlemont (1728-99), commander-in-chief of the Volunteers, and Frederick Augustus Hervey (1730-1803), who was both Bishop of Derry and Earl of Bristol, all used their positions with the Volunteers to advance their political positions (although they did not all agree with one another).

The Volunteers never directly threatened government but the sight of their parades and conventions exercised sufficient pressure to assist the Patriot arguments in favour of free trade (by which was meant full participation for Ireland in free trade with the British colonies) and later for legislative independence. A spectator at the original exhibition of Wheatley's painting would have known that on 4 November 1779 the Volunteers were shouting "Free trade or else!"

Spalding's Diving Bell
Monday 2 June 1783

> *"His friends and acquaintances, having so many proofs of the trifling danger with which this wonderful visitation of the deep was attended, many of them ventured at times to accompany him."*
> Dublin Evening Post, 11 June 1783

The East Indiaman, *Belgioso*, left Liverpool on 4 March 1783, bound for China by way of Lisbon. She was not expected to approach the Irish coast, but a combination of strong south-easterly winds with snow and poor visibility drove the large ship westward, and she struck and was wrecked on the Kish Bank, in Dublin Bay. A total of 147 people were reported drowned.

The cargo declared consisted of cloth, ginseng (imported from Canada and fetching a guinea for a pound in weight on London markets, and exported at five times this value to the East), flints, silver bullion, Spanish dollars packed in chests and worth £40,000, and lead. The value of the cargo was estimated at between £130,000 and £150,000.

The cargo was evidently valuable, and the underwriters decided to hire a salvage company. They chose Spalding & Co. of Edinburgh, which had recently been involved in recovering guns from the wreck of the *Royal George* at Spithead.

Charles Spalding, born in Edinburgh, was a confectioner by trade. He had worked for some time on improvements to Dr. Halley's diving bell, and he developed what became known as "Charles Spalding's Diving Bell". It was 200 gallons in size and could accommodate two men. It was weighted and had a system of ropes for varying signals. The air was replenished by barrels lowered from a vessel above, and delivered into the bell by a hose. The bell had several small windows with strong glass.

Spalding sailed to Dublin with his nephew and colleague, Ebenezer Watson, and their equipment, and began work salvaging the *Belgioso* in five to seven fathoms on the Kish Bank on 1 June. The underwriters were defraying their expenses, and in the event of a successful operation, Spalding & Co were to receive one-quarter of recovered silver and one-half of the rest of the cargo.

In Dublin Spalding met with James Dinwiddie, LL.D., a celebrity scientist, itinerant lecturer, and fellow Scot, whose passion for experiment and for scientific equipment left him permanently in debt. Dinwiddie descended at least once in Spalding's diving bell, for he left a record of the sensations experienced by a diver. On the morning of 2 June, when Dinwiddie accompanied Spalding and Watson out to Kish Bank, he planned to descend again with an air pump and some other apparatus, to try experiments in condensed air, particularly related to sound. Dinwiddie remained in the boat while Spalding and Watson made the first three dives of the day, in seven fathoms of water. From the third dive they did not return. Dinwiddie waited for agreed signals on the ropes to pull them up, but the signals never came. When the bell was hauled up it was found that the signal ropes had become entangled. Moreover, the last barrel of air sent down to the men had not reached them. They had suffocated.

The bodies of the two divers were returned to George's Quay in Dublin, where they lay until 8 June, when they were buried in St. Mark's Church, Westland Row.

Dinwiddie contributed to discussions on the cause of death. The role of oxygen was not well understood in the early 1780s, with the work of Lavoisier just beginning to be translated from the French. Newspaper reports on Spalding's death suggest that he may have been killed by "putrid air" coming from the corpses on the *Belgioso*, perhaps mixed with the odour of ginseng.

Dinwiddie gave a series of successful lectures on the ill-fated salvage attempt, and in July he advertised that he would have Spalding's actual diving bell in his lecture room. Dinwiddie's lectures indicate the ways in which science was entering the popular imagination in late eighteenth-century Ireland. The bell itself certainly seems to have remained in Dublin because in the following years there were several renewed attempts to salvage the *Belgioso*, and some of them were described as having used Spalding's bell. In the summer of 1783 two African divers well known for recovering treasure also died at the wreck of the *Belgioso*, as did an unnamed Irishman. The underwriters took out a new contract, but in spite of recorded efforts to recover the treasure through the 1780s there were no successes, and presumably the treasure is still out there, at Kish Bank.

Flood Challenges Grattan to a Duel
Tuesday 28 October 1783

"Among other qualifications for public station, the gladiatorial is one of the most essential."
Lord Townshend.

"You can be trusted by no man—the people cannot trust you—the minister cannot trust you; you deal out the most impartial treachery to both. You tell the nation that it is ruined by other men, while it is sold by you. You fled from the embargo, you fled from the mutiny bill, you fled from the sugar bill! I, therefore, tell you in the face of your country, before all the world, and to your beard, you are not an honest man."
Henry Grattan.

While the settlement of disputes through single combat was not unknown in medieval Ireland, it was the new English in the sixteenth century who introduced into Ireland the idea of duelling predicated on European ideas of a code of honour amongst gentlefolk. As a social practice the spread of duelling in Ireland seems to have lagged behind that in England, where the code of honour was a marked feature of the court culture whose excesses contributed to provoke the revolution of the mid-seventeenth century. It was only in the late seventeenth century that duelling really seems to have taken hold in Ireland, but throughout the following century, as it was more and more widely condemned by Church, state and moralists in England, it was becoming increasingly fashionable—or addictive—in Ireland.

Not surprisingly, duels were common among military men. A duel was a meaningless affair unless the combatants had some claim, at least in their own minds, to gentility and honour. Among Catholics the defence of such pretensions through the duel seems to have been influenced by the experience of Irish exiles in continental European armies, where duelling was a common practice. Among Protestants the heavy military presence from the 1640s and the new access to wealth and social pretension through the Cromwellian plantations seems to have been significant. One might therefore be tempted to represent duelling as meaning two rather different things for the various adherents to the Jacobite and Williamite causes. For Jacobites duelling was a way of demonstrating breeding and class in the absence of the property and wealth that might once have given substance to claims of social superiority. For many settler "gentlemen" it was a way of asserting a claim to gentility for which the acquisition of property was not always sufficient guarantee.

However one might schematize the origins of duelling, by the middle of the eighteenth century it so permeated the mindset of the Irish gentry as to have become ingrained as the habitual response to certain conflicts over courage, sexual conduct and political disputes. But duelling also became a recourse for significant differences between men—differences that might have been settled through words, and where the willingness to risk one's life, or to murder another person, seemed largely beside the point.

One of the most famous affairs of honour in eighteenth-century Ireland took place when the relationship between two former allies, Patriot politicians Henry Flood and Henry Grattan, began to deteriorate. Following the success in 1782 of the Patriot campaign for legislative independence for the Irish parliament, Grattan had become associated with a more moderate wing of the Patriots, satisfied with the concessions achieved, while Flood became leader of a more radical group determined to force the British government into renouncing its right to legislate for Ireland. This difference in strategy fuelled the personal differences already existing between the two men. In 1783 the government made further concessions to Flood, and Grattan committed himself to association with the British Whig administration and Dublin Castle. Flood became ever more popular as the defender of Irish interests, whilst Grattan, formerly the people's darling, began to be viewed with suspicion.

On 28 October 1783, Grattan launched an attack on Flood during a debate in the Irish House of Commons. Grattan represented Flood as a politician by turns intemperate, seditious and corrupt: "you were silent for years and you were silent for money." He accused his fellow MP of abandoning principles to court public opinion. Eventually, when Grattan had paused in his attack, Flood rose to defend himself and launch a counter-attack in which he accused Grattan of being "a mendicant patriot who was bought by his country for a sum of money and sold his country for prompt payment." Flood hinted that a duel was the only possible outcome to the day's proceedings. The Speaker of the House, who had been apparently mesmerized by the events of the day, at last intervened, instructing Flood to say no more. Flood angrily left the chamber and had gone from the building by the time John Foster, MP for Louth, had persuaded the house that the two men should be taken into custody to prevent the argument continuing outside.

In fact, Flood quickly issued a challenge to Grattan and the two men agreed to meet and fight at a spot in Blackrock two days later, on Thursday 30 October. The duel never took place. The sheriff of Dublin had stationed lookouts on all the main roads leading from the city and one of these spotted the duelling party. Grattan and Flood were brought before a judge who bound them to official recognizances of £2,000 each (an enormous sum) to keep the peace.

There was some surprise that the matter ended here. In August 1769 Henry Flood had killed his antagonist, James Agar, in a celebrated duel at Dunmore, County Kilkenny. The Agar family clamoured for a prosecution, but in the event Flood was found guilty only of manslaughter in his own defence, and was set free. Grattan was also willing to defy anti-duelling laws. In 1797, for example, he challenged Patrick Duigenan, a notorious defender of Protestant ascendancy, over remarks published by Duigenan in a pamphlet. Other thwarted duellists had made the short journey across the Irish sea to Holyhead to fight duels forbidden in Dublin, and it was not uncommon to carry these matters further, to prearranged meetings in France or Holland.

Jonah Barrington, the great, if unreliable (or rather, great because unreliable) memoirist of eighteenth-century Ireland gives a number of humorous and haunting accounts of duels, including the duel in which his brother was killed, and in nineteenth-century accounts of eighteenth-century Ireland the fiery duellist rapidly became a literary stereotype.

The Arrest of Lord Edward Fitzgerald
Saturday 19 May 1798

"I would rather be Fitzgerald, as he is now, wounded in his dungeon, than Pitt at the head of the British Empire."
Wolfe Tone.

At about 10 o'clock on the evening of 18 May, William Putnam McCabe, an Ulster activist in the United Irishmen who was also known as the "emerald Pimpernel", and who was Lord Edward Fitzgerald's agent and *ipso facto* bodyguard, sent two parties along Bridgefoot Street and Watling Street towards Usher's Island. Lord Edward was in hiding, at the Yellow Lion public house in Thomas Street, and his friends, having had a tip-off that the Yellow Lion was to be searched, were trying to move him to another safe-house at 20 Usher's Island. They did not then know that the resident of this house, Francis Magan, was an informer on the payroll of Dublin Castle. The advance parties met Major Sirr and his troops, engaging in a scuffle. Miss Moore, the daughter of the Yellow Lion's publican, and a group of bodyguards, who were accompanying Lord Edward in a third party, realized they could not reach their destination, and took him further down Thomas Street, to number 135, where she asked Nicholas Murphy, a feather merchant, who had previously lodged Fitzgerald, to take him in again. Murphy prepared a back attic room and Fitzgerald, who had a bad cold, went up to sleep.

Lord Edward Fitzgerald (1763-98) was born at Carton House, County Kildare, into Ireland's premier aristocratic family. His father (d. 1773) was Earl of Kildare and the first Duke of Leinster. His mother's family was highly connected to the English aristocracy and involved in British political circles. Lord Edward was a younger son, who served in the British army during the American War of Independence. His radicalism developed in America and increased in travels to revolutionary France. From 1783 he was a member of the Irish parliament. In the 1790s he joined the United Irishmen and in 1797 he renounced his title and gave up his parliamentary seat. In 1792 he married Pamela, the adopted (or illegitimate) daughter of the French writer, Mme. de Genlis. Whatever the truth of her origins it was widely believed that Pamela was the daughter of the Duc d'Orléans, known as Philippe Égalité, a cousin of the King of France who had espoused the revolution. From the summer of 1797 Fitzgerald became the prime military strategist for the United Irishmen planning their rebellion. He narrowly escaped arrest on 12 March 1798, and on 18 May he was just five days from the planned uprising on the 23rd.

The next day, 19 May, Francis Magan went to call on Miss Moore. She told him where they had moved Fitzgerald, and he hastened off to pass on this information to the Castle. That day there were searches in Thomas Street, starting with the pub. Murphy, hearing the commotion, moved Fitzgerald onto the roof of his warehouse for several hours during the day. At four o'clock he was brought down to dinner with the Belfast journalist, Samuel Neilson, one of the executive of the United Irishmen's Society. After dinner Neilson left and Fitzgerald went up to the attic to lie down.

At 7 o'clock Murphy went up to the attic to invite Lord Edward down to tea. Fitzgerald was lying on the bed, reading Le Sage's *Gil Blas*. As Murphy was standing speaking to him Sergeant Swan burst in and addressed Fitzgerald: "You are my prisoner." Fitzgerald grabbed his dagger and slashed at Swan. Captain Ryan, hearing the commotion, rushed upstairs and threw himself at Fitzgerald in an attempt to restrain him. Ryan wrapped his arms round Fitzgerald's waist, to which he clung, as Fitzgerald stabbed him repeatedly. Fitzgerald then tried to get out through the door, but he was still dragging Ryan, who was bleeding heavily, but would not release his grip. At this point Major Sirr appeared, took aim with his pistols, and shot Fitzgerald twice in the shoulder, causing the dagger to fall. Several soldiers then rushed in and battered Fitzgerald to the floor with their muskets, cutting him across the neck in the fray.

There were two hundred soldiers in the street, prepared to quell a riot, as Ryan and Fitzgerald were carried out of no. 135. Ryan was taken to a surgeon, and Fitzgerald was carried in a sedan chair to the Castle, where he was laid across some chairs in the office of the Secretary for War, while the Surgeon General, George Stewart, dressed his wound. Lord Camden's private secretary, Mr Watson, entered and spoke with him, asking if he had any message for his wife. There was none, except a request to break the news gently.

Fitzgerald was then removed to Newgate Gaol, where he was placed in a private room with an armed guard. For the first night only, another United Irishman prisoner, Thomas Russell, was allowed to stay with him.

Lord Edward Fitzgerald died as a result of his injuries on 4 June 1798. A few days previously Captain Ryan had died. Fitzgerald's family blamed his death on neglect by the authorities, who failed to have his wound treated by surgery.

Francis Magan was paid £1,000 reward and an annuity for the next thirty years for his role as informant.

The arrest of Lord Edward was the subject of many pictorial representations, both pious and caricatural, throughout the nineteenth century.

Chapter Three
A PROMENADE ON THE SOUTH SIDE

"You wou'd smile, Madam, if you had the Picture of your quondam friend at the black Raven, like an over-grown Oaf newly come to Town, staring and gazing at all the Signs, and every thing else in the Streets; pacing out their length, and enquiring ever and anon, What call ye this Street? Who dwells in yon great House? Whose fine coach is that?"

John Dunton, from *The Dublin Scuffle* (1699)

When the Lumière brothers came to Dublin in 1897, they filmed O'Connell Bridge. O'Connell Bridge is the place where the pulse of Dublin is felt most strongly. The river is at its most dramatic as it widens towards the sea, past Gandon's magnificent Custom House, the view of which is sadly obscured by a railway bridge. Nevertheless, downriver one sees the watery coastal light and smells the ocean. Upriver the sequence of bridges and the tall quayside buildings suggest the intimacy of the old city centre. Walk north of the river onto O'Connell Street, which has been undergoing refurbishment in recent years to create more of the atmosphere of a Parisian boulevard and less of Time Square in the 1980s, and one is on the city's main thoroughfare, with its monuments and sites of historic interest. Stand at either end of the bridge at rush-hour, and you will be aware of the traffic crisis that has hit the city in the last decade.

College Green

Walk south across the river over O'Connell Bridge and one comes first onto Westmoreland Street, home to one of the Bewley's Oriental Cafés, the one favoured by James Joyce. You also pass Beshoff's fish and chip restaurant. Ivan Iylanovich Beshov was originally from the Ukraine and was part of the crew of the Russian vessel, the famous battleship *Potemkin*, which mutinied at Odessa in 1905. He arrived in Ireland in 1911 with the intention of travelling on to Canada. He missed his boat connection and decided to stay. When he married an Irish woman,

Beshov changed name to Beshoff. The first Beshoff's fish and chip shop opened in 1922. There is another branch at 6 Lower O'Connell Street. Westmoreland Street comes round to College Green, the centre of Georgian Dublin. Another old shop front is that of The Irish Yeast Company on College Street. This small shop, over a century old, opposite Trinity College Dublin, was originally founded by a Dublin barrister in the 1890s to supply fresh yeast to Dublin's bakeries. It changed direction when it was taken over by its present owners, the Morelands, in the 1940s. Although it still supplies fresh yeast, its main business now is cake decoration.

The streets and square between College Green and the Grand Canal are peppered with plaques to Dublin's famous residents. The universities, the museums, libraries and academies of culture and science developed in this area. These are the streets that are first pounded by most visitors to the city.

The Bank of Ireland on the corner opposite Trinity College was originally designed by Edward Lovett Pearce, Ireland's leading Palladian architect, and built between 1729 and 1739 to house the Irish parliament, being enlarged by the architect James Gandon and others later in the century. In earlier centuries the Irish parliament had met in the Assembly Room at Dublin Castle. Chichester House, on College Green, was purchased to house the parliament, which first met there at the restoration of the monarchy in 1660. Chichester House was demolished to make way for Pearce's building. The Irish parliament building was the first purpose-built bicameral parliament house in the world. After the Act of Union the building was sold to the Bank of Ireland on condition that the interior be so transformed that it could never be used as a parliament again. There is an arts centre in the old armoury in Foster Place. The old House of Lords building is well preserved and is occasionally used for receptions, conferences and meetings. In the House of Lords chamber still hang original tapestries by Jan van Beaver of the Siege of Derry and the Battle of the Boyne. The chamber is surprisingly small, and its intimacy must have contributed to the sense of drama during some of the scenes enacted there.

Thomas De Quincey visited Dublin to stay with a school friend, the son of Lord Altamont, at the period when the Union was ratified. He described the last session of the House of Lords, which he attended:

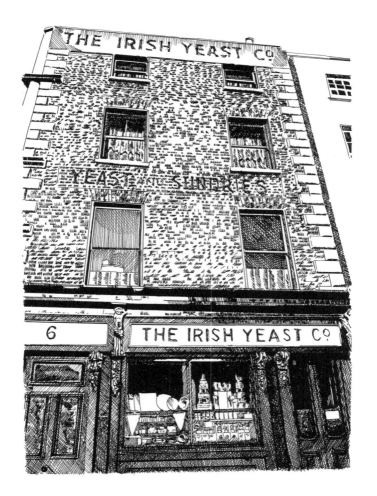

Gradually the house filled: beautiful women sat intermingled among the peers;... Next came a stir within the House, and an uproar resounding from without, which announced the arrival of his Excellency. Entering the house, he also, like the other peers wheeled round to the throne, and made to that mysterious throne a profound homage. Then commenced the public business, in which, if I recollect, the Chancellor played the most conspicuous part—that Chancellor (Lord Clare) of whom it was affirmed in those days, by a political opponent, that he might swim in the innocent blood which he had caused to be shed. But nautical men, I suspect, would have demurred to that estimate. Then were summoned to the bar—summoned for the last time—the gentlemen of the House of Commons; in the van of whom, stood Lord Castlereagh... At which point in the order of succession came the royal assent to the Union Bill, I cannot distinctly recollect. But one thing I do recollect—that no audible expression, no buzz, nor murmur, nor susurrus even, testified the feelings which, doubtless, lay rankling in many bosoms. Setting apart all public or patriotic considerations, even then I said to myself, as I surveyed the whole assemblage of ermined peers, "How is it, and by what unaccountable magic, that William Pitt can have prevailed on all these hereditary legislators and heads of patrician houses to renounce so easily, with nothing worth the name of a struggle, and no reward worth the name of an indemnification, the very brightest jewel in their coronets? This morning they all rose from their couches Peers of Parliament, individual pillars of the realm, indispensable parties of every law that could pass. Tomorrow they will be nobody—men of straw—terrae filii. What madness has persuaded them to part with their birthright, and to cashier themselves and their children forever into mere titular Lords?"

One of the incidental glories of the last days of the Irish parliament was Sir Boyle Roche (1743-1807). Roche was a enemy of Catholic relief and a supporter of the Act of Union, but he is most remembered for his verbal blunders. Many of Roche's sayings are recorded by fellow MP Jonah Barrington, in his memoirs, *Personal Sketches of his Own Time* (1827-32) and the polemic *Rise and Fall of the Irish Nation* (1833). Barrington uses Roche to illuminate the perverted logic and self-delusions necessary to sustain his opponent's position, but most of Roche's "bulls" are now remembered out of context. Probably the best-known is the occasion when he asked the Commons "Why should we put ourselves out of our way to do anything for *posterity*;—for what has *posterity* done for *us*?"

Roche is quoted as having said on another occasion about the Act of Union: "Gentlemen may titther, and titther, and titther, and may think it a bad measure; but their heads at present are hot, and will so remain till they grow cool again; and so they can't decide right now; but when the *day of judgment* comes, *then* honourable gentlemen will be satisfied at this most excellent Union. Sir, there is no Levitical degree between nations, and on this occasion I can see no shame in *marrying our own sister*." A final example, not inappropriate to our own day, occurred when Roche was arguing for the suspension of Habeus Corpus: "It would surely be better, Mr. Speaker, to give up not only a *part*, but, if necessary, even the *whole*, of our constitution, to preserve the remainder!"

Outside Trinity College and facing the old parliament building is a statue of Henry Grattan (1746-1820), one of the great Patriot orators of late eighteenth-century Dublin. His advocacy of legislative independence had the consequence that the years between 1782 and the Union in 1800 have since the late nineteenth century been known as the period of "Grattan's parliament". His statue was erected in 1876. Beside the statue are two of the original four gas lamp standards, decorated with carved seahorses.

From 1701 until it was destroyed by a nationalist bomb in 1929, there was an equestrian statue of William III by Grinling Gibbons on College Green. The statue was the focus of loyalist celebrations, particularly on the king's birthday (4 November) and from the 1790s onwards on the anniversary of the Battle of the Boyne (12 July). There were many student pranks associated with it, and many attempts to deface it before its eventual destruction. In the early part of the eighteenth century Trinity students were inclined to be Tories, and—especially when drink was taken—they protested by defacing William's statue with mud and hay, or mounting a scarecrow behind the king. Between 1779 and 1792 the focus of attention changed with the Volunteers taking over the celebration of William's birthday. They gathered around the statue with placards demanding "Relief to Ireland" or "The Glorious Revolution", claiming a link between their own protests and William's "glorious revolution".

The rise of the United Irishmen brought a new republicanism, antagonistic to all monarchs, and in the 1790s the celebration of William's birthday and the anniversary of the Boyne were taken over by newly formed Orange societies. The Orangemen painted the statue white, dressed it in a cloak and sash, and adorned it with orange lilies. The horse was decked with orange streamers and green-and-white ribbons were placed beneath its raised foot, symbolizing the crushing of the Jacobites. Naturally these demonstrations attracted new antagonism towards the statue, and in 1798 Watty Cox, the periodical editor, broke off the king's sword and attempted to file off his head. Through the nineteenth century the statue was regularly defaced, and in 1836 alone three attempts were made to blow it up. From 1882, celebrations around the statue were banned because of the sectarian conflicts that arose between the Orangeman and their opponents.

Trinity College Dublin

Trinity College was founded by Elizabeth I in 1592 on the site of the Augustinian priory of All Hallows, which was suppressed in 1538. It was established as a Protestant college but admitted Catholics and Dissenters until 1637, when restrictions were placed on attendance by Catholics, which lasted for a hundred and fifty years. In the nineteenth and twentieth centuries the Catholic Church opposed attendance of its members at Trinity, objecting to the college's Anglican orientation. This "ban" was lifted in 1970.

Among the first cohort of students at the college was that "miracle of learning", James Ussher (1581-1656). Ussher went on to become Professor of Divinity and Vice-Provost. From 1625-56 he was Archbishop of Armagh and Anglican Primate of All Ireland. He created a 10,000-volume library, now housed at Trinity, and moved to England in 1640 to pursue his scholarly interests. He was the first known Irish supporter of a Keplerian view of the universe, with its understanding of the relationship between the sun and planets. He also used modern astronomical methods alongside his biblical knowledge to date the creation to 4004 BC, a theory which gained popular support.

The college is fronted by an impressive grey stone neo-classical façade (1752-1759), attributed to Theodore Jacobsen. On either side of the gate are statues by Foley of two famous Trinity graduates, Edmund Burke (1729-97) and Oliver Goldsmith (1728-74).

Edmund Burke, the philosopher and politician, was born at 12 Arran Quay, and educated at Trinity between 1743 and 1748. When Burke arrived at Trinity he sent descriptions of his experience to his old school friend, Richard Shackleton, whose father ran the school in Ballitore where Burke had been a pupil. This is his first meeting with his tutor, Dr. Pellasier:

> *We were admitted into his rooms, and he had three very grand ones. He and Jack Baily had a good deal of chat and a couple of men were setting up a barometer in his room—so he could not for a while examine me. At last he brought out Francis's Horace, Dauphine's Virgil and Homer, with I don't know whose notes; he made me construe* Scriberius Vario &c Eheu fugaces, Postume *&c and in Virgil I began the 103rd line of the Sixth Aeneid, and in Homer with the 227th line of the Third Iliad, and the 406th of the Sixth and he was pleased to say (what I would not say after him unless to a particular friend) that I was a good Scholar and understood the Authors very well, and seemed to take pleasure in them (yet by the bye, I don't know how he could tell that) and that I was more fit for the College than three quarters of my class; but he told me I must be examined again by the Senior Lecturer.*

While he was at Trinity Burke began work on his remarkable early treatise, *A Philosophical Enquiry into the Origins of Our Ideas of the Sublime and the Beautiful* (1757). He trained as a barrister in London, returning to Ireland for a few years in the early 1760s as a private secretary in Halifax's administration. In 1765 he was elected to the Westminster parliament, where he served until 1794. In the 1770s Burke supported the American colonists and in 1786 he proposed the removal from office of Warren Hastings, Governor-General of Bengal. Burke's speeches about Hastings' abuse of power during the impeachment are among his clearest statements on the virtues of custom and tradition, and the evils of colonial misgovernance. His *Reflections on the Revolution in France* (1790) put the case against the revolution. He lived for most of the last thirty years of his life on his estate at Beaconsfield in Buckinghamshire.

Oliver Goldsmith was originally from County Longford. After Trinity College he travelled in Europe before settling in London in 1756. From 1760 he was associated with the literary circle of Samuel Johnson. Goldsmith is remarkable for having made a distinguished contribution across the most prestigious literary genres of his period. His novel, *The Vicar of Wakefield* (1766), his poem, *The Deserted Village* (1770), his play, *She Stoops to Conquer* (1773) and his commercial natural history, *A History of Earth and Animated Nature* are all among the best examples of their kind in the period.

Passing through the main gate under the archway, one enters the wide cobbled quadrangle called Parliament Square. Directly ahead is the Campanile, donated in 1853 by the Archbishop of Armagh, Lord Beresford. It was placed on a spot supposed to be at the centre of the medieval priory. Beyond the Campanile, at the far end of the square, is a row of red brick buildings, the Rubrics, which date from 1700 and are the oldest surviving buildings in the College. Goldsmith had his chambers here.

The Examination Hall on the right was built between 1779 and the mid-1780s to designs by Sir William Chambers (1723-1796). Chambers was responsible for the design of several important Dublin buildings, including Charlemont House and the Casino at Marino, but there is no evidence that he ever visited the city. Instead, he produced designs and sent builders to execute them. The gilt oak chandelier in the Examination Hall hung formerly in the old Irish House of Commons in College Green. The impressive organ case is believed to have been built in Dublin in 1684 by Lancelot Pease, who also did work for King's College, Cambridge. The only surviving example of Pease's work known anywhere, it is the oldest existing Irish-made organ case and one of the most important in Britain and Ireland.

The chapel designed by Chambers to match the Examination Hall, features plasterwork by Michael Stapleton (c.1740-1801). Stapleton was a Dublin master-builder and stuccodore, who ran a workshop famous for its neo-classical plasterwork. As a Catholic he was not a guild member. Many examples of his work survive and there is a large collection of his drawings and engravings in the National Library. The chapel was built to Chambers' design by Christopher and Graham Myers. Behind the chapel is a tiny graveyard named Challoner's Corner (after Luke Challoner, who was buried there in 1613), reserved for the burials of Provosts of the College. Beside the chapel is the dining hall, designed in 1743 by Richard Cassels. The building suffered badly from a fire in the early 1980s but has since been restored.

The library, designed by Thomas Burgh and built between 1712 and 1732, contains the Long Room, the largest single chamber library in Europe. On the ground floor is The Colonnades exhibition gallery, displaying some of the college's great treasures. *The Book of Kells* is on display in a purpose-built treasury, along with other early Christian manuscripts. Also on display is Ireland's oldest harp, dating from the fifteenth or sixteenth century and made of willow with 29 strings. Known as the Brian Bórú harp, from a mistaken belief in its antiquity, its design is typical of Irish harps produced over a period of eight hundred years.

Beyond the Rubrics is the New Square (built 1838-1844), containing the Printing House with its Doric portico, built in 1734, and the museum building designed by Deane and Woodward in 1853, which has animal and plant carvings around the windows.

The Provost's House on the corner of Trinity College, built in 1760, is one of the grandest of Dublin's Georgian mansions, with a coved ceiling in the salon which runs the entire length of the building. Among its more celebrated occupants were George Salmon (1819-

1904), the mathematician and theologian, and the classical scholar John Pentland Mahaffy (1839-1919), who befriended Oscar Wilde and Oliver St. John Gogarty. Wilde described Mahaffy as "my first and best teacher" and "the scholar who showed me how to love Greek things." In 1874, before Wilde went up to Oxford, he spent several weeks helping Mahaffy edit his forthcoming book, *Social Life in Greece*, which was one of the earliest texts to describe and discuss Greek love (although Mahaffy describes it as "that strange and to us revolting perversion").

Mahaffy disapproved of James Joyce, a student at University College, the Catholic institution on St. Stephen's Green and cited him as proof that "it was a mistake to establish a separate university for the aborigines of this island—for the corner-boys who spit in the Liffey."

For much of the nineteenth and twentieth centuries Trinity was associated with an anti-Catholic ethos and was perceived to be hostile to Irish language and Gaelic traditions.

The year 2004 was the centenary of the admission of women to Trinity. Today, women constitute sixty per cent of the student population. Alice Oldham (1850-1907) was among the first nine women graduates of the Royal University of Ireland in 1884. She was a school teacher at Alexandra College and a campaigner for women's university education. In 1897 she wrote:

> [T]here are causes other than the need for bread. We have seen in our own day a great advance made by all the subject and more helpless classes towards a freer richer life, and fuller personal development. Women share in this democratic advance, and I can no more see how we can arrest it—were it desirable to do so—in their case, than we can in the case of the working classes. We cannot and should not hinder the aspiration for more active life and greater mental acquirement; but we can and should train and direct this new energy and growth, so that it may become a blessing and not a detriment to society. Without education this activity may produce mere eccentricity, political faddism, philanthropic hysteria, and busy-body shallow restlessness in women. We can as yet hardly estimate the good which solid intellectual training will enable it to effect in public and private life.

Women were admitted to lectures in 1899 and subsequently argued for full equality. In James Joyce's story "The Dead" (Dubliners,

1914), Gabriel Conroy dances with Miss Ivors, a young nationalist woman with whom he studies at university. Many of Joyce's female contemporaries became activists in nationalist and suffrage movements, notably Hanna Sheehy Skeffington, whose husband Frank had published, in 1901, a pamphlet on women's education in tandem with a pamphlet by Joyce on Irish literature and the university question.

The James Ussher Library, Trinity's first twenty-first-century building, was officially opened by the President of Ireland, Mary McAleese, in April 2004. It is the third library to be opened in Trinity's 400-year history. The eight-storey, €27-million building provides 9,500 square metres of accommodation for staff and students of the College, and moved a large percentage of the library's printed book holdings from closed to open access. The James Ussher Library also houses the Glucksman Map Library, Ireland's largest map collection, with more than 650,000 printed and digital items in its care, dating from the sixteenth century to the present day. Designed by McCullough Mulvin Keane Murphy Duff, a collaboration of two Dublin architects' firms, the library won the Downes Bronze Medal from the Architectural Association of Ireland.

Exit Trinity into Nassau Street and follow the wall and railings of Trinity College past the entrance to the new Arts Building. To the left is College Park with its playing fields and the cricket pitch from which, tradition claims, W. G. Grace once hit a six clear over the railings and through a window of the Kildare Street Club, to the alarm of its members.

Streets around Trinity
The first building in South Leinster Street, at the end of the railings, was once Finn's Hotel, where James Joyce's wife Nora Barnacle worked as a chambermaid. Left in Lincoln Place is the Dental Hospital of Ireland, established in 1879 and moved to Lincoln Place in 1895. To the left is Westland Row with Pearse Station, formerly known as Westland Row Station, the terminus for the first commuter train in the world, which made its maiden voyage from Dublin to Kingstown (Dún Laoghaire) on 17 December 1834. 21 Westland Row was the birthplace of Oscar Wilde (1854-1900), although Wilde sometimes later claimed to have been born at his parents' later, more prestigious address, 1 Merrion Square.

36 Westland Row, on the opposite side of the street, built in 1771, has been the home since 1871 of the Royal Irish Academy of Music, which was founded in 1848 as the Irish Academy of Music. The academy offer degree courses in conjunction with Trinity College Dublin and Dublin City University. The interior has fine plasterwork by Michael Stapleton and decoration in the style of Peter de Gree and Angelica Kaufmann.

Sweeney's Pharmacy at 1 Lincoln Place is where, in *Ulysses*, Leopold Bloom obtains the cake of lemon soap which travels with him for the rest of the day. The shop is still fitted as it was in 1904, and lemon soap remains available.

Merrion Square
A right hand turn leads towards Merrion Square, which was planned in 1762 for Lord Fitzwilliam. Many of the houses still have their fine Georgian railings, and a few have the ironwork balconies which became fashionable along with the floor-length windows of the late Georgian period. The houses are faced with handmade bricks produced in brickworks around the city. The public park in the centre belonged for some time to the Church and was presented to Dublin Corporation by Archbishop Dermot Ryan, after whom it is named. In the Great Famine of the 1840s soup kitchens were set up in the park to help alleviate the suffering.

1 Merrion Square, the corner house, was the residence of Sir William Wilde (1815-76), a prominent eye-surgeon and antiquarian, with his wife, Jane (c. 1821-96), who in her early adult life published nationalist poetry in *The Nation* under the name, "Speranza". This address was the childhood home of their son Oscar Wilde, the playwright. The Wilde parents had their own share of scandal when Sir William was accused of drugging and raping a patient. Mary Travers did not make the charge to the police, but sued Lady Wilde for libel in 1864. Travers won, but was awarded only a farthing in damages. Whatever the justice of the charge, it seems to have met with some scepticism. There is a colourful sculpture of Oscar Wilde languishing across a boulder in Merrion Square.

Among other notable residents of the Square were Sir Jonah Barrington (no. 42); the lawyer and politician Daniel O'Connell, who secured Catholic emancipation in 1829 (no. 58, now owned and

refurbished by the University of Notre Dame, Indiana); the novelist, Joseph Sheridan Le Fanu (no. 70); the sculptor Andrew O'Connor (no. 77); the discoverer of wave mechanics and Nobel Prize winner for Physics, Erwin Schrodinger (no. 65); and another Nobel Prize winner, the poet and playwright William Butler Yeats (no. 82).

The National Gallery of Ireland on Merrion Square West was built from 1859-1864 as a public testimonial to William Dargan (1799-1867), the designer of Ireland's railways and organizer of the Dublin Exhibition of 1853. Dargan's statue stands outside. The playwright George Bernard Shaw (1856-1950), who bequeathed one-third of the royalties from his literary estate to the gallery as an acknowledgement of its role in his education, is also commemorated by a statue. (The Shaw birthplace at 33 Synge Street is now open to the public). Another benefactor was Sir Alfred Chester Beatty (1875-1968), who in addition to establishing the Chester Beatty Library of Oriental Art, donated many works to the National Gallery. The Gallery was built to the design of Francis Fowke (1823-1865), an engineer in the Science and Art

Department in London, who based his plans on those earlier submitted by Charles Lanyon. The building has been extended several times, most lately into the Millennium Wing in 2002.

The gallery has a good selection of European painting since the Renaissance, with Italian baroque and Dutch painting both particularly well represented. The collection of Irish paintings since the eighteenth century is very extensive. The work of Jack B. Yeats (1871-1957), brother of W. B. Yeats, is especially prominent and the gallery has recently established a Yeats Museum.

Among Irish painters Yeats is one who has produced many scenes of the city. One of his best-known images is *The Liffey Swim* (1923). Yeats was a competitor for Ireland at the VIII Olympiad in Paris in 1924, although not in sport. From 1912 to 1948, in addition to athletic competitions, artists could compete in the areas of architecture, sculpture, painting, music and literature. Each work had to be related to sport, and Yeats won the Silver Medal for Painting for *The Liffey Swim*. The picture places the implied spectator among a group of Dubliners, leaning over the quayside walls and watching the swimmers approaching through the water. Yeats was deeply interested in the tension between individual and group identities, as felt in crowds, and by the particular forms of forgetting and remembering the self that occur during sporting events and other moments of spectatorship. Several of his paintings of horse and dog racing show crowds dispersing, and could be described as meditations on disappointment. In *The Liffey Swim* the backs and side faces of the viewers are still rapt in hope and attention, but by placing the spectators at a significant distance from the swimmers, Yeats queries the meaning of this involvement.

Opposite the gallery, the Rutland Fountain was designed in 1791 by H. A. Baker, a pupil of James Gandon. The fountain depicts "The Marquis of Granby relieving a distressed soldier and his family." The medallions and figurative panels on the fountain are decorated with Coade stone, the invention of George and Eleanor Coade, who made casts using a secret recipe which produced a very tough material. Coade stone was at the height of its popularity in the 1780s, and other examples can be seen decorating the Rotunda.

Merrion Square is celebrated for its fine Georgian doors, which provide one of the city's iconic images. Many of the door cases are carved from Portland stone, a fine, easily carved white limestone quarried in the South of England. These doorways, with their columns, fanlights, recesses and decorative carving, are the most elaborate features of the otherwise simple, elegant façades of the houses in the square. The fanlights are particularly lovely, not least because each one, handmade, is different, and so one gets the pleasure of an extraordinary variety within the simple structure. The original glass was hand-blown and where it survives the fanlights have a subtle reflection. The square retains its antique granite pavement. An act of parliament in 1774 regulated the paving of the city's streets, and many pavements from that period are heavy granite quarried at Dalkey, Ticknock or other small local quarries.

Leinster House, beside the National Gallery, was designed by Richard Cassels in 1745 for the Earl of Kildare. The projecting bow on the northern side of the house is said to be the prototype for the bow-fronted White House in Washington, DC. The architect of the White House was James Hoban (1762-1832), who studied architecture at the Dublin Society's School, where he won a prize in 1780. In 1792 Hoban won the competition for the design of the White House. Originally, Leinster House had two small wings but these have been replaced with the large blocks of the National Library and Museum.

In the 1740s the north side of the city was the most fashionable area, and Lord Kildare's friends questioned the advisability of his building a town house in what was then almost open country. "Wherever I go," said the Earl, "they will follow." In 1785 Richard Crosbie (1755-1800) became the first Irishman to succeed in making an ascent in a hot air balloon—others had tried. Crosbie set off from the lawn of Leinster House. The land to the north and east of the square remained relatively underdeveloped in the eighteenth century, and it was reported that in the high tides and floods of 1792 the Duke of Leinster succeeded in sailing a boat from Ringsend through a breach in the river wall as far as the Holles Street corner of Merrion Square.

The Fitzgerald family, who were Earls of Kildare and Dukes of Leinster, lived at Leinster House for nearly seventy years. One famous resident was Lord Edward Fitzgerald, the leader of the United Irishmen, fatally wounded while being arrested for his part in the 1798 rebellion.

In 1814 Leinster House was acquired by the Royal Dublin Society, from whom it was bought by the Irish government in 1925 to become the seat of the national parliament, Oireachtas na hÉireann. The

Oireachtas consists of two chambers, the Dáil (lower house) and the Seanad (upper house or senate). The granite memorial outside on Leinster Lawn commemorates Arthur Griffith, Kevin O'Higgins and Michael Collins, who were among the founders of the modern Irish state.

Leinster House has two main entrances. One is on Kildare Street, where it is flanked to the left by the National Library, and to the right by the National Museum. The official entrance is the Garden Front, the original main door of the building, which looks across a broad lawn, Leinster Lawn, to Merrion Square. Viewed from here, to the left is the National Gallery with the Natural History Museum to the right. The original building comprises three storeys over a basement, is rectangular in shape, with a circular bow projecting on the north (Trinity College) end. All the ornamental parts and the Kildare Street front of Leinster House are of Portland stone. The greater part of the building is of limestone from Ardbraccan, County Meath.

In the entrance hall hangs an original framed copy of the Easter 1916 Proclamation of the Irish Republic, alongside portraits of two founders of the Irish state, Michael Collins and Cathal Brugha. The Dáil Chamber was originally the lecture theatre of the Royal Dublin Society. The room is octagonal in shape, and its original seating capacity was 700. Little alteration was needed to adapt it for parliamentary purposes: the floor was raised and the seating capacity reduced. The Seanad Chamber was once used as a ballroom when owned by the Duke of Leinster. The walls of the chamber are plain, reflecting its use by the Royal Dublin Society as a picture gallery. In each chamber the speaker uses a reproduction of an ancient Irish bell: in the Dáil it is a copy of a bell from Lough Lene Castle now in the National Museum, and in the Seanad is a reproduction in somewhat less than half size of a bronze bell formerly known as the Clog Beannaighthe (blessed bell) and now more generally as the Bell of Armagh.

On the foundation stone of Leinster House the architect, Richard Cassels, placed a Latin inscription which reads in translation:

The house,
of which this stone is the foundation,
James, twentieth Earl of Kildare,
caused to be erected in Molesworth's field,

in the year of our Lord 1747.
Hence learn, whenever, in some unhappy day,
you light on the ruins of so great a mansion,
of what worth he was who built it,
and how frail all things are,
when such memorials of such men cannot outlive misfortune.
By Richard Castle, Architect

Next to Leinster House is the Natural History Museum. The building was designed by Sir William Frederick Clarendon and opened to the public in 1857. It has been nicknamed the "The Dead Zoo". The collection includes hundreds of stuffed and imaginatively mounted animals, birds and insects—many of them hunting trophies—as well as giant deer (Irish Elk) skeletons and the fine Blaschka glass models of marine life. Recent renovations have restored it to some of its Victorian splendour as a cabinet museum, but with a new message fostering the celebration of biodiversity.

Merrion Street continues up towards Baggot Street. No 24 is one of the several reputed birthplaces of Arthur Wellesley, Duke of Wellington and the victor of the Battle of Waterloo. Sigmund Freud discusses a joke about Wellington in his *Jokes and Their Relation to the Unconscious* (1905):

Von Falke brought home a particularly good example of representa-
tion by the opposite from a journey to Ireland, an example in which
no use whatever is made of words with double meaning. The scene
was a wax-work show (as it might be, Madame Tussaud's). The
guide was conducting a company of old and young visitors from figure
to figure and commenting on them: "This is the Duke of Wellington
and his horse," he explained. Whereupon a young lady asked: "Which
is the Duke of Wellington and which is his horse?" "Just as you like,
my pretty child," was the reply. "You pays your money and you takes
your choice."

24 Merrion Street is now part of the five-star Merrion Hotel, which occupies four former town houses, built in the 1760s by Lord Monck (Charles Stanley Monck) for wealthy Irish merchants and nobility. He lived in no. 22, which became known as Monck House. 24

Upper Merrion Street was leased to Garrett Wellesley, Earl of Mornington, in 1769; it has since been known as Mornington House. The Merrion Hotel houses a remarkable art collection, one of the most important private collections in Ireland. Work by Paul Henry (1876-1958), Nathaniel Hone (1831-1917), Mainie Jellet (1897-1944), Sir John Lavery (1856-1941) Louis le Brocquy (1916 -), William Leech (1881-1968), Daniel Maclise (1806-70), Jack B. Yeats (1871-1957) Roderic O'Conor (1860-1940), Mary Swanzy (1882-1978), William Scott (1913-1989) and Daniel O'Neill (1920-1974) can be seen in the hotel's restaurants and reception rooms.

From Merrion Square South one can walk along Mount Street Upper. No. 29 (the corner house on Fitzwilliam Street) has been refurbished with a collection of artefacts and works of art of the period 1790-1820 to create the atmosphere and appearance of a typical middle-class home of the time.

St. Stephen's Church, known because of its shape as the "pepper canister", was designed in 1824 by John Bowden in neo-classical style. Inside is a handsome canopied pulpit carved in Italian rosewood and walnut. Outside there is an unusual decorated tripod oil lamp standard, one of Dublin's many beautiful pieces of ironwork.

Continuing to the left of the church you will come to the Grand Canal. Beside the canal is a seat dedicated to the memory of Patrick Kavanagh, who lived near here and wrote "O commemorate me where there is water, canal water preferably..." There is, rather disconcertingly, a life-size sculpture of Kavanagh, sitting on his seat. Directly opposite the Kavanagh seat is one in memory of Percy French (1854-1920), the songwriter., whose lyrics include the immortal *Are Ye Right There, Michael?*

> *Are ye right there, Michael, are ye right?*
> *Do you think that we'll be there before the night?*
> *Ye've been so long in startin',*
> *That ye couldn't say for sartin*
> *Still ye might now, Michael, so ye might!*

Close to the canal is Herbert Place, birthplace of the novelist Elizabeth Bowen (1899-1973). Her memoir *Seven Winters* describes the house at Herbert Place, where her family spent their winters, while their summers were spent in their big house at Bowen's Court, County Cork. Her other Dublin book is a history of the Shelbourne Hotel on St. Stephen's Green.

Fitzwilliam Street, together with Merrion Square East and Fitzwilliam Place, was the longest complete Georgian thoroughfare in Europe until the 1960s, when a row of houses was replaced by a modern office block. Fitzwilliam House at no. 6 was for some years the home of Margaret Burke Sheridan (1889-1958), the Irish prima donna. After hearing her in *Madame Butterfly* in Milan, Puccini coached her in 1923 for the title role in *Manon Lescaut*, which became her most famous part. From then she became famous for her renditions of Puccini's work. Toscanini called her the "Empress of Ireland". She retired in 1936 and came back to Ireland, where she established a school for singers. John Ryan describes her in her later years:

> *Margaret Burke Sheridan, the famous soprano, was a delightful ornament of the scene. Brought up as an orphan by the Dominican nuns in the West of Ireland (who were intelligent enough to know that she had a unique gift for singing) she was, thanks to their encouragement, able to study music and singing in Dublin. In time she became a professional, joining the La Scala opera while yet scarcely more than a girl. It was said that she was a great pet of Puccini and his favourite "Butterfly".*
>
> *Once, to my amazement, she sang the whole of the aria One Fine Day for Miss Whelan, the manageress, and myself in the downstairs lounge of the Monument Café in Grafton Street. It was a thrilling experience and, even after so many years, I find it hard to convince myself that it really took place. Ethereal happenings did not seem to belong in such mundane surroundings—but she would not have agreed with me there.*
>
> *Opera is a Tower of Babel in which the Italian tongue predominates. While Margaret Burke Sheridan spoke—or rather sang (for she was a thrush really)—in the five or six languages in which divas communicate—hopping from one linguistic branch to another—her shapely hands sculpted the missing parts of the conversation. She had lost little of her legendary beauty at this time (it was said that one of her lovers had thrown himself from the top of the Savoy Hotel in*

*London) so that physical proximity with her radiant beauty was
enough to make a green young man giddy.*

Fitzwilliam Square

The earliest houses in Fitzwilliam Square date from 1714, but the
square was the last of Dublin's Georgian squares to be completed,
taking its final form in 1830. Most of the houses have their original
fanlights, some still with box-shaped glass recesses in which a lamp
would have been placed. The houses have elaborate door-knockers and
iron foot-scrapers. There are some examples of a simple security device
in the form of a fan-shaped arrangement of spikes set into the wall
beside a window. Fitzwilliam Square also displays a great range of
ornamental iron balconies in a variety of styles. The park in the centre
of the square is private and is reserved for the use of the residents. The
artist Mainie Jellett lived at no. 36, on the west side and William
Dargan, the railway designer, lived at no. 2, on the east.

Mary Harriet (Mainie) Jellett (1897-1944) was born in the house
on Fitzwilliam Square, the eldest of four daughters. She was educated at
home and then with various art teachers in Dublin and London. From
1923 she regularly exhibited her abstract art in Dublin, and became the
leader of the Modern Movement in Ireland. Some of her paintings can
be seen in the National Gallery. She died of cancer at the age of 47 and
is buried at St. Fintan's Churchyard in Sutton.

On the corner of the square as you return to Fitzwilliam Street is
no. 18, once the studio of Jack B. Yeats. The final stretch of the street
is called Fitzwilliam Place. Sir Richard Griffith lived here at no. 2 and
the naturalist, Robert Lloyd Praeger at no. 19. Sir Richard Griffith
(1784-1878) has been described as the father of Irish geology. He had
a number of jobs in engineering, road-building and surveying, and in
1811 he began the construction of a pioneering geological map of
Ireland, which was published in 1838-9. Praeger (1865-1953) was a
leading Irish naturalist, who moved in 1893 from Belfast to Dublin,
where he worked at the National Library, becoming its director in
1920. He was also President of the Royal Irish Academy in the 1930s.
He was a botanist who explored many previously unsurveyed parts of
the country. He was also a gifted writer who was able to produce
popular as well as more scholarly accounts of his interests, and he was a
founding member of the monthly periodical, *Irish Naturalist*.

28 Fitzwilliam Place, with its curious neo-gothic design, was the city home of Edward Martyn (1859-1923), the playwright who was a co-founder of the Abbey Theatre.

St. Stephen's Green

Earlsfort Terrace, on the corner of St. Stephen's Green, contains the National Concert Hall, formerly the principal building of University College Dublin. It was built between 1863 and 1865 as the central hall for the Great Exhibition and acquired by the university in 1908.

The central park of St. Stephen's Green is one of three ancient commons in the city. The area was levelled and walled in 1678 and a ditch dug round it. The four sides, each a quarter of a mile in length, were known as Leeson's Walk, French Walk, Beaux' Walk and Monks' Walk. There was no overall plan to the buildings as there was in the Fitzwilliam developments, and the Green is notable for the variety in age and style of its houses. The south and west sides were the earliest built and the soonest replaced. The park had by the end of 1814 deteriorated to such a state that the Corporation allowed the residents of the Green to rent it and take over its maintenance. The present railings were then erected, together with the series of granite bollards (originally linked by iron chains) around the outside.

Further improvement took place inside, and the park remained private until 1880 when Sir Arthur Guinness (1840-1915), Lord Ardilaun, bought out the lease, had the present lake and gardens laid out, and opened the 22-acre park to the public. Opposite the College of Surgeons is a seated statue of Lord Ardilaun looking in the direction of the Guinness brewery at St. James' Gate.

The Green has a W. B. Yeats memorial garden with a sculpture by Henry Moore, a bust of James Joyce facing his former university at Newman House, a memorial to the Fenian leader Jeremiah O'Donovan Rossa near the Grafton Street corner, and a group representing the Three Fates inside the Leeson Street gate, a gift from the German people in thanks for Irish help to refugees after the Second World War. The Merrion Row corner features a bronze statue of Theobald Wolfe Tone, the republican leader of 1798, and a memorial to the great famine of 1845-50. Near the centre of the park is a garden for the blind, with a curved seat commemorating Louie Bennett and Helen Chenevix. Louie Bennett (1870-1956) was a feminist, trade union activist and novelist. She was a member of the Irish Women's Suffrage Federation, secretary of the Union of Democratic Control, an editor on the *Irish Citizen*, and a member of the Irish Women Workers' Union, which she restructured with Helen Chenevix (1890-1963). Both came from prosperous Protestant families (Chenevix was the daughter of a bishop). Both attended Alexandra College, though twenty years apart. Chenevix was one of the first female graduates of Trinity College Dublin.

In 1918 the two women undertook the re-organization of the Irish Women Workers' Union, following the imprisonment, after 1916, of Helena Molony, its General Secretary, who had taken part in the Easter Rising. Louie Bennett's work with the IWWU, despite the nearly forty years she was to spend at the helm, was less as an organizer in a day-to-day sense than as a leader who, despite many endeavours to do so, was unable to secure any significant alternative position of public power. Bennett and Chenevix were part of an influential network of lesbians living in Dublin, many of whom met each other through their involvement with the suffrage movement and many of whom later became actively involved in the Revolution, in trade unions, local government and issues related to poverty such as healthcare and social housing. These Irish lesbians visited and were in contact with other lesbians and feminists in Europe and America and the UK who were also involved in addressing social inequities and were hence part of a broader network that shared ideas, information and encouragement. Most notable among them are Dr. Kathleen Lynn and her partner Madeleine ffrench-Mullen, suffragists, members of the Irish Citizen Army, founders of the pioneering hospital St. Ultan's; nurse Elizabeth O' Farrell and her partner Julia Grenan, buried together in the Republican grave plot at Glasnevin; Helena Moloney, republican revolutionary, trade unionist, Abbey actress and her partner, psychiatrist Dr. Evelyn O'Brien. Elizabeth O'Farrell, incidentally, was famously cut out of the photograph of Patrick Pearse's surrender from the GPO in 1916.

Iveagh House and Newman House

Nos. 80 and 81 St. Stephen's Green South mark the site of Iveagh House. No. 80 was originally built in 1736 as a town mansion for Robert Clayton, Bishop of Cork and Ross. It was acquired in 1856 by Benjamin Lee Guinness (father of Lord Ardilaun) who amalgamated it with the adjoining house, no. 81, to build the present Iveagh House. In 1939 the second Earl of Iveagh presented it to the government and it now houses the Department of Foreign Affairs.

Guinness, for visitors the Dublin drink *par excellence*, dates from the eighteenth century. The founder of the brewery was Arthur Guinness (1725-1803), who moved into a small brewery in James's Street in 1759. The dark-coloured beer brewed by Guinness became known as stout in the 1820s. The founder's son Arthur (1768-1855) took over the business in the 1790s and built it up into a large enterprise. Arthur was also a governor of the Bank of Ireland and active in politics and philanthropy. He was a Liberal who supported Catholic Emancipation and the 1832 Reform Bill. The third generation of Guinness entrepreneurs was led by the brothers Richard Samuel Guinness (1797-1857) and Benjamin Lee Guinness (1798-1868). Richard became an MP and Benjamin was Lord Mayor of Dublin in 1851, and Conservative MP for Dublin 1865-8. Benjamin contributed large sums of money for the restoration of St. Patrick's Cathedral. In 1868 the brewery and business was taken over by his two sons Arthur (1840-1915) and Edward Cecil (1847-1927). Arthur became Conservative MP for Dublin in 1874 and was created Baron Ardilaun in 1880. His philanthropic projects in the service of the city included the building of the Coombe hospital, the donation of St. Stephen's Green as a public park and the restoration of Marsh's Library.

This, the oldest public library in Ireland, was founded by Archbishop Narcissus Marsh (1638-1713) in 1701 and housed in a Georgian brick building beside St. Patrick's Cathedral. The interior has changed very little over three centuries, and the wire cages in which readers were locked with rare books have been retained. The library houses an important collection of three hundred Irish manuscripts and over 25,000 books relating to the sixteenth, seventeenth and early eighteenth centuries.

Arthur Guinness withdrew from the business which was then managed by Edward Cecil, who was created Baron Iveagh in 1891, and Earl Iveagh in 1919. Guinness became a public company in 1886, but the Guinness family remained prominent in the business until the 1980s. The Guinness brewery is now part of the giant drinks company, Diageo. As a drink Guinness has been through many incarnations, with bottles, cans, draught stout, warm and cold beer all having their day and their advocates. The notion that Guinness does not travel has been part of an Irish tourist campaign, and Guinness' own clever marketing strategy has produced some of the most successful advertising campaigns in history.

Nos. 85 and 86 together are known as Newman House, home of the Catholic University (later University College), which was founded in 1850 with Dr. (later Cardinal) John Henry Newman as its rector. The priest and poet Gerard Manley Hopkins (1844-99) was a lecturer here. No 85 is among the oldest surviving houses on this side of St. Stephen's Green and contains admired plasterwork by the Lafranchini brothers, Paolo (1695-1770) and Filippo (1702-1779), Swiss stuccodores who brought Italian baroque figurative plaster work to Ireland in 1739 and had a huge influence on Irish plaster workers later in the century. It was built for Hugh Montgomery, a wealthy landowner and member of parliament for County Fermanagh. This was one of the first town houses built by Richard Cassels (a.k.a. Castle, c.1690-1751), the Huguenot architect from Germany, who came to Ireland to work on Edward Lovett Pearce's parliament building, and who also designed Leinster House and, later, the Dining Hall at Trinity College. This is a smaller house on a more intimate scale.

No 86 was built in 1765 for Richard "Burnchapel" Whaley. Whaley was a virulent anti-Catholic who swore never to let a Papist across his threshold and earned his nickname by burning chapels in County Wicklow. His son, "Jerusalem" Whaley, was a founder of the Hellfire Club. Legend tells that Jerusalem threw a crucifix through the front window of no. 86 on Maundy Thursday, and ever since on the same day its image is still to be seen there. It is larger and more airy than its neighbour. It has good plaster work attributed to Robert West (d. 1790), one of a Dublin family of stuccodores, who was associated with the creation of stucco variants of French rococo *boiserie* or wainscoting. The lion over the door is by John van Nost the Younger (c.1712-1780), a sculptor who moved to Dublin in about 1750 and created a number of important works, including an equestrian statue of George II that stood in St. Stephen's Green for nearly two centuries until it was destroyed by dynamite in 1937, and a life-size statue of George III as a Roman emperor, now in the National Gallery of Ireland.

Newman House, which belongs to University College Dublin, has recently been restored and is open to the public.

John Henry Newman (1801-90) famously converted from Anglicanism to Catholicism and was ordained a priest in 1847, returning from Rome to establish oratories at Birmingham and London. In 1845 the British Prime Minister Robert Peel had passed a statute to establish colleges at Belfast, Cork and Galway, to be known as Queen's Colleges. This provision was designed to satisfy Catholic demands for access to university education, and undermine the repeal movement. In order to appease Protestants the act placed restrictions on theological teachings, and thus alienated the Catholic hierarchy. In April 1851 Newman received a letter from Paul Cullen, Archbishop of Armagh, asking advice on the setting up of a university in Dublin. Cullen had been directed towards Newman by the Pope. Later that summer Cullen visited Newman at his oratory in Birmingham and persuaded him to come to Ireland in the autumn. During the first week in October Newman attended meetings on the university at Thurles and on 12 November he recorded in his diary that he had been "Appointed Head of the new University". Between 10 May and 7 June Newman delivered in Dublin the first five of his Discourses on the Scope and Nature of University Education, later to form part of his Idea of a University. The lectures were given on five successive Mondays, beginning on 10 May, in the Rotunda Hospital. Newman wrote to his friend, Ambrose St. John: "The lecture, I suppose has been a hit... all the intellect, almost of Dublin, was there." Later in a letter to another of his friends he wrote, "I have prospered here in my lectures beyond my most sanguine expectations."

In 1852 Cullen was installed as Archbishop of Dublin, and Newman was formally appointed Rector of the Catholic University of Ireland, which opened on 3 November 1854 at 86 St. Stephen's Green. There were faculties of theology, philosophy and letters, and science. The Catholic University Medical School was opened the following year in Cecilia Street and the University Church on St. Stephen's Green was opened in 1856. Newman was rector for seven years, during which time he came into conflict with Cullen and the Catholic hierarchy, who did not share his vision for education and the involvement of the laity. He eventually resigned and returned to the oratory in Birmingham.

Manley Hopkins was another Englishman who converted to Catholicism, in his case at Oxford. He became a Jesuit priest and came to Ireland as a lecturer at the Catholic University towards the end of his career, when he was a lonely figure with no great interest in Irish affairs. When he first arrived in Dublin he wrote to his friend the poet Robert Bridges:

> *The house we are in, the College, is a sort of ruin and for purposes of study very nearly naked. And I have more money to buy books than room to put them in.*
>
> *I have been warmly welcomed and most kindly treated. But Dublin itself is a joyless place and I think in my heart as smoky as London is: I had fancied it quite different.*

Hopkins is buried in the Jesuit plot at Glasnevin cemetery.

On the pavement opposite Newman House is a seat dedicated to James Joyce, one of the university's more famous students, and his father, John Stanislaus Joyce (1849-1931).

The Irish Universities Act (1908) established University College Dublin (successor to the Catholic University) as one of the constituent colleges of the National University of Ireland. In 1964 the university moved to a site at Belfield, Mount Merrion, which is now the largest university campus in Ireland. In 1997 The Universities Act conferred independent university status on the college.

The Royal College of Surgeons and the Shelbourne Hotel

The Royal College of Surgeons in Ireland, halfway along the west side of the Green, was originally designed in 1806 by Edward Parke, but twenty years later was redesigned and extended by William Murray (whose son designed the College of Physicians in Kildare Street). Figures representing Medicine and Health stand above the pediment. In the Easter Rising of 1916 the college was occupied by rebel troops under Constance Markievicz. There was fighting here, and at the Shelbourne Hotel, and bullet-scars can still be seen on the columns. The Shelbourne Hotel is a prominent Victorian building with striking figures of Nubian princesses and their slaves. The constitution of the Irish Free State was drafted in the Shelbourne. Elizabeth Bowen wrote its history in the 1940s, presenting it as Dublin's Algonquin:

> *Dublin is full of oddities—and is it not something to be so spry, inquisitive, gay? In this majestic drawing room, genius as well as*

fashion has held its court—Yeats here sat, reading his poems aloud to a friend. The coffee-room rings and has rung with grand racy talk. Through the Hall flow and have flowed prelates, peers, politicians, sportsmen, soldiers, tourists, journalists, financiers, athletes, aesthetes, diplomats, debutantes, dramatists and all the rest of us. In the pageant of figures, the sea of faces today and yesterday merge.

The Huguenot Cemetery

Close to the Shelbourne is a tiny cemetery, the oldest Huguenot non-conformist burial ground in Europe. Huguenots were French Protestants who adopted the Calvinist form of the Reformed faith in the sixteenth century. Louis XIV's 1685 Edict of Fontainebleau, closing Huguenot churches and schools, drove about a third of the Huguenot population of France into exile. Under the patronage of the Lord Lieutenant, the Duke of Ormond, who had spent much of the interregnum in exile in France, a group of Huguenot settlers came to Dublin and were employed as weavers. An Act to Encourage the Settlement of Huguenots in Ireland was passed on 3 November 1692. Later Huguenots, notably the La Touche family, became prominent in banking. Le Fanu, Rocque, D'Olier and Boileau are among other well-known Dublin Huguenot family names.

In the seventeenth century the Huguenots worshipped at the Chapel of St. Brigide's, in a private house in Wood Street, and at the Chapel of Lucy Lane. The former congregation moved to Peter Street in 1711. Over the entrance to the Huguenot Cemetery the date 1693 is etched in granite. On the left hand side by the entrance is a limestone triptych carved with the family names of all those believed to be buried in the cemetery. Many Huguenots did not favour headstones, so the location of plots is obscure. There is also a memorial to Jacques Fontaine (1658-1728), who established a classical school on St. Stephen's Green in 1709: "His memoirs stand as a remarkable testimony of the Huguenot experience. This stone given by descendants in America 15th May 1999." There are further Huguenot burial grounds in Dublin at Cabbage Garden (Cathedral Lane) and at St. Luke and St. Nicholas Without (The Coombe).

Dawson Street
Dawson Street runs north off St. Stephen's Green. The Mansion House was built in 1710 for Joshua Dawson, after whom this street was named, and was purchased from him in 1715 by Dublin Corporation to become the official residence of the Lord Mayor of Dublin. The dining room has a handsome fireplace, decorated with caryatids and a reclining sphinx. The Round Room to the left was built in 1821 for a reception for George IV, and saw the first assembly of Dáil Éireann, the Irish parliament, on 21 January 1919, when the Declaration of Independence was adopted. It is now mainly used for receptions and exhibitions.

At no. 19 is the Royal Irish Academy, founded in May 1785 by the Royal Dublin Society, with Lord Charlemont as its first president. In 1851 it moved from its first premises on Grafton Street to the present building. Housed in the Academy is a remarkable library of Irish manuscripts, among the most precious of which is the Psalter of St. Columcille, an incomplete copy of the Vulgate version of the Psalms. Many of the objects donated to the Academy are on show in the National Museum, where they were transferred in 1890. These include the Cross of Cong, a twelfth-century processional cross containing a relic allegedly of the True Cross, and first recorded at Cong (Co. Mayo) in the seventeenth century, often described as the finest example in metalwork of the medieval Irish *Urnes* style; and the Ardagh Chalice, an eighth-century communion cup composed of gold, silver, brass, bronze, copper and lead, with an exceptionally fine filigree decoration. In its early years the Academy pioneered scholarship into the Irish language and culture, and early members included Charles O'Conor (1710-91), antiquarian and founder member of the Catholic Association, and George Petrie (1790-1866), the antiquarian scholar and collector of Irish traditional music. The RIA is the country's leading learned society and has numbered many outstanding scholars in its membership. Among its honorary members in the past have been Goethe, Jakob Grimm, Albert Einstein and Max Born. It is now financed by the government through the Higher Education Authority.

19 Dawson Street is a mid-eighteenth-century house, originally built for Lord Northland. The reading room and meeting room were added at the rear in 1852-4. The president's chair was formerly the Lord Chancellor's throne in the Irish House of Lords; the chandelier once hung in the Hall of Requests, and some of the benches from the Lords and Commons are also here.

Next to the Academy, St. Anne's Church was built in 1720 to the design of Isaac Wills. The present façade dates from 1868 when it was rebuilt by Deane and Woodward. Lord Newtown left a bequest to the church in 1723 to buy bread for the poor, and a special shelf erected beside the altar for this bread may still be seen today.

Felicia Hemans (1793-1835), born in Liverpool but having lived most of her life in Wales, with which country she is most closely associated, spent the last four years of her life at 21 Dawson Street, and is buried in St. Anne's. There is a stained glass window dedicated to her in the church. Hemans was one of the most important literary figures of the early nineteenth century. A best-selling poet in England and America, she was regarded as leading female poet in her day and celebrated as the epitome of national "feminine" values. Charles Dickens refused to subscribe to the window appeal, saying "I would rather read Mrs Hemans by her own light than through the colours of any painted window that ever was or will be contracted for." For most of the twentieth century Hemans suffered critical neglect and was best remembered through parodies of her most famous poem, "Casabianca" ("The boy stood on the burning deck") but her star is rising again.

Two notable marriages took place in St. Anne's. On 21 July 1785, 21-year-old Theobald Wolfe Tone married 16-year-old Martha

Witherington (whom he later renamed Matilda). Tone first saw Witherington sitting in the window of her home at 68 Grafton Street, and struck by her beauty, he determined to be introduced to her. He knew her brother from Trinity and soon became a frequent caller at the house of her father, William Witherington, a woollen draper. The two young people fell in love and "one beautiful morning in the month of July", only a few months after their first meeting, they walked the short distance from Grafton Street to Dawson Street to be married. In spite of this short distance, Martha's family viewed the marriage as an elopement and it caused a breach with the Witherington family that was never really healed. Within a year their first child was born, and the Tones were obliged to spend much of their early married life living with his parents.

On 4 December 1878 Bram Stoker, author of *Dracula* (1897), married Florence Balcombe. Stoker lived nearby at 30 Kildare Street, and also in the elegant Marino Crescent at Clontarf, and there is now a Dracula/Stoker exhibition and heritage centre on Clontarf Road. Florence Balcombe had previously been courted by Oscar Wilde. He wrote about her to a friend: "I am just going out to bring an exquisitely pretty girl to afternoon service in the Cathedral. She is just seventeen with the most perfectly beautiful face I ever saw and not a sixpence of money. I will show you her photograph when I see you next." When Wilde heard of her intended marriage to Stoker, he asked her to return a little gold cross he had given her. Three years later, when Florence was about to make her debut on the stage in London, Wilde asked Ellen Terry to give her a crown of flowers as if they were from Terry herself:

I should like to think that she was wearing something of mine the first night she comes on the stage, that anything of mine should touch her. Of course if you think—but you won't think she will suspect. How could she? She thinks I never loved her, thinks I forget. My God, how could I?

Dawson Street is linked to the parallel Kildare Street via Molesworth Street. Freemasons' Hall has been the home since 1865 of the Grand Lodge of Freemasons in Ireland, the autonomous governing body of the organization, which was established around 1724 and is the second oldest Grand Lodge in the world. The society grew rapidly in the eighteenth century, and there was an explosion of membership in the 1790s after the French Revolution had shown the potential of masonry as a cloak for revolutionary political activity. Henrietta Battier was commissioned to write a poem in honour of freemasonry in 1791, and she took the opportunity to poke a bit of fun at the masons:

> *For the want of integrity some keep at bay,*
> *For Free-Masons always perform what they say;*
> *Unanimous, grateful, pure-hearted, and just,*
> *A Free-Mason always is true to his trust.*
>
> *CHORUS*
> *The dictates of honour still ruling their lives,*
> *No order on earth like Free-Masonry thrives.*

Four major rooms are on view at the Freemasons' Hall, each designed in a different style: classical, ancient Egyptian, medieval gothic and Tudor. There is also a museum with a permanent display on the history of the Order.

Kildare Street

The approach from Molesworth Street leads to the front of Leinster House, flanked by the matching rotundas of the National Museum and National Library. Originally the whole group was owned by the Royal Dublin Society and the central courtyard was open.

The National Museum was built between 1884 and 1890, as was the National Library opposite, to the design of Sir Thomas Deane, the younger (whose father, also Thomas Deane, was Woodward's partner). It has a collection of Celtic antiquities and artefacts from the Iron Age and Bronze Age, together with a range of items excavated from Viking sites in Dublin.

The treasury houses a permanent exhibition of the greatest treasures of early Irish art, including the Ardagh and Derrynaflan Chalices, the Cross of Cong, the Tara Brooch, the Clonmacnois Crozier and St. Patrick's Bell. Opposite the museum, on the other side of Kildare Street, a plaque marks a former residence of Bram Stoker, at no. 30.

The National Library was established under the Dublin Science and Art Museum Act (1877), but its origins can be traced to the library of the Royal Dublin Society. In 1877 a substantial portion of the RDS library was purchased by the State as the foundation of a new national library. The main building opened to the public in 1890. The domed reading room is a comfortable, old-fashioned space, and regular users of the library are well known to one another.

Lady Morgan

Sydney Owenson, Lady Morgan (1783-1859), the novelist, lived at 35 (now 39) Kildare Street. After the publication of her novel, *The Wild Irish Girl* (1806) she became something of a celebrity. She was taken up by an aristocratic couple, the Marquis and Marchioness of Abercorn, who gave her a home. They introduced her to their friend Dr. Charles Morgan, a young widower also brought into the household, and put her under some pressure to marry him. They also managed to secure Morgan a knighthood. In 1812-13, after their marriage, the Morgans set up their own home in Kildare Street, where they lived for 25 years. Morgan was appointed physician to the Marshelsea Prison and also undertook private practice. Lady Morgan's sister, Lady Olivia Clarke, who was also a writer, lived north of the river at a house in Great George Street, and the two women were great entertainers. Lady Morgan was a campaigner for Catholic emancipation and she held salons in her Kildare Street home, gathering together many of the city's liberal opinion-makers. In her *Memoirs* she mentions a street ballad from the late 1820s, which celebrated her fame:

Och, Dublin city there's no doubtin'
Bates every city upon the say;
'Tis there you'll hear O'Connel spoutin';
An' Lady Morgan making tay.

Chapter Four

FROM THE UNION TO THE FAMINE

After the Union

In the early nineteenth century Dublin was transformed from a city confident in itself and its role, full of money and projects, into what Lady Morgan described as "dear dirty Dublin". The vice-regal court was dramatically reduced in pomp, and the absence of the parliament had symbolic as well as literal influence on the city's self-imaginings. Many of the owners of the great houses and estates became greater absentees. Serving the aristocracy was a declining occupation, but there was more call on services for the middle classes. The professions increasingly dominated the city. More Catholics moved into Dublin from what was the perceived over-population of the countryside, and as Catholic political demands became more central to Irish politics Catholic influences on the city's life became more obvious. There had been a majority of Catholic residents in the city since the middle of the eighteenth century, but only after Catholic emancipation in 1829 did this begin to translate into local or national political influence on governance. The energies that had gone into great houses and civic buildings at the end of the previous century were diverted into church building and domestic architecture.

The Act of Union came into effect on 1 January 1801, but perhaps only with the crushing of Robert Emmet's rebellion in 1803 were the revolutionary aspirations of the United Irishmen suppressed for a generation. The emergence of Daniel O'Connell as a Catholic leader changed the aims and strategies of political activism. From the mobilization of the movement for Catholic emancipation nineteenth-century Irish patriotism was to be reformed into a nationalism which placed the needs of the Catholic majority at the centre of its aspirations. After the achievement of Catholic emancipation in 1829, and his election at the head of a small group of 39 Irish anti-Union MPs in 1832, O'Connell turned his attention to a campaign to repeal the Act of Union.

The most significant Irish novelists in the first fifty years of the nineteenth century—Maria Edgeworth, Sydney Owenson (Lady Morgan), Charles Robert Maturin, William Carleton, Gerald Griffin, John and Michael Banim—had relatively little to say about Dublin life, apart from Maturin's (1782-1824) under-rated achievement in *Women; or, Pour et Contre* (1818), which explores Methodist society in Dublin in 1813 through a remarkable description of interiors and dialogue, compensating for the more melodramatic and predictable aspects of the plot. A distinctively Dublin, rather than merely Irish, culture was developed, on the other hand, in the newspapers and periodical press. On the Protestant side, the *Dublin University Magazine* was founded by six Tory dons and undergraduates at Trinity in 1833. It was committed to the intellectual heritage of Protestant Ireland. It was ambivalent about the matter of the Act of Union but interested in asserting the cultural independence of Ireland. Through the 1830s the *DUM* published the work of Samuel Ferguson, James Clarence Mangan, Charles Lever, William Carleton and Sheridan Le Fanu, whose differences make evident the fact that the magazine was committed to a high quality of argument and writing.

In the 1840s the Young Ireland movement focused on *The Nation*, a weekly newspaper founded and owned by Charles Gavan Duffy, in collaboration with Thomas Davis and John Blake Dillon. The writers at *The Nation* believed in a non-sectarian cultural nationalism, and promoted national literature and the Irish language. One of the writers for *The Nation* was Jane Elgee, who later married William Wilde and became the mother of Oscar Wilde. Elgee published some of her poetry and essays under the pseudonym "Speranza". She was not, however, embarrassed to claim authorship of risky pieces. Her article "Jacta Alea Est" (July 1848) was attributed to Gavan Duffy and mentioned in sedition charges against him. When Duffy was interrogated about the article in his prosecution, Elgee rose in the public gallery to claim authorship.

In July 1848 *The Nation* was suppressed because of its revolutionary articles. There was a brief and completely unsuccessful rising by Young Irelanders in July 1848. Thomas Francis Meagher and William Smith O'Brien were deported after the rising; John Mitchel had been deported for treason-felony earlier that year. Mitchel (1815-75) was a solicitor who wrote editorials for *The Nation* and later established the more radical journal, *United Irishman*. Traumatized by the events of the Famine, he became an advocate for revolution. The *United Irishman* was established in February 1848 specifically as an organ of revolution. In May Mitchel was convicted and transported to Tasmania, He escaped to America in 1853 and the following year published his *Jail Journal*, which became a hugely influential text for Irish nationalists.

Between 1845 and 1850 approximately 1.1 million people in Ireland (an eighth of the population) died from famine-related diseases, and a further million emigrated. The famine was triggered by a potato blight, and spread easily though a country with a weak infrastructure. The government's failure to make appropriate interventions aggravated the situation. The greater Dublin area was the only part of the country to see a population rise in the famine decade. People moved into the city in flight from the deprivation in the countryside. Many departed for America on "coffin ships", poorly equipped and rife with disease. The increase in Dublin's population in the famine years exacerbated a nineteenth-century trend for more prosperous citizens to move out to the expanding suburbs whilst the inner city was given over to increasingly dense and impoverished tenement slums. Dublin Corporation governed the city proper alone and was unable to draw on the resources of the independent wealthier suburbs. Many public health projects were thwarted by the Corporation's inability to tax or exploit in other ways wealthier workers and residents.

It is easy to think of Dublin as a miserable, deprived backwater in the nineteenth century, but in areas including medicine, astronomy and engineering, as well as in the arts, there were remarkable achievements.

Emmet's Rebellion
Saturday 23 July 1803

> *"Let my character and my motives repose in obscurity and peace, till other times and other men can do them justice; Then shall my character be vindicated. – Then may my epitaph be written."*

Robert Emmet, Speech from the Dock

On the morning of 23 July Robert Emmet's agents rode from Dublin City into County Dublin, and the adjacent counties of Kildare and

Wicklow to alert his allies that a rising was about to take place and that they were to hold themselves in readiness for the forthcoming fight. Thousands of rebels from the countryside were needed to mass at the White Bull Inn on Thomas Street at 6pm that evening. According to Emmet's plan they would be given weapons and final instructions for the rising itself, scheduled to begin with a strike on Dublin Castle at 9pm.

Robert Emmet (1778-1803) was the son of a prosperous Munster physician, Dr. Robert Emmet. In 1770 Dr. Emmet was appointed state physician and the family moved to 35 Molesworth Street, Dublin. By 1777 the family had moved to a large house on St. Stephen's Green West, where the future revolutionary was born. (A statue of Emmet now stands on St. Stephen's Green opposite the site of his demolished birthplace.) He was the fourth child to survive infancy, and his elder siblings, Christopher Temple, Thomas Addis and Mary Anne were all to influence his political development. It was probably while he was a pupil at Whyte's English Grammar School on Grafton Street that Emmet met the young Thomas Moore of Aungier Street, who later memorialized his friend in poetry. During the American War of Independence the Emmet family sympathized with the rebels and this heightened the growing nationalist tendency in the family's politics. In 1788 Temple Emmet, a brilliant young barrister, died suddenly from smallpox and Thomas Addis Emmet abandoned medicine to retrain as a barrister (he later became Attorney-General of New York State).

In the early 1790s the Emmet home on St. Stephen's Green was a regular meeting place for the leaders of the new Society of United Irishmen, whose objective was to institute a democratic government on the model of revolutionary France or America in Ireland, overturning the sectarian Irish parliament and the English administration. Thomas Addis Emmet joined the United Irishmen and brought Theobald Wolfe Tone, Archibald Hamilton Rowan, William Drennan and Thomas Russell into the Emmet circle. The Emmet home was only a few hundred yards from Leinster House, the Dublin home of the Fitzgerald family. The arrest of Lord Edward Fitzgerald and other leaders in the days before the United Irish rebellion was planned to erupt in Dublin in May 1798 contributed to the low impact of the insurrection in the city itself. Robert Emmet seems to have been active in recruiting for the United Irishmen at Trinity College in this period. Thomas Addis

Emmet was one of the leaders arrested in 1798. He was imprisoned at Fort George in Scotland until 1802. During 1799 Robert Emmet was in hiding as a member of the Executive Directory of the United Irishmen. He seems to have spent some of this time thinking about military tactics.

In 1800 Robert Emmet visited France and in January 1801 he met Napoleon to assure the French leader that the Irish were still ready to support an invasion. Nonetheless, he was to some extent disillusioned with the level of French interest in Ireland. While he was living in Paris he befriended an American inventor, Robert Fulton, who furthered Emmet's interest in military technology. Emmet returned to Ireland in October 1802, when it seemed that war between Britain and France was likely soon to recommence. He contacted other conspirators and they began to plan a *coup d'état* to take place in Dublin when the French invasion landed.

Emmet's father died in December 1802, leaving his son £2,000, which was put towards planning the revolution. The revolutionaries began to lease buildings in which to stockpile weapons. The main depot was on Marshal Lane South, to the rear of the White Bull Inn on Thomas Street.

By the start of July 1803 preparations in the city were well under way, but communication with the French was frustrating and the rebels decided that they had to take the risk of an insurrection in the capital as a first step in a national uprising. They reasoned that it would be very difficult for the authorities to retake the city and that the French would respond to this signal, while the rest of the country would rise. What was not appreciated was whether, following the terrible losses of 1798, other parts of the country would be prepared to rise up without the presence of the French invasion.

On 16 July a rebel depot at 26 Patrick Street accidentally blew up, with two men killed. It was clear that the authorities could not remain in ignorance of the plot for much longer, and this drove the rebels on. The date was fixed for 23 July and messengers were sent around the country to signal the plan. It was crucial to the plot's success that thousands of rebels from Counties Dublin and Kildare should enter the city on 23 July and mass on Thomas Street by 6 o'clock. The rebels were unaware of how advantageous their situation was. Although there had been some intelligence warnings to Dublin Castle about the proposed unrest, there was a failure of communication and planning between the Castle and the army, so that many parts of the city were relatively undefended. Emmet was to lead the attack in the city with an elite band of veteran United Irishmen. On the day of the proposed rising these men became worried about failures in communication and lack of discipline amongst their followers and they abandoned some of their more ambitious objectives to concentrate on storming the castle. They thus missed the chance to disable various parts of the administration.

As the evening approached Emmet became convinced that the rising was doomed, and to save as many of his followers as possible he decided to countermand the order for the rising. A solitary rocket was launched according to pre-arranged signal. Hundreds of people who had gathered round the city dispersed, while rebels gathering in Wood Quay, Ship Street, Thomas Court and elsewhere left their stations.

Emmet determined to go ahead himself with a symbolic gesture that would at least make clear the political motivation for those acts of rebellion still bound to take place. Dressed in the green and white uniform he had designed for himself, he read extracts from the proclamation he had printed by John Stockdale in 62 Abbey Street on the afternoon of the rebellion, and entitled "The Provisional Government to the People of Ireland". It set out the political motives and agenda of the United Irishmen and their statement on human rights. He then led a column of about 200 men towards Dublin Castle. As they moved from Thomas Street, the rear end of this column met with a carriage carrying Lord Kilwarden, the 64-year-old Lord Chief Justice of Ireland, his daughter Elizabeth and his nephew, Reverend Richard Wolfe, who were on their way to the castle to seek refuge. They had already been offered shelter in the Guinness compound at James' Gate, but decided to press on. Kilwarden was dragged from his carriage and killed by the rebels, demonstrating Emmet's lack of authority over the mob once the action was under way. Richard Wolfe was also piked to death. These murders were subsequently given iconic status in the loyalist imagination as a rebel atrocity that indicated that a reign of terror would have succeeded their victory. It is described by Charles Robert Maturin in his great gothic novel, *Melmoth the Wanderer* (1820):

In the year 1803, when Emmett's [sic] insurrection broke out in
Dublin—(the fact from which this account is drawn was related to
me by an eye-witness)—Lord Kilwarden, in passing through Thomas
Street, was dragged from his carriage, and murdered in the most
horrid manner. Pike after pike was thrust through his body till at last
he was nailed to a door, and called out to his murderer to "put him
out of his pain." At this moment, a shoemaker, who lodged in the
garret of an opposite house, was drawn to the window by the horri-
ble cries he heard. He stood at the window, gasping with horror, his
wife attempting vainly to drag him away. He saw the last blow
struck, he heard the last groan uttered, as the sufferer cried, "put me
out of pain" while sixty pikes were thrusting at him. The man stood
at his window as if nailed to it; and when dragged from it, became—
an idiot for life.

Following the death of Kilwarden, Emmet and most of his senior
leadership abandoned the assault on the castle and retreated to
Rathfarnham.

As the evening went on there were several skirmishes fought
between small groups of rebels and the regular soldiers of the 21st
regiment. In each case the army withdrew to barracks in the face of the
enemy attack. This was one of the few occasions in Dublin's history
when there was street fighting between regular and irregular soldiers in
the city.

The abortive rising was followed by mass arrests over several
counties and searches through the Dublin area for the leaders and for
their arms supplies. On 26 July Anne Devlin, Emmet's assistant at
Rathfarnham, was arrested with her sister and tortured by the yeomanry
searching for Emmet. Many years later she told the story of her part in
the rebellion and her experiences in prison to the historian of the
United Irishmen, R. R. Madden and to Brother Luke Cullen, who
wrote them as a first-person narrative. Devlin achieved posthumous
fame as a heroine of the rising, and one of the best historical films to
come out of Ireland, Pat Murphy's *Anne Devlin* (1984) is based on her
narrative.

Emmet was arrested at the home of the Palmer family off Mount
Drummond Avenue, Harold's Cross, on 25 August by Town Major
Henry Charles Sirr, the same man who had arrested and shot Lord

Edward Fitzgerald. Sirr was an ex-army officer and Dublin's *de facto* chief of police. When Emmet was apprehended he tried to make an escape but Sirr pursued him across several gardens, and opened fire. When Emmet was finally apprehended, he was taken to Dublin Castle, where he was interviewed by members of the Privy Council. He was then taken to Kilmainham gaol on 30 August. On 19 September Emmet went on trial in Green Street Courthouse, charged with high treason. The trial lasted for over twelve hours. Emmet offered no defence and accepted more than his fair share of responsibility, probably in order to protect his subordinates and his secret fiancée, Sarah Curran, who had been implicated in correspondence with him. He seems to have entered into an agreement with the prosecutor, Chief Secretary William Wickham in order to protect Curran. The most celebrated part of the trial was Emmet's speech from the dock, which exists in several versions, put out by competing interests after his death. It would appear that the Judge, Lord Norbury, felt its rhetorical effectiveness, for he several times interrupted Emmet, these interruptions occasioning some of Emmet's most famous sallies.

Though you, my Lord, sit there as a judge; and I stand here a culprit; yet, you are but a man;—and I am a man also. And when you, or any other judge, speak against the motives of a dying man, I do conceive it to be the right of the dying man, —that it is his duty, to vindicate his character and his views from aspersion.

On the following day Emmet was taken under heavy guard to a scaffold in Thomas Street, where his rising had begun. Outside St. Catherine's Church he was hanged and beheaded in front of a large crowd. His body was taken back to Kilmainham gaol where it was put on display, before it was removed to the burial ground at Hospital Fields (Bully's Acre). Some days later the body was removed to St. Michan's Church, from which it seems to have been removed once more to a final, unknown grave. Through the twentieth century there were many attempts to discover the location of the final grave, with excavations at several sites in Dublin, but these proved unsuccessful.

Emmet's fiancée, Sarah Curran (1782-1808) was the daughter of John Philpot Curran, a barrister who defended many of the United Irishmen in 1798. He refused to defend Emmet, furious when he discovered the rebel's relationship with his daughter. She left home after Emmet's execution, living with friends in the south of the country. Her father's hostility and the shock of Emmet's death contributed to weakening her health. In 1805 she married Captain R. H. Sturgeon, and three years later died of tuberculosis. A poem by Thomas Moore, "She is Far From the Land Where Her Young Hero Sleeps" and a story by Washington Irving, "The Broken Heart", contributed to the romantic mythology that gathered around Curran after her death, when she became a type for fidelity and grief. A number of nineteenth-century illustrations represented her visiting Emmet in prison on the eve of his execution, or visiting his grave before she left Ireland.

Thomas Moore, Emmet's childhood friend, wrote the most famous of many poems that took their cue from the speech from the dock:

Oh! breathe not his name, let it sleep in the shade,
Where cold and unhonour'd his relics are laid:
Sad, silent, and dark, be the tears that we shed,
As the night-dew that falls on the grass o'er his head.

But the night dew that falls, though in silence it weeps,
Shall brighten with verdure the grave where he sleeps;
And the tear that we shed, though in secret it rolls,
Shall long keep his memory green in our souls.

When R. R. Madden discovered that Anne Devlin had been buried in a pauper's grave at Glasnevin in 1851, he had her remains removed to "that part of the cemetery, which is in the most request—very near the spot where the remains of O'Connell are deposited." He erected to her a monument of a cross standing on a bank of shamrocks, where an Irish wolfhound is lying. The inscription reads:

To
the memory
of
Anne Devlin
(Campbell)
the faithful servant of
ROBERT EMMET

who possessed some rare
and noble qualities
who lived in obscurity and poverty
and so died
on the 18th day of September 1851
Aged 70 years
May she rest in Peace. Amen

Dublin Zoo Opens in Phoenix Park
Thursday 1 September 1831

> *"Some of them live for thirty years*
> *and die dangling. They hang on*
> *like the leaves they pretended to be,*
> *then like dying leaves turn dry.*
>
> Suspicions amongst thoughts are like bats
> amongst birds, *Francis Bacon writes,*
> they fly ever by twilight. [...]"
> Caitríona O Reilly, from "A Lecture upon the Bat"

The oldest existing zoo in Europe is Vienna's Tiergarten Schönbrunn, founded in 1752 and opened to the public in 1765, in a tradition of royal menageries or collections of animals dating back at least to the Middle Ages. In 1793 the Paris Ménagerie du Jardin des Plantes was established by a naturalist and laid out in a garden designed to reveal scientific principles of classification. It transformed the notion of the menagerie as spectacle into a more Enlightenment-influenced concept of pedagogical display. The Garden and Menagerie of the Zoological Society of London were established in 1828 and the following year opened to members of the Society for scientific study and inspection of animals. Only in 1847 did London Zoo open its doors to the public.

At a meeting called and chaired by the Duke of Leinster in the Rotunda Hospital, Dublin, on 10 May 1830, it was decided to establish The Zoological Society of Dublin to form a collection of living animals, on the plan used by the Zoological Society in London. Within a year the Lord Lieutenant, the Duke of Northumberland, had arranged for five-and-a-half acres of land to be donated from the Phoenix Park, then known as "The Garden", for the establishment of a zoological garden. Dublin Zoological Gardens, the third oldest public zoo in the world, opened to the public on 1 September 1831, with its first animals mainly supplied by the London Society. In the first 14 months there were 36,497 visitors who contributed £508 in subscriptions and £912 in entrance fees. The zoo had 46 mammals, including 15 monkeys, and 72 birds. By the first general meeting of the Society, in 1832, the collection was reported to include 123 species: 47 mammals, 72 birds and 4 reptiles.

The meeting of the Zoological Society was held in November that year, and the first president was Philip Crampton (1777-1858), a Dublin surgeon, elected in 1833. Crampton's interest in zoology was related to his scientific research—he is remembered for publishing in 1813 a paper in Volume 1 of Thomas Thomson's *Annals of Philosophy: or Magazine of chemistry, mineralogy, mechanics, natural history, agriculture, and the arts* describing the organ in the eyes of birds used for accommodation, now known as *Musculus Cramptonianus*, or Crampton's muscle.

There were three buildings on the original site: a house, later known as the Director's Residence and rebuilt in 1866, an outhouse, and a small cottage. In the early 1830s the cottage was occupied by a Mrs. O'Rourke. Relations between Mrs. O'Rourke and the zoo soured, and on 20 April 1832 entry from the lodge into the Zoological Gardens was cut off. A later letter cautioned her "not to hang any more of her washing within sight of the visitors to the Garden." In 1833 the entrance lodge to the zoo was built in the style of a thatched cottage at a cost of thirty pounds.

The zoo held an open day in 1838 to celebrate Queen Victoria's coronation; 20,000 people visited, which is still the highest number of visitors in one day. The name of the society was changed to the Royal Zoological Society of Ireland, and Victoria became its patron. In 1844 the zoo received its first giraffe and in 1855 bought its first pair of lions, which bred for the first time in 1857. The first permanent enclosures were a bear pit and a house for carnivores. Nesbitt House, built in 1877 as an aviary, is now used as a bat house. Reptiles received their own house in 1876, and the first tea-rooms were built in 1898.

One of the zoo's most famous residents was Cairbre (1927-44), a product of the zoo's successful lion-breeding programme. He was filmed, roaring, on the original introductions to Metro-Goldwyn-Mayer films.

In the nineteenth century city zoos established on scientific principles gradually began to replace travelling menageries, in which animals were exhibited as curiosities. One proprietor of a travelling menagerie was Thomas Atkins, founder of Liverpool Zoo, who came to Dublin in the 1830s with a bull rhinoceros that he had purchased in Calcutta in 1834 for £1,000. It was exhibited in Dublin, Glasgow, Edinburgh and Liverpool as an Indian rhinoceros, although it may have been a specimen of the rare Javan rhinoceros, one of at most half a dozen specimens ever seen alive in Europe. A one-month stay in 1835 at Dublin Zoo alone brought in £140.

In 1876 Dublin and London newspapers reported the death of a reptile keeper at the zoo after "a bite from a python". John Supple of 6 West Liffey Street was found unconscious in the reptile house and was removed to Steeven's Hospital where he died. The inquest jury, however, shared the scepticism of the attending doctor, and recorded that the death was due to an already established pulmonary congestion.

During the Easter Rising of 1916, it became difficult to enter and leave Phoenix Park and meat ran out. In order to keep the lions and tigers alive, some of the other animals in the zoo were killed and used as food. During the Second World War coal was hard to come by, so older trees were cut down and used to heat the tropical houses.

In 1911 Dr. B. B. Ferrar was appointed superintendent at the zoo and professionalized the role of superintendent (later director), taking much of the day-to-day management out of the hands of the Zoological Society's board. The original site of the zoo was expanded several times, most recently in the 1990s. In 1994 the government of Ireland granted Dublin Zoo IR£15 million to help it reach commercial self-sufficiency so that future government subsidies would be unnecessary. As part of the plan, drawn up by the Zoological Society of Ireland and the Office of Public Works, a number of themed areas were developed: the World of Primates, the Fringes of the Arctic, the World of Cats, the City Farm, and the African Plains. In the summer of 2000 the zoo opened the African Plains, a savannah for large African animals. The zoo was given 32 acres that had been part of the grounds of Áras an Uachtaráin, the presidential residence, to accommodate the new area. The addition of the African Plains doubled the size of the zoo.

A story about the zoo circulates as an urban myth on the internet. A family spending the day at Dublin Zoo lost their small son. After frantic searching he was discovered near the penguin enclosure, dirty, dishevelled and unwilling to talk about what had happened. His mother had no success in coaxing from him what had befallen him in the missing hour and took him home, where he rushed unbidden to the bathroom. He locked the door and ran a bath, asking his mother to stay outside. She grew increasingly concerned at this uncharacteristic behaviour and eventually burst into the bathroom, where she found her little boy playing with a live baby penguin, which he had smuggled home in his backpack.

Frederick Douglass at Conciliation Hall
Monday 29 September 1845

> *"My sympathy with distress is not confined within the narrow bounds of my own green island. No—it extends itself to every corner of the earth. My heart walks abroad, and wherever the miserable are to be succored, or the slave to be set free, there my spirit is at home, and I delight to dwell."*
> Daniel O'Connell

In the summer of 1845 the American abolitionist, former slave Frederick Douglass, travelled to Europe to promote his autobiography and to speak to abolitionists, asking for their support in the campaign to end slavery in the United States. He arrived by ship in Liverpool, after a difficult voyage, and at once travelled on to Dublin, where his tour began. He stayed in Ireland from September 1845 until the following January, visiting Cork, Limerick and Belfast as well as Dublin and other smaller towns. In July 1846 he revisited Belfast from Scotland. He returned to America in April 1847. During his visit he wrote letters back to America, many of which were intended for publication in the abolitionist newspapers and periodicals. On 29 September 1845 in Dublin he attended a meeting of the Repeal Association at Conciliation Hall, addressed by Daniel O'Connell and wrote about it to William Lloyd Garrison. The letter was published in *The Liberator*, 24 October, 1845.

Douglass was born into slavery in Maryland in 1818. He passed through the ownership of several slave holders, until he was living in

Baltimore, from where he escaped on his second attempt in September 1838. He travelled to New York and shortly after his arrival married Anna Murray, a free black woman he had met in Baltimore. During their marriage they had five children together. By 1841 Douglass had begun his life as a public figure. He first became active in the cause for the abolition of slavery. After Douglass spoke at an anti-slavery meeting about his experience as a slave, he was urged by William Lloyd Garrison to become a lecturer for the American Anti-Slavery Society. In 1845, he wrote about his life as a slave in the *Narrative of the Life of Frederick Douglass, An American Slave*. After its publication, he spoke out against slavery in England, Scotland, and Ireland. Upon his return to the United States in 1847, he settled in New York and published the weekly paper, *North Star*.

Daniel O'Connell (1775-1847) was a passionate abolitionist and frequently linked the condition of the Irish to that of slaves in the United States. When he was raising money for Ireland in America he refused contributions from slave owners. Frederick Douglass was also an advocate of temperance and one of the places he found common cause in Ireland was with the temperance societies there, which had gained particular strength in the 1830s under the leadership of Father Theobald Mathew (1790-1856). It was plausible for both black Americans and Irish Catholics to identify alcohol abuse as a mechanism by which the under-classes soothed their social and economic deprivation and were vitiated from any energy for resistance. Alcoholism also pandered to the negative stereotypes used to denigrate both groups.

The best way to describe Frederick Douglass's visit to Conciliation Hall is in his own words, excerpted from his letter to Garrison:

If the labor of the last two weeks be a fair sample of what awaits me, I have certainly sought repose in the wrong place. I have work enough here, on the spot, to occupy every inch of my time, and every particle of my strength, were I to stay in this city a whole six months. The cause of temperance alone would afford work enough to occupy every inch of my time. I have invitation after invitation to address temperance meetings, which I am compelled to decline. How different here, from my treatment at home! In this country, I am welcomed to the temperance platform, side by side with white speakers, and am received as kindly and warmly as though my skin were white.

I have but just returned from a great Repeal meeting, held at Conciliation Hall. It was a very large meeting—much larger than usual, I was told, on account of the presence of Mr. O'Connell, who has just returned from his residence at Derrynane... When I entered, one after another was announcing the Repeal rent for the week. The audience appeared to be in deep sympathy with the Repeal movement, and the announcement of every considerable contribution was followed by a hearty round of applause, and sometimes a vote of thanks was taken for the donors. At the close of this business, Mr. O'Connell rose and delivered a speech of about an hour and a quarter long. It was a great speech, skilfully delivered, powerful in its logic, majestic in its rhetoric, biting in its sarcasm, melting in its pathos, and burning in its rebukes. Upon the subject of slavery in general, and American slavery in particular, Mr. O'Connell grew warm and energetic, defending his course on this subject. He said, with an earnestness which I shall never forget, "I have been assailed for attacking the American institution, as it is called,—Negro slavery. I am not ashamed of that attack. I do not shrink from it. I am the advocate of civil and religious liberty, all over the globe, and wherever tyranny exists, I am the foe of the tyrant; wherever oppression shows itself, I am the foe of the oppressor; wherever slavery rears its head, I am the enemy of the system, or the institution, call it by what name you will. I am the friend of liberty in every clime, class and color. My sympathy with distress is not confined within the narrow bounds of my own green island. No—it extends itself to every corner of the earth. My heart walks abroad, and wherever the miserable are to be succored, or the slave to be set free, there my spirit is at home, and I delight to dwell."

...I have heard many speakers within the last four years—speakers of the first order; but I confess, I have never heard one, by whom I was more completely captivated than by Mr. O'Connell. I used to wonder how such monster meetings as those of Repeal could be held peaceably. It is now no matter of astonishment at all. It seems to me that the voice of O'Connell is enough to calm the most violent passion, even though it were already manifesting itself in a mob. There is a sweet persuasiveness in it, beyond any voice I ever heard. His power over an audience is perfect.

...On being introduced to Mr. O'Connell, an opportunity was afforded me to speak; and although I scarce knew what to say, I managed to say something, which was quite well received.

After Douglass's five months in Ireland, when he had seen some of the effects of the Famine he wrote again to Garrison from Scotland:

[T]hough I am more closely connected and identified with one class of outraged, oppressed and enslaved people, I cannot allow myself to be insensible to the wrongs and sufferings of any part of the great family of man. I am not only an American slave, but a man, and as such, am bound to use my powers for the welfare of the whole human brotherhood. I am not going through this land with my eyes shut, ears stopped, or heart steeled.

Douglass says that he had heard much of the misery and wretchedness of the Irish people before leaving the US, and was prepared to witness much on his arrival in Ireland, but that his experience convinced him that the half had not been told.

I supposed that much that I heard from the American press on this subject was mere exaggeration, resorted to for the base purpose of impeaching the characters of British philanthropists, and throwing a mantle over the dark and infernal character of American slavery and slaveholders. My opinion has undergone no change in regard to the latter part of my supposition, for I believe a large class of writers in America, as well as in this land, are influenced by no higher motive than that of covering up our national sins, to please popular taste, and satisfy popular prejudice; and thus many have harped upon

the wrongs of Irishmen, while in truth they care no more about Irish-
men, or the wrongs of Irishmen, than they care about the whipped,
gagged, and thumb-screwed slave. They would as willingly sell on
the auction-block an Irishman, if it were popular to do so, as an
African. For heart, such men have adamant—for consciences, they
have public opinion. They are a stench in the nostrils of upright men,
and a curse to the country in which they live. The limits of a single
letter are insufficient to allow any thing like a faithful description of
those painful exhibitions of human misery, which meet the eye of a
stranger almost at every step. I spent nearly six weeks in Dublin, and
the scenes I there witnessed were such as to make me "blush, and
hang my head to think myself a man."

I speak truly when I say, I dreaded to go out of the house. The
streets were almost literally alive with beggars, displaying the great-
est wretchedness—some of them mere stumps of men, without feet,
without legs, without hands, without arms—and others still more
horribly deformed, with crooked limbs, down upon their hands and
knees, their feet lapped around each other, and laid upon their backs,
pressing their way through the muddy streets and merciless crowd,
casting sad looks to the right and left, in the hope of catching the eye
of a passing stranger—the citizens generally having set their faces
against giving to beggars...The spectacle that affected me most, and
made the most vivid impression on my mind, of the extreme poverty
and wretchedness of the poor of Dublin, was the frequency with
which I met little children in the street at a late hour of the night,
covered with filthy rags, and seated upon cold stone steps, or in
corners, leaning against brick walls, fast asleep, with none to look
upon them, none to care for them. If they have parents, they have
become vicious, and have abandoned them. Poor creatures! they are
left without help, to find their way through a frowning world—a
world that seems to regard them as intruders, and to be punished as
such.

Meagher of the Sword
Tuesday 28 July 1846

"Abhor the sword? Stigmatise the sword? No, my lord…"
Thomas Francis Meagher.

It was only in the 1830s, after the achievement of Catholic emancipation, that a movement developed in favour of repealing the Act of Union. The Repeal Movement was led by Daniel O'Connell, and featured a "repeal rent" modelled on the successful Catholic rent of the 1820s.

In 1841-2 O'Connell was preoccupied with his position as Lord Mayor of Dublin, but towards the end of 1842 there was an economic downturn and also pressure from the weekly *Nation* newspaper, recently founded by Charles Gavan Duffy and Thomas Davis.

O'Connell declared that 1843 would be repeal year. A series of huge open-air demonstrations, known as monster meetings, were organized from the start of the year. There were plans that the agitation would climax in the election of a council of 300 at the end of the year, and that this would be a shadow parliament to plan a repeal bill. The British Prime Minister, Sir Robert Peel, stood firm, however, and when the government banned the meeting planned for October at Clontarf, O'Connell backed down. A week later O'Connell and the other leaders were arrested on charges of conspiracy. They were convicted and imprisoned in 1844. On their release they attempted to revive the Repeal Movement, but with the famine taking its toll and the more militant stance of the Young Irelanders, O'Connell was never able to revive the mass movement of 1843.

On 11 July 1846 O'Connell put forward a "peace resolution" to the Repeal Association at a meeting in Conciliation Hall on Burgh Quay, the usual venue for Dublin's repeal meetings. It was an attempt to heal the growing rift between himself and the "Young Irelanders" by obliging them to back down. O'Connell's statement proposed "that to promote political amelioration, peaceable means alone should be used, to the exclusion of all others…" The aim of O'Connell's resolution was to press the Young Irelanders into an abandonment of their arguments in favour of physical force as an acceptable means in the struggle for repeal. The resolution involved an attack on *The Nation*.

During the debate 23-year-old Thomas Francis Meagher (1823-67) rose to speak to the resolution. Meagher, originally from Waterford, had been educated by the Jesuits, first in Clongowes Wood College, Co. Kildare, and then at Stonyhurst College in Lancashire, England. At school he was a brilliant student, particularly excelling at literature. Thanks to Stonyhurst he spoke with an Anglo-Irish accent. When he returned to Waterford in 1843 he became a zealous advocate of repeal like his father, Thomas Meagher, who was mayor of the city in that year—the first Catholic mayor of Waterford since the time of Cromwell. In 1844 Meagher went to Dublin with the intention of becoming a lawyer. He became a contributor to the *Nation* and a friend of the other writers.

Meagher's address was delivered with the slight English drawl that characterized his speech. He struck observers as conceited and rather a fine gentleman. But on this evening his eloquence warmed the audience. He began with attacking the compromises proposed by the Whigs, suggesting that the more prosperous Ireland became the more, not less, vital would be independence. He praised the aged patriot, Robert Holmes, for an address to the Queen's Bench and went on to assert the centrality of repeal to the aims of the movement.

> But we, my lord, who are assembled in this Hall, and in whose hearts the Union has not bred the slave's disease— we have not been imperialised—we are here to undo that work, which forty-six years ago dishonoured the ancient peerage, and subjugated the people of our country.

He praised O'Connell:

> No, my lord, I am not ungrateful to the man who struck the fetters off my arms, whilst I was yet a child; and by whose influence my father—the first Catholic who did so for two hundred years— sat for the last two years, in the civic chair of an ancient city.

Meagher repudiated any suggestion that he was arguing for armed rebellion:

> In the existing circumstances of the country an incitement to arms would be senseless, and, therefore, wicked... But, my lord, I dissented from the resolutions before us, for other reasons... for I felt that, by assenting to them I should have pledged myself to the unqualified repudiation of physical force in all countries, at all times, and in every circumstance. This I could not do; for, my lord, I do not abhor the use of arms in the vindication of national rights.

From this point the speech launched its final rhetorical flourish, calling on biblical authority in the example of Judith and Holofornes, and recent historical precedent in Belgium:

From that night in which, in the valley of Bethulia, He nerved the arm of the Jewish girl to smite the drunken tyrant in his tent, down to the hour in which He blessed the insurgent chivalry of the Belgian priests, His Almighty hand hath ever been stretched forth from His throne of light, to consecrate the flag of freedom—to bless the patriot sword. Be it for the defence, or be it for the assertion of a nation's liberty, I look upon the sword as a sacred weapon... Abhor the sword? Stigmatise the sword? No, my lord, for at its blow, and in the quivering of its crimson light a giant nation sprang up from the waters of the Atlantic, and by its redeeming magic the fettered colony became a daring, free Republic.

Example followed example until John O'Connell interposed to prevent Meagher being further heard and said that any members who refused to accept Daniel O'Connell's interpretation of the "peace resolutions" were opposed to O'Connell's leadership. At this, William Smith O'Brien and several members, including John Mitchel, Meagher and Gavan Duffy, walked out of the meeting and the Young Irelanders, in a body, quit Conciliation Hall.

The speech earned Meagher the sobriquet "Meagher of the Sword" and led to the secession of the Young Irelanders from the Repeal Association, and to the foundation of the Irish Confederation, headed by John Mitchel, Smith O'Brien and Gavan Duffy.

Meagher took part in the uprising of 1848 and was transported to Van Dieman's Land. In 1852 he escaped to the United States, where he spent the rest of his life, fighting for the Union in the American Civil War and becoming a general. There was rather a discrepancy between the highfalutin defence of military action in the Young Ireland rhetoric, and the actual events of their rebellion.

The First Use of General Anaesthetic in Ireland
Friday 1 January 1847

"I regard this discovery as one of the most important of the century. It will rank with vaccination and other of the greatest benefits that medical science has bestowed on man... it offers an occasion beyond measure more worthy of Te Deums in Christian cathedrals and for thanksgiving to the Author and Giver of all good, than all the victories that fire and sword have ever achieved."
John MacDonnell, *The Dublin Medical Press*

Mary Kane of County Meath pricked her arm on a hawthorn branch. In Ireland the hawthorn is a fairy tree and sometimes it brings bad luck. It was an unlucky prick for Mary Kane. The literature on her case does not tells us how and why, but the prick on the arm led to suppurative arthritis of the elbow joint, and that in turn led her to Dr. John MacDonnell of the Richmond Hospital, Dublin. MacDonnell (1796-1892) was born in Belfast, son of Dr. James MacDonnell who was a major figure in medicine in the north, and one of the founders of the Belfast General Dispensary and Fever Hospital. Dr. MacDonnell placed Mary Kane on his list for surgery on New Year's Eve, 1846. The arm was to be amputated.

The Richmond Hospital was the surgical unit of the four state-financed hospitals connected with the Dublin House of Industry (founded 1773), all in and around New Brunswick Street. There had been a Royal College of Surgeons in Dublin since 1784, and in the nineteenth century there were some outstanding medical practitioners in Dublin who gained world-wide recognition. These included Robert Adams, Denis Burkitt, Abraham Colles, Dominic Corrigan, Sir Peter Freyer, Arthur Jacob, John Maconchy, Terence Millin, Sir Thornley Stoker (bother of novelist, Bram Stoker), William Stokes and William Wilde (father of Oscar).

None of the forms of anaesthetic used in early nineteenth-century surgery rendered the patient unconscious during the operation. There are extraordinary extant accounts from surviving patients of the sensations experienced during an operation—Frances Burney's description of her mastectomy in 1811 is one of the best-known.

*Yet—when that dreadful steel was plunged into the breast—
cutting through veins—arteries—flesh—nerves—I needed no
injunctions not to restrain my cries. I began a scream that lasted
unintermittingly during the whole time of the incision—& I
almost marvel that it rings not in my Ears still? So excruciating was
the agony...*

Over the Christmas period in 1846 Edward Hutton, a surgeon at
the Richmond Hospital, read the newly arrived *British and Foreign
Medical Review*, which contained accounts from Boston of a series of
operations recently performed using ether anaesthesia. The editor of the
Review, Sir John Forbes, added a postscript describing how he had
witnessed two pioneering operations under ether anaesthetic at
University College Hospital in London. Hutton showed the articles to
John MacDonnell, who decided that they should test the procedure on
Mary Kane. He postponed her surgery for twenty-four hours in order
to construct an ether dispenser, which he tested several times on
himself, "rendering myself insensible for some seconds, five or six
times."

On New Year's Day, observed by several eminent physicians and
surgeons of Dublin, and a class of medical students, John MacDonnell
gave the anaesthetic to Mary Kane, and proceeded with the
amputation. Mary felt nothing until she came round in time to see
MacDonnell put a thread in her arm. Eight days later he reported her
quite safely recovered. So, eleven days after its first use in London,
Dublin surgeons operated for the first time under general anaesthetic.
On the evening of the operation MacDonnell returned to his home at
4 Gardiner's Row and wrote up the case for *The Dublin Medical Press*,
edited by Arthur Jacob from his home across the Liffey, at 23 Ely
Place.

John MacDonnell went on to a distinguished career as professor of
descriptive anatomy at the Royal College of Surgeons, and Poor Law
Medical Commissioner. His son Robert MacDonnell (1828-1889) also
became a surgeon, and performed the first human blood transfusion in
Ireland in 1865.

The Death of James Clarence Mangan
Wednesday 20 June 1848

"In my boyhood I was haunted by an indescribable feeling of something terrible."
James Clarence Mangan, *Autobiography*

"—great wits jump you know—"
Mangan, Letter to Charles Gavan Duffy, 1840 or 1841

"Et moi, I like various
contrarious
    Assemblies – both
    punchdrinking bawlers
And sighers of sighs—both
    your grinners and
    grumblers.
Mangan, from "Pathetic Hypothetics"

One of the many monuments to the memory of the dead in St. Stephen's Green is a bust of the poet James Clarence Mangan (1803-1849) by Oliver Sheppard. The head of Mangan sits on a plinth fronted by a carved woman's face. She is *Róisín Dubh*, a representation of an image from one of his best-known poems, "Dark Rosaleen". Sheppard's face of Mangan is modelled on a drawing of the poet made just after his death, and on Mangan's death mask.

The last three or four years of Mangan's life were ones of desperate poverty and misery. While Ireland was suffering its worst ever famine, the Dublin poet was eking out a living from writing and was largely dependent on the generosity of friends who were themselves under pressure. He lived in squalor, in an alcoholic haze, with a brother who was incapable of helping either of them. He wrote in tap-rooms and public houses, emerging to deliver his poems and translations and plead for instant payment. He was often seen in the Bleeding Horse pub, which survives on Camden Street. The country was ravaged with poverty and disease and Mangan's way of life made him vulnerable. In May 1849 he was admitted to the cholera sheds at Kilmainham. When he was released, it was to destitution. In June friends found him in a desperate state and took him to the Meath Hospital, which had been erected in 1822 on the site of Jonathan Swift's former garden beside the Deanery at St. Patrick's Cathedral. Mangan died on 20 June.

At the Meath hospital he had been recognized by William Stokes, a physician, and in one of those instances that draw attention to a possible rift in sensibility between those times and these, Stokes instantly sent for the respected portrait painter, Sir Frederic Burton, suggesting that he might wish to make a sketch of Mangan. One of Burton's versions of this well-known sketch was taken just after the poet's death, and the artist later made his own copy. The portrait emphasizes Mangan's fine features and his wild, romantic hair. Although the body is not sketched in, the place where the neck would meet the body suggests nakedness and vulnerability, stressing the poet's poverty and relative youth. Mangan's death mask is an altogether more stern and challenging image of the poet.

Mangan was the nearest thing Ireland had to a romantic poet in the style of Keats or Shelley, and Burton's sketch resembles portraits of Keats and of Thomas Chatterton. Mangan was a poseur, albeit a serious poseur, and one does not imagine him objecting to his own public exposure at death. His death has come to seem haunting to readers for another reason, since it cannot be dissociated from the context of the famine years in which it occurred. If the poet, struck down by cholera, admitted anonymously into the overcrowded fever hospital, is at first glance an Everyman of his period, the attention paid to his body in death only serves to remind us of the numberless corpses piling up across the countryside and in the famine ships leaving Ireland. In 1849 there were 11,357 cholera burials at Glasnevin, the cemetery where Mangan was buried.

> *In Siberia's wastes*
> *No tears are shed,*
> *For they freeze within the brain.*
> *Nought is felt but dullest pain,*
> *Pain acute, yet dead;*
>
> *Pain as in a dream,*
> *When years go by*
> *Funeral-paced, yet fugitive,*

When man lives, and doth not live,
Doth not live, nor die.
(from "Siberia")

James Clarence Mangan was the son of a grocer and a hedge-schoolmaster, a member of Dublin's early nineteenth-century Catholic *petite-bourgeoisie*. When James Mangan married Catherine Smith she was running a grocery at 3 Fishamble Street and the couple continued in this business, but James Mangan senior also entered into property speculation and lost their fortune. Young James was educated at various schools in and around the Liberties of Dublin. By the time he was fifteen his family was in financial trouble and young Mangan was apprenticed to a scrivener, the career he was to follow for most of his adult life, supporting his parents until their deaths in the 1840s. He seems to have approached his employment with all the enthusiasm of Bartleby. For twenty years he was a legal scrivener and then a copyist for the Ordnance Survey, and finally a cataloguer for the library at Trinity College Dublin.

He began to write in his teens and published poems in almanacs. By the early 1830s he had become associated with the Comet Club and was published in the *Comet* magazine. From 1824 to 1846 he published articles on, and translations from, German romantic poets in the *Dublin University Magazine*. He also published Turkish, Arabic and Persian translations—"Literae Orientales"—although these were not actually translations from the oriental languages, but either inventions of his own, or translations of versions in the European languages known to Mangan: French and German. The 1830s was also a great period of Celtic scholarship in Dublin, and Mangan made friends with men like George Petrie and Owen Connellan, who talked to him about the Irish manuscripts they were studying and gave him translations from the Irish to versify and make his own.

Mangan was an admirer of another eccentric Dublin writer, Charles Robert Maturin, the author of the remarkable gothic novel *Melmoth the Wanderer* (1820). To some extent, Mangan reinvented Maturin in his own image, describing the sociable cleric as a loner, almost an outcast. When he looked at Maturin, he saw Melmoth, although with typical perversity Mangan claims that *Melmoth the Wanderer* is nothing like so fine a book as Maturin's least-appreciated

novel, *The Milesian Chief,* and describes the diabolical wanderer as "a bore of the first magnitude, who is always talking grandiloquent fustian, and folding his cloak about him." This sounds rather like Mangan himself. Charles Gavan Duffy described him "dressed in a blue cloak (mid-summer or mid-winter), and a hat of fantastic shape, under which golden hair as fine and silky as a woman's hung in unkempt tangles, and deep blue eyes lighted a face as colourless as parchment."
Mangan gives a wonderful description of an occasion (possibly invented, of course) when he followed Maturin into St. Peter's Church in Aungier Street, and watched him recite the burial service. At the end of the service Maturin gazes around the congregation and his eye falls on Mangan, who "reddened up to the roots of my hair at being even for a moment noticed by a man that ranked far higher in my estimation than Napoleon Bonaparte."

In his sketch on Maturin, Mangan goes on to write somewhat plangently about the gothic novelist's tragic early death, due to "an apothecary's blunder" (Maturin drank the wrong medicine in the night and poisoned himself), and his hurried burial in obscurity. This is quite untrue of Maturin, but prophetic of Mangan's own death in poverty, and the funeral at Glasnevin attended by only five people. The nationalist allegories discovered by readers of his later poems ensured that it would be Mangan, rather than Maturin, who is better remembered in their native Dublin.

Chapter Five
KILMAINHAM

Heuston is the most handsome of Dublin's railway stations and is a portal to Kilmainham, an area of exceptional interest in terms of social and political history, architecture and the other visual arts. Kingsbridge Station, as it was originally named, was commissioned in 1846 from Sancton Wood, an English architect. It is based on the design of an Italian palazzo. A central block of nine bays is used to mask the train shed, designed by Sir John McNeill, and its features include projecting Corinthian columns, balustrades and an attic storey decorated with carved swags and urns. To either side of the main block are domed campaniles and to the south is the main entrance block built along the side of the railway shed. Funds ran out before the interior and the rear of the station could be completed, but recent restoration work is smartening up the interior. The station was renamed to honour Seán Heuston, a republican who led rebels at the Mendicity Institute in the 1916 Easter Rising, and who was shot by firing squad at the nearby Kilmainham gaol on 8 May 1916.

The history of Kilmainham dates back to 606AD when St. Maigneann founded a church here, giving the site the Irish name Cill Maigneann. One reminder of those monastic origins is a tenth-century decorated granite cross shaft, possibly the remains of a boundary cross, now located in Bully's Acre. In 1174 Richard, Earl of Pembroke (Strongbow) founded a priory for the Knights of St. John of Jerusalem, also known as Knights Hospitallers. These knights cared for pilgrims and the poor at their priory, known as the "castle of Kilmainham", and their foundation survived until the English reformation, when Henry VIII destroyed the monasteries in 1540. The English Viceroy confiscated the priory and its lands, which were adjacent to and incorporated within Phoenix Park. One can still walk easily from Kilmainham, past Heuston Station, and cross the river to enter the park close to the Wellington monument.

In 1671 William Robinson became "surveyor-general of all fortifications, buildings etc in Ireland". Robinson was one of the earliest identifiable architects to make his mark on Dublin. He carried out work at Dublin Castle, Phoenix House and Chapelizod House and he designed Marsh's Library (1703). His best-known building is the Royal Hospital, Kilmainham (1680-87), the first classical public building in Ireland, built under the patronage of the Lord Lieutenant, the Duke of Ormond, and under charter from the English King Charles II. The old priory was demolished in 1670. The Royal Hospital was a home for retired soldiers, built on 64 acres of the former lands of the Knights Hospitallers. It opened two years earlier than the Royal Hospital at Chelsea in London, which had a similar mission. Ormond was inspired by Les Invalides, a hospital for retired soldiers built by Louis XIV in Paris in 1670.

For over two centuries the Royal Hospital, with its elegant façade and beautiful interiors, was a major Dublin landmark and served its philanthropic purpose. The first pensioners arrived at Kilmainham in 1684, and the earliest casualties from the Battle of the Boyne were treated there in 1690. James Ward, in around 1720, described the feelings inspired by a view of the hospital from Phoenix Park:

A Fabrick rais'd in peaceful Charles's Reign,
Where vet'ran Bands, discharg'd from War, retire,
Feeble their Limbs, extinct their martial Fire:
I hear methinks, I hear the gallant Train,
Recount the Wonders of each past Campaign:
Conquests, and Triumphs in my Bosom roll,
And Britain's glory fills my wid'ning Soul:
Here blest with Plenty, and maintain'd at ease,
They boast th'Adventures of their youthful Days;
Repeat exhausted Dangers o'er again,
And sigh to speak of faithful Comrades slain.
(James Ward, from "Phoenix Park", 1724)

A rather different sense of the life of an eighteenth-century soldier appears in the memoirs of an Irish pensioner in the Chelsea Hospital. Christian Davies was born in Dublin in 1667, the daughter of a brewer. After the death of her parents she lived with an aunt, from whom she inherited a public house. She had been married a few years and had some small children, when her husband was press-ganged and she took the decision to disguise herself as a man and follow him to Holland:

I was not long deliberating, after this thought had possessed me, but immediately set about preparing what was necessary for my ramble; and disposing of my children, my eldest with my mother, and that which was born after my husband's departure, with a nurse (my second son was dead), I told my friends, that I would go to England in search of my husband, and return with all possible expedition after I had found him. My goods I left in the hands of such friends as had spare house room, and my house I let to a cooper. Having thus ordered my affairs, I cut off my hair, and dressed me in a suit of my husband's, having had the precaution to quilt the waistcoat, to preserve my breasts from hurt, which were not large enough to betray my sex, and putting on the wig and hat I had prepared, I went out and bought me a silver-hilted sword, and some Holland shirts: But was at a loss how I should carry my money with me, as it was contrary to law to export above 5l. out of the kingdom; I thought at last of quilting it in the waistband of my breeches, and by this method I carried with me fifty guineas without suspicion.

I had now nothing upon my hands to prevent my setting out; wherefore, that I might get as soon as possible to Holland, I went to the sign of the Golden Last, where Ensign Herbert Laurence, who was beating up for recruits, kept his rendezvous. He was in the house at the time I got there, and I offered him my service to go against the French, being desirous to show my zeal for his majesty King William, and my country. The hopes of soon meeting with my husband, added a sprightliness to my looks, which made the officer say, I was a clever brisk young fellow; and having recommended my zeal, he gave me a guinea enlisting money, and a crown to drink the king's health, and ordered me to be enrolled.

She retained her male disguise until she was reunited with her husband, at which point she realized that she was keen on the soldier's life and so they persisted together in the army. As a retired pensioner she dictated her memoirs which were published in 1740.

Kilmainham pensioners came from all over Ireland and Britain, and in the nineteenth century there were veterans of Waterloo and of the campaigns in India and Afghanistan. In the nineteenth century the building grew in military significance. It became the headquarters of the Commander-in-Chief of the Army, who combined this role with that of Hospital Master. In 1922 the Hospital became the property of the new Irish Free State. A few old soldiers lived on there, while others were relocated to England. The departure of the final residents in 1927 saw the beginning of a process of decay, although the building was used as Garda headquarters from 1930 to 1950. For a long period after 1950 the hospital was virtually abandoned. Then, in the 1980s, restoration work began and in the 1990s it was re-opened, restored and adapted, as the Irish Museum of Modern Art, the home of collections of twentieth-century Irish and international art. IMMA's strength is in its Irish collection and in its imaginative use of exhibition space, particularly as it has developed a programme of site-specific art. Critics of the restoration have complained that the space is not well suited to contemporary art, particularly because the rooms are so small. Judge for yourself. It is Dublin's most exciting gallery for anyone who wants to get a quick sense of what interests younger and emerging artists.

Burial Grounds

Located to the left of the Kilmainham Gate entrance to the Royal Hospital Building, in the grounds of the Royal Hospital are two interesting burial grounds (mind you, as Samuel Beckett says at the start of *First Love*, "Personally I have no bone to pick with graveyards, I take the air there willingly, perhaps more willingly than elsewhere, when take the air I must."). The hospital burial ground itself is the cemetery of the old soldiers who resided here over the centuries. The area is separated into the space for privates and the space for officers, because death abolishes many things, but not rank. There is a stone plaque on the south wall which reads:

Within the precincts of this cemetery have been laid
To rest the remains of 334 pensioners who have died
In the Royal Hospital Kilmainham. Their names regiments
and dates of decease will be found inscribed on brass
tablets in the respective chapels of the Institution.

Those brass plaques are now on the wall outside the hospital's deconsecrated chapel. The 334 pensioners died between 1880 and 1905. A further 305 people were buried here between 1905 and 1931. There are curious and moving life-stories associated with each of these graves. There is also a certain poignancy attached to the memorials for some British soldiers killed during the 1916 Rising. In a city that naturally does so much to commemorate the revolutionary heroes of the Rising, a few families have chosen to mark the victims on the other side of the struggle. The officer's burial ground has fewer memorials and also contains some of the earliest stones: Hive and Elizabeth Hackett (1652), Corporal William Proby (1700) and Lt. David Buchanan (1720). Proby was wounded at the Battle of the Boyne and was one the earliest inmates of the hospital. Among the medical staff buried here is George Renny (1757-1848), a Scotsman who came to Kilmainham in 1783 as a surgeon, and who was instrumental during his career in alleviating some of the miseries of the Irish poor, through his work at Kilmainham and at other hospitals in the city. He was particularly interested in fevers and epidemics and promoted study into their causes. He realized the importance of water supplies for public health and was responsible for the erection of street fountains in poor areas. Renny was

75 when the terrible Asiatic cholera epidemic of 1832 swept across Dublin, but he was still active in tending to sufferers.

It was the cholera epidemic which finally closed the main cemetery at Bully's Acre to public burials. During the six months of the epidemic 3,200 victims were buried at Bully's Acre, and it became clear by the end of that period that the graveyard was overcrowded and posed a risk to public health. Bully's Acre has served as a cemetery since the sixth century when St. Maigneann was buried here. Brian Bóroimhe's son Murcadha was said to have been buried here after the battle of Clontarf and the remains of a Great Celtic Cross are still to be seen. By the eighteenth century Bully's Acre was one of the most popular spots for burials in Dublin, being common land and thus free. An attempt to close it in the eighteenth century caused riots. Many of the city's leading citizens are buried here, and it is also the site of numberless unmarked graves of the poor.

The headless body of Robert Emmet was briefly interred here by soldiers of the Roscommon Militia in 1803. Denis Lambert Redmond, Felix Rourke, John McIntosh, Thomas Keenan, and Henry Howley were definitely buried here, as were in all probability the others executed for participating with Emmet. Redmond and Rourke were buried halfway between the Kilmainham Gate Lodge and the Celtic Cross seen above, both close to Robert Emmet's original place of burial.

Other notable features of Kilmainham include the early eighteenth-century gardens and the former stable buildings, now the local Garda barracks. The West Gateway was designed by Francis Johnston as an addition to Watling Street Bridge (now Rory O'More Bridge) in 1812. It is a mock medieval gateway constructed from limestone. In its original location it became a hindrance to traffic and was dismantled and removed to Kilmainham. The nearby Dr. Steeven's Hospital, built in 1720, is a small architectural replica of the Royal Hospital.

Lunatics and Prisoners

Yet another hospital has made an appeal to the imagination over two and half centuries. On 19 October 1745 Jonathan Swift died, leaving his entire estate, derived from royalties from his writings, for the founding of a hospital for the mentally ill, the first of its kind in Ireland.

St. Patrick's Hospital was granted a Royal Charter by George II on 8 August 1746. St. Patrick's was built by architect George Semple following Swift's detailed instructions. One of its earliest governors, a treasurer to the board and visiting state physician to the hospital, was Dr. Robert Emmet, father of the revolutionary, who led his assault on Dublin Castle from nearby Thomas Street. It is now the oldest, purpose-built psychiatric hospital continuously functioning on its original site in Britain and Ireland.

At the end of the nineteenth century, St. Patrick's hospital purchased St. Edmundsbury, four miles upriver in Lucan. Together, St. Patrick's and St. Edmundsbury Hospitals admit some 2,300 patients each year while assessing and treating a further 10,000 patients on an out-patient basis.

Swift's sly comment on his own munificence (presented as the assessment of an indifferent observer) is one of his most famous verses, and characteristic of his self-deprecating humour and his rigorous critique of his native city:

He gave the little Wealth he had,
To build a House for Fools and Mad:
And shew'd by one satyric Touch,
No Nation wanted it so much:...
("Verses on the Death of Dr. Swift, D.S.P.D.")

For all the grandeur of its architectural heritage, Kilmainham is a prime location in which to reflect on the history of Dublin's poor and sick, its vagabonds and dispossessed. Kilmainham gaol is also now a museum, one which attempts to give the visitor an insight into what is was like to have been confined in a prison between 1796, when it opened, and 1924, when it closed. Leaders of the rebellions of 1798, 1803, 1848, 1867 and 1916 were detained here and the names of Robert Emmet, Charles Stewart Parnell, the leaders of the 1916 Rising and de Valera are associated with the gaol. Pearse, Clarke, MacBride and Connolly were executed at the prison and one of the last prisoners to die there, Erskine Childers, was executed by the Free State government in 1922. There is an excellent exhibition on the history of the prison, with imaginative use of documents, photographs and artefacts, and the building has an extraordinary atmosphere.

The gaol was probably originally a bridewell attached to a court, where prisoners were held waiting for the arrival of circuit judges. The prison was a holding cell, not a place of punishment, and the arrival of the circuit court would clear rather than fill the cells. Punishments included fines, flogging, torture, death or transportation. In the eighteenth century, however, more and more people were confined for bad debts. These debtors had to pay for their confinement and they were expected to raise money to pay off their fines and debts without the means to do so, and so people began to remain in prisons over several years, often with their families also in the gaol or the surrounding area. When the British penal reformer John Howard visited Kilmainham in the late eighteenth century, he found hunger, poverty, overcrowding and systematic cruelty by warders to prisoners. In 1796 the old bridewell was replaced by a major prison, part of the general prison expansion of the period. The prisoners captured in 1798 were among the first to be detained, and in many cases executed. In 1863 a new east wing was opened, built according to the panopticon principle outlined by Jeremy Bentham. Prisoners were held individually in 101 single cells, and the whole three-storey wing could be viewed from one vantage point.

Prisons have been the setting for a number of literary and dramatic works and films, with two of the best-known examples being John Mitchel's autobiographical *Jail Journey* (1854), which frames the narrative of his transportation from Ireland with a history of the country and an attack on British imperialism, and Brendan Behan's *The Quare Fellow* (1956), set in Mountjoy Jail in the hours leading up to an execution. Behan drew on his own experiences in prisons in Britain and Ireland.

One of Dublin's most celebrated ballads dates from the eighteenth century and describes the lead-up to a hanging. Here are the first, third, fifth and eighth stanzas from "The Night Before Larry Was Stretched":

The night before Larry was stretched
   The boys they all paid him a visit;
A bait in their sacks, too, they fetched;
   They sweated their duds till they riz it:
For Larry was ever the lad,
   When a boy was condemned to the squeezer,

Would fence all the duds that he had
    To help a poor friend to a sneezer,
       And warm his gob 'fore he died.
....

"I'm sorry dear Larry," says I,
    "To see you in this situation;
And, blister my limbs if I lie,
    I'd as lieve it had been my own station."
"Ochone! it's all over,' says he,
    For the neckcloth I'll be forced to put on,
And by this time tomorrow you'll see
    Your poor Larry as dead as a mutton,
       Because, why, his courage was good."
....

Then the clergy came in with his book,
    He spoke him so smooth and so civil;
Larry tipped him a Kilmainham look,
    And pitched his bag wig to the devil;
Then sighing, he threw back his head
    To get a sweet drop of the bottle,
And pitiful sighing, he said:
    "Oh, the hemp will be soon round my throttle,
       And choke my poor windpipe to death."
.....

When he came to the nubbling chit,
    He was tucked up so neat and so pretty,
The rumbler jogged off from his feet,
    And he died with his face to the city;
He kicked, too—but that was all pride,
    For soon you might see twas all over;
Soon after, the noose was untied;
    And at darky we waked him in clover,
    And sent him to take a ground sweat.

Chapter Six
DUBLIN AFTER THE FAMINE

After the famine roads, which went nowhere, came the railroads, linking the suburbs to the city centre, the north to the south, the capital to the countryside. Some of the great entrepreneurs of late nineteenth-century Dublin were railway men, and they brought other manufacturing and engineering projects to the city. The state held back from interfering in the development of the city in this period, and the Corporation had very little power. The late nineteenth-century projects were those of determined individuals, businessmen turned philanthropists or patrons of the arts. At the same time, the population of the city was coming to be imaginatively refigured not as a community but as the "masses". The poverty of the working classes in late nineteenth-century Dublin had a great deal to do with traditions of casual labour in a city with what has been described as a warehouse economy. While Irish parliamentary politics were largely dominated by the land question, city politics had a lot to do with the resistance to syndicalism and trade unionism. After the failure of the Repeal Movement in the 1840s the later century was dominated by campaigns for land reform and Home Rule. Charles Stewart Parnell was the dominant parliamentary leader in the period.

In parallel with parliamentary politics there was more violent agitation, much of it associated with the Fenians. Fenianism was a revolutionary movement which had begun in the Irish immigrant communities in the United States following the collapse of the Repeal and Young Ireland movements and the devastation of the Famine in the 1840s. On St Patrick's Day 1858 James Stephens (1824-1901), a veteran of the failed 1848 rising who had subsequently fled to Paris, set up a revolutionary society in Dublin dedicated to establishing a democratic Irish republic. This secret society had no name to begin with; the name Fenian, referring to the warriors of ancient Ireland, was adopted by a parallel branch of the organization in America headed by John O'Mahony (1816-77). It was gradually extended to encompass the Irish movement. In 1867 there was an unsuccessful

Fenian rising in County Dublin. Fenianism also began to develop terrorist tactics in this period. Towards the end of the century a significant number of women began to become involved in political action, some on the national question (as unionists or nationalists), some as feminists, many as both. The Ladies Land League was the first major political organization run by women. In the two decades before the Easter Rising women became involved in a variety of political organizations, though in many cases they complained of discrimination.

The Irish Literary Revival

During the period from the 1880s to the 1920s writers in both the English and Irish languages began to look to the past for inspiration, and to draw on images from Irish folklore and mythology. Standish James O'Grady's English versions of ancient Irish bardic tales influenced Yeats and other poets. Lady Gregory collected folklore as a means to access indigenous Irish culture, and J. M. Synge visited the remote Aran Islands as part of the same project. The revival gave impetus to the foundation of the Irish Literary Theatre (later the Abbey Theatre) with its commitment to Irish drama. The Arts and Crafts Movement in Ireland also developed a distinctly Irish flavour. Popular historians revived interest in the Brehon Laws, Ireland's medieval legal system, and used an interpretation of those laws to suggest that indigenous Irish culture was more inclined to co-operative organization, and was significantly less patriarchal than the imposed British culture. The literary revival was part of a broader attempt to re-Gaelicize Irish culture, which saw people with nationalist sympathies take up study of the Irish language, and support the Gaelic Athletic Association, with its function to preserve and cultivate the national pastimes of Ireland and encourage a boycott of "garrison" sports such as rugby and cricket.

In some ways the Irish revival was the cultural wing of the independence movement, but there were many people who espoused cultural nationalism and yet rejected the violent overthrow of British rule. By the outbreak of the First World War in 1914 a Bill providing for Irish Home Rule had finally been enacted in the British parliament, but it was suspended for the duration of the war. Although the 1916 Easter Rising was better organized and supported than any rising since that of Robert Emmet, it did not claim widespread support in Dublin until British executions and reprisals alienated public opinion and propelled a full-scale revolution.

The Great Dublin Exhibition
Thursday 12 May 1853

William Dargan (1799-1867), the railway contractor, was the genius behind the decision to provide a showcase for Irish industry at the Great Dublin Exhibition of 1853. Dargan was born near Carlow, and educated in England. He joined a surveyor's office and was employed under Thomas Telford on the construction of the Holyhead road in 1820. He then returned to Ireland to start his own contracting business and in 1831 built the first railway in Ireland, the Dublin to Dún Laoghaire line. The business prospered, and by 1853 he had constructed over six hundred miles of railway as well as the Ulster Canal, connecting Lough Erne and Belfast.

The exhibition was sited on the lawn of the Royal Dublin Society outside Leinster House, facing Merrion Square. It lasted from 12 May to 31 October. Queen Victoria, Prince Albert, and the Prince of Wales, then a boy of twelve, paid an official visit on 29 August. When the exhibition opened, the architect, John Benson, was given a knighthood. Queen Victoria visited Dargan at his house, Mount Anville, Dundrum, and he was offered a baronetcy, which he declined.

In the immediate context of post-famine Ireland, Dargan's exhibition was an important attempt to restore some sense of national pride and to promote Irish manufactures in a way that would counteract the sense that Ireland's troubles had made the country some kind of pariah for business. It would also and provide some short term employment in a city of high unemployment and poverty.

The iron, timber, and glass exhibition pavilion had three domed halls and four other exhibition rooms with gallery promenades. It was one-third the size of the Crystal Palace, built to house London's Great Exhibition in 1851. There was a Fine Art Court, a Machinery Court, and a space for foreign exhibits.

The Illustrated Dublin Exhibition Catalogue contrasts the London Exhibition with the Great Irish Industrial Exhibition:

We consider the Great Exhibition held in Dublin in the year 1853, as even a larger contribution to the wealth of these kingdoms, than the Great Exhibition which took place in London in the year 1851; and we do not doubt that His Royal Highness Prince Albert, on visiting the Irish Capital, will earnestly rejoice that his indefatigable exertions and enlightened policy—which made that year memorable—have again borne rich fruitage, and again advanced the best interest of his country (Virtue).

Dargan lost £20,000 of his own money on the exhibition. One notable outcome, however, was the founding of the National Gallery of Ireland the following year. The gallery opened a decade later, largely thanks to Dargan's efforts. His contribution to the nation was recognized by the statue of him by Sir Thomas Farrell on the lawn outside the gallery, adjacent to the place where his exhibition once stood. Moreover, the city went on to host several more industrial exhibitions through the nineteenth century.

Dargan's later business ventures outside construction work did not prosper. In 1866 he was injured in a fall from his horse, and his inability to attend to his affairs brought acute financial difficulties. He died at 2 Fitzwilliam Square the following year.

Donnybrook Fair
21 August 1854

"O you lads that are witty, from famed Dublin city
And you that in pasttime take any delight,
To Donnybrook fly, for the time's drawing nigh
When fat pigs are hunted, and lean cobblers fight;
When maidens so swift, run for a new shift;
Men, muffled in sacks, for a shirt they race there;
There jockeys well booted, and horses sure-footed,
All keep up the humours of Donnybrook Fair.

Brisk lads and young lasses can there fill their glasses
With whisky, and send a full bumper around;

Jig it off in a tent till their money's all spent,
   And spin like a top till they rest on the ground.
Oh, Donnybrook capers, to sweet cat-gut scrapers,
   They bother thy vapours, and drive away care;
And what is more glorious – there's naught more uproarious –
   Huzza for the humours of Donnybrook Fair."
Charles O'Flaherty, from "The Humours of Donnybrook Fair"

Donnybrook Fair, an annual event since 1204, was held for the last time on 21 August 1854. The following year it was suppressed. This was part of a pattern of regulating and suppressing fairs and other outdoor festivities in the nineteenth century.

In 1204 King John granted a licence to the Corporation of Dublin for the holding of an annual eight-day fair in the village of Donnybrook, and under Henry III, this was extended to fifteen days. Originally, opening day was 3 May, the Feast of the Finding of the True Cross. This was later changed to 21 March, the feast of St. Benedict and finally settled in August.

During the Middle Ages, the fair was of little importance to Dublin, since it was dangerous to leave the protection of the city walls and brave the bands of outlaws who would attack, rob and murder defenceless citizens. The Corporation disposed of the Donnybrook Fair licence to the Ussher Family in the sixteenth century; in 1756 the Usshers gave it to Sir William Wolsely, who in turn leased it to Joseph Madden in 1778. The Madden family kept the licence until 1855, when they resold it to the Corporation for £3,000. The Corporation instantly suppressed the fair.

As it had grown and become more popular, the fair had become a by-word for disorder and drunkenness. In 1779 *Faulkner's Dublin Journal* noted that "[T]he fair continued until yesterday, and will probably last until it shall grow into such an enormity of riot and outrage as shall end itself." The phrase "a donnybrook" entered the language, meaning a scene of uproar. The Fair Green was covered in booths made of sods covered with rags, old sheet and petticoats. Most of these sold drink, but some sold "neat victuals", mainly salt beef and cabbage, potatoes and Dublin Bay herrings. There were horse dealers, games, boxing and wrestling exhibitions, and usually some kind of half-organized fighting. An 1836 licensing act specified that traders had to close their outdoor booths from 6pm to 9am in summer. Drinking and fighting were generally reported to be at their worst in late afternoon and early evening, when the more respectable pursuits of the fair had been exhausted. The real problem started after dark when there was dancing to very loud music, which in turn gave rise to a lot of fighting and brawling.

Charles O'Flaherty (c.1794-1828) is the author of a poem that captures the teeming activity of the fair, with the range of occupations and classes to be met with, the games such as sack races and toss-throwing, the music and dancing, the smells of food and drink, the ballad-singers, hawkers and traders, and the circus animals.

> *'Tis there are dogs dancing, and wild beasts a-prancing,*
> *With neat bits of painting in red, yellow, and gold;*
> *Toss-players and scramblers, and showmen and gamblers,*
> *Pickpockets in plenty, both of young and of old.*
> *There are brewers, and bakers, and jolly shoemakers,*
> *With butchers, and porters, and men that cut hair;*
> *There are mountebanks grinning, while others are sinning,*
> *To keep up the humours of Donnybrook Fair.*

Contemporary records agree that the most objectionable thing about the fair was the noise and as the area grew more residential, the cry for its abolition became stronger. This eventually led to a formation of a committee led by the local Catholic Curate Fr. P. J. Nowlan. This committee conducted a very strong publicity campaign against the fair, calling it a place where no respectable person would go and citing it as a means of corrupting and depraving the people of Dublin. Finally the campaign succeeded, and in 1855 when the Corporation of Dublin regained the licence, the fair was suppressed.

The Phoenix Park Murders
Saturday 6 May 1882

> *"The new Chief Secretary, Lord Frederick Cavendish, remained in*
> *the offices of his own department, engaged in business, till past seven*
> *o'clock, when he set out for his lodge in Phoenix Park, which is about*
> *the centre of that inclosure. His Lordship went on foot. He knew the*

way well, for he had been there before when his brother, Lord Hart-
ington, was Chief Secretary. He had arrived from England but at
noon of that fatal day.

Mr Burke, the Under-Secretary, left the Castle on a car some
minutes later, and overtook Lord F. Cavendish about the Park gate.
The Under-Secretary then got off the car, which he dismissed, and the
Under-Secretary and Chief Secretary walked together on the left-
hand path. It is presumed that Lord Cavendish was going merely to
look in at his own house, for he and the Under-Secretary were to
dine with Lord Spencer at the Viceregal Lodge. About two hundred
yards from the Phoenix Column, they were murderously attacked. It
was then nearly half-past seven o'clock, but it was still broad daylight.
The attack was so sudden and silent that it scarcely attracted any
notice. A common hackney car appears to have driven up and four
fellows jumped off it, the driver remaining in his seat. Lord Freder-
ick Cavendish was on the outside of the path, and Mr Burke was next
the grass. The assailants rushed upon them with daggers, and a fierce
struggle for life took place. But the murderers killed their victims in
a few moments, and then drove off by a side road in the direction of
Chapelizod, and rapidly disappeared."

The Illustrated London News, May 1882

The new Chief Secretary for Ireland, Lord Frederick Cavendish (1836-
1882), arrived in Dublin at noon on 6 May 1882, in the train of the
new Lord Lieutenant of Ireland, Earl Spencer. Spencer made a formal
entry into the city and rode on horseback to Dublin Castle, where he
was sworn in. A fifteen-gun salute in Phoenix Park announced that the
ceremony was complete.

The office of Chief Secretary to the Lord Lieutenant was one of the
principal offices of state in Ireland and by the end of the nineteenth
century carried more weight than that of the Lord Lieutenant himself.
The Chief Secretary was the main exponent of government policy on
Ireland in the House of Commons, and as such he was responsible for
the work of 29 government departments. Cavendish, the second son of
the Duke of Devonshire, had been an MP for seventeen years before his
posting to Ireland.

At seven o'clock that evening, Cavendish was walking in Phoenix
Park with his Under-Secretary, T. H. Burke. A group of assassins armed

with surgical knives approached the two men and brutally stabbed them to death.

The second murdered man was Thomas Henry Burke (1829-1882), a Galway man. Burke entered Dublin Castle as a clerk in 1847 and worked in various departments attached to the Chief Secretary's Office. In 1869 he became Under-Secretary for Ireland and he was closely associated with the policy of government coercion during the Land War.

The background to the murders was precisely the Irish Land War, fought on and off between 1879 and 1903. In 1879 the Irish National Land league was formed in Dublin by Michael Davitt (1846-1905), a nationalist leader who was himself the son of an evicted tenant farmer from Mayo. Davitt spent his youth in England where he lost an arm in a factory accident in Lancashire. He came back to Ireland fired up with concern for farmers and for industrial labourers. He joined the Fenian movement in 1865 and in 1870 he was sentenced to fifteen years of penal servitude for gun-running.

The Fenian movement was a revolutionary movement partly originating among the Irish immigrant population in the United States, which dramatically increased in the years after the famine. The collapse of the Repeal Movement and of the Young Irelanders after the failed rising of 1848 sent many activists overseas and left a leadership vacuum in Ireland, only partially filled by the constitutional movement for independence. The originally nameless secret society founded in Dublin on St. Patrick's Day 1858 by James Stephens, evolved into the Fenian organization or "brotherhood". The name "Fenian" was adopted from a parallel American organization led by John O'Mahony.

There was a small Fenian rising at the beginning of March 1867. Although it was poorly supported as it happened, there was a mobilization of nationalist sympathy for the Fenians after they had been put down. In September 1867 an attempt to rescue two Fenian prisoners from a police van in Manchester resulted in the death of a policeman. In November five men were convicted of his murder and three of these were executed. The deaths of the "Manchester martyrs" increased the Irish public's sympathy for Fenianism and softened the attitude of the influential Catholic Church towards the Fenians.

When Davitt came out of prison in 1877 he became an architect of the so-called New Departure, a compact with the Home Rule politician, Charles Stewart Parnell and Fenian leader John Devoy, in which the three men asserted the indivisible link between the land question and the national question. This proved a springboard from which they could launch the Irish Land League and the agrarian campaign of 1879-82. Parnell became president of the League, widening its support base. Tenants were demanding rent abatements to take account of a serious economic downturn. Since the Famine there had been an increase in the number of annual tenancies with the result that tenants had to face significant annual rent increases and could lose their farms at six months notice. The Land League transformed the campaign for rent reductions into a campaign against the systematic abuses of the Irish landowning system. When landlords did not concede, rents were withheld, evictions impeded and landlords and their agents boycotted (a term coined in response to the treatment given to Captain Charles Boycott, an agent in County Mayo who came into conflict with the League and was consigned to what Parnell described as "moral Coventry"). There was also an increase in agrarian crime during the Land War. Meanwhile, the League boosted its own supporters with mass meetings and with aid for evicted tenants.

When William Ewart Gladstone became Prime Minister of the United Kingdom in 1880 he acknowledged the need for concessions on the land question and established a parliamentary commission of enquiry. The Irish Land Act (1881) gave Irish tenants the "three Fs": fair rents, fixity of tenure and free sale. This might have defused tensions over land more significantly if Gladstone had not also introduced coercive legislation to curb agrarian protests. The Land League bitterly opposed William Edward Forster's Coercion Bill early in 1881. The government arrested Parnell and most of the leaders of the Land League, who had rejected the terms of the Land Act as inadequate, imprisoning them in Kilmainham gaol in October 1881, and suppressing the League. Agrarian crime increased in protest at these arrests. Early in 1882 the Kilmainham Treaty between Gladstone and Parnell offered release from prison and increased concessions to poorer farmers in the Land Act in return for support for the Act from the League leaders and their influence in quelling unrest.

Parnell was released from Kilmainham on 2 May 1882. On 6 May the Phoenix Park murders took place. The killings produced widespread shock and disgust. The culprits were the Irish National Invincibles, a

Penny Dreadful name for a small fanatical group of Fenians. The assassins were James Carey, Dan Curley, James Mullett and Edward McCaffrey. By July 1882 Carey was already a police suspect. Carey was a Dubliner, the son of a bricklayer and himself a bricklayer turned master-builder. He had been a member of the Fenians since the early 1860s, and was a veteran of the 1867 rising. But he was also a figure of some social respectability, not merely a prosperous tradesman and property owner, but active in his local Catholic church, and recently elected to the Dublin Corporation.

Under arrest Carey turned Queen's evidence, and as a result of his testimony five of his co-conspirators were hanged, and a further eight were sentenced to penal servitude. The men he betrayed were of a humbler class—artisans, labourers, cab drivers and publicans—and hatred of their crime did not prevent Carey from being loathed with the contempt usually felt for those who save themselves at the expense of former comrades.

When the trial ended Carey was kept for his own safety in Kilmainham prison, while his wife and seven children were moved by the authorities to London. In return for his evidence Carey was to be relocated in Natal. He joined his wife and children on the *Kinfaus Castle*, a ship bound for Cape Town. The family travelled under Mrs. Carey's maiden name of Power. On board the ship "the Power family" was befriended by another Irish passenger, Patrick O'Donnell, who was travelling with a young woman relative (who later emerged as a girlfriend) to Natal. O'Donnell was only booked as far as Cape Town, but the two families became so close that O'Donnell decided to travel on with the Powers to Natal. At Cape Town they all transferred to a coastal steamer, *The Melrose*, which set off on 28 July 1883. The next day, at about 3.45 pm, O'Donnell and Power were having a drink together when O'Donnell pulled out a revolver and shot his friend. The first shot hit Carey in the neck. He staggered towards his wife's cabin and O'Donnell fired a second shot into his back. Carey's wife came out and as she held him O'Donnell fired his third and final shot. Mrs. Carey and her children gathered around the dying man, covered in his blood. O'Donnell approached Mrs. Carey and told her, "I had to do it."

Both O'Donnell and his victim were brought ashore at Port Elizabeth. O'Donnell was brought before a magistrate to be charged with the murder, and Carey was buried.

The news of Carey's murder was greeted with widespread joy in Dublin. There were bonfires in Abbey Street and in Temple Bar. In the usual bonfire night tradition children went around begging pennies "to burn James Carey."

The immediate assumption in the popular press was that O'Donnell was an Invincible who had tracked Carey with the intention of murdering him. O'Donnell was a Donegal man who had worked for several years in America and who had decided to go to South Africa to try his luck in the diamond mines. On the way from America to South Africa he had made a visit home to Gweedore in the early summer of 1883, at the time when Carey's associates were being executed, and been made aware of the violent animosity against Carey in Ireland. On the voyage to South Africa several passengers had recognized the Carey family, who were not heavily disguised, and O'Donnell, who carried a gun from his years in America, seems to have felt it a duty to act as executioner. He may have been drunk at the time of the shooting.

O'Donnell was brought to England for trial and in spite of the large sums raised for his defence fund in Ireland and especially in America, he was convicted and hanged in London on 17 December 1883. There are memorials for him—casting him as a nationalist martyr—in his native Derrybeg, and in Glasnevin. Also in Glasnevin is a memorial to James FitzHarris, known as Skin-the-Goat, the Dublin jarvey who drove the Invincibles to the scene of the murder. He was offered £10,000 and a pardon to inform on the men, but refused, and was sentenced to penal servitude for life. He is mentioned in the Eumaeus episode of *Ulysses*. The National Graves Association erected his memorial plaque in 1968. Thomas H. Burke is also buried at Glasnevin.

Transit of Venus Watched from Dunsink Observatory
Wednesday 6 December 1882

"The sun was already beginning to put on the ruddy hues of sunset, and there, far in on its face, was the sharp, round, black disc of Venus. It was then easy to sympathise with the supreme joy of Horrocks, when, in 1639, he for the first time witnessed this spectacle. The intrinsic interest of the phenomenon, its rarity, the fulfilment of the prediction, the noble problem which the transit of Venus helps

us to solve, are all present to our thoughts when we look at this pleasing picture, a repetition of which will not occur again until the flowers are blooming in the June of A.D. 2004.

Sir Robert Ball

Among Robert Ball's earliest memories was his recollection of being thrust from an upstairs window of the family home to look down on the passing funeral of Daniel O'Connell. Robert Stawall Ball (1840-1913) was born in Dublin and grew up through the famine years. He was the son of Robert Ball (1802-57), a botanist and naturalist, sometime secretary of Dublin Zoological Society. Robert Ball senior married Amelia Gresley, the daughter of a Bristol merchant, and they lived for many years at 3 Granby Row, near Rutland Square. In the house was a library largely devoted to natural history and philosophy, and a small museum of artefacts collected by Ball. The family often provided a temporary home for animals on their way to the zoo—a Brazilian sloth and a tortoise from the Galapagos were sometime inhabitants of 3 Granby Row.

Ball attended school first in Dublin, at North Great George Street, and then at a small boarding school in England, before entering Trinity College Dublin after his father's sudden early death. While he was at Trinity he read the work of Charles Darwin and became an advocate of evolutionary theory. After his graduation he was offered a position as tutor to the children of the Earl of Rosse. He accepted on condition he might use the astronomical facilities at Birr Castle, the Earl's seat in County Offaly.

William Parsons, the third Earl of Rosse (1800-1867) had begun building telescopes in the 1820s. In the 1840s Rosse made the "Leviathan of Birr"; with its 72-inch mirror the Leviathan remained the world's largest telescope for over seventy years until 1917. In 1867 Ball became professor of applied mathematics at the Royal College of Science, in Dublin, and the following year he married Frances Steele. His theoretical work earned him the fellowship of the Royal Society and the Cunningham Medal of the Royal Irish Academy. From 1874 he was Andrews Professor of Astronomy at Trinity and director of the Dunsink Observatory. (Dunsink is the principal astronomical observatory in Ireland and part of the Dublin Institute for Advanced Studies. It was founded by Trinity College in 1783 and is situated four miles north-west of the city centre.) The Dunsink position gave Ball a good residence, only yards from the Observatory, plus 14 acres of farmland. Here the Balls raised a family; when he moved to Cambridge in 1892 he noted with gratitude the provision of piped gas and water, both absent in the Dunsink residence.

During the period 1874-84 Ball gave over 700 public lectures in Ireland and Britain. He was a talented popularizer of scientific theories, and his first book, *The Story of the Heavens*, was published in 1885. In 1886 he was knighted for his services to science and education.

A transit of Venus is the observed passage of the planet across the disk of the sun. The planet Venus, orbiting the sun catches up with and passes the slower earth. The first recorded observation of a transit was by young Jeremiah Horrocks in 1639, about three decades after the invention of the telescope. Since then, transits have been witnessed in 1761, 1769, 1874, 1882 and 2004. The next will be in 2012. The pattern of frequency for transits of Venus is such that there will be a long gap (between 100 and 121 years), followed by an eight-year gap, then the pattern repeats.

When Robert Ball arrived at Dunsink in 1874, his assistant, Dr. Ralph Copeland, was in Mauritius observing the transit of Venus. Eight years later Ball made scrupulous preparations for the observation of the next transit on 6 December 1882. When he realized that his view of the transit would be blocked by a tree on a neighbouring farm, he asked permission to have it felled. But there was little he could do about the winter weather. In *The Story of the Heavens* he describes the day of the transit:

> *The morning of the eventful day appeared to be about as unfavourable for a grand astronomical spectacle as could well be imagined. Snow, a couple of inches thick, covered the ground, and more was falling, with but little intermission, all the forenoon. It seemed almost hopeless that a view of the phenomenon could be obtained from that observatory...*
>
> *The snow was still falling when the domes were opened; but, according to our prearranged scheme, the telescopes were directed, not indeed upon the sun, but to the place where we knew the sun was, and the clockwork was set in motion which carried round the telescopes, still constantly pointing towards the invisible sun.*
>
> *... The tourmaline was all ready, but up to one o'clock not a trace of the sun could be seen. Shortly after one o'clock, however, we noticed that the day was getting lighter; and, on looking to the north, whence the wind and the snow were coming, we saw, to our inexpressible delight, that the clouds were clearing. At length, the sky towards the south began to improve, and at last, as the critical moment approached, we could, detect the spot where the sun was becoming visible. But the .predicted moment arrived and passed, and still the sun had not broken through the clouds, though every moment the certainty that it would do so became more apparent.*
>
> *... To my delight, I saw the small notch in the margin of the sun showing that the transit had commenced, and that the planet was then one-third on the sun... While steadily looking at the exquisitely beautiful sight of the gradual advance of the planet, I became aware that there were other objects besides Venus between me and the sun. They were the snowflakes, which again began to fall rapidly. I must admit the phenomenon was singularly beautiful. The telescopic effect of a snowstorm with the sun as a background I had never before seen. It reminded me of the golden rain which is sometimes seen falling from a flight of sky-rockets during pyrotechnic displays; I would gladly have dispensed with the spectacle, for it necessarily followed that the sun and Venus again disappeared from view. The*

clouds gathered, the snowstorm descended as heavily as ever, and we hardly dared to hope that we should see anything more; 1 hr. 57 min. came and passed, the first internal contact was over, and Venus had fully entered on the sun. We had only obtained a brief view, and we had not yet been able to make any measurements or other observations that could be of service. Still, to have seen even a part of a transit of Venus is an event to remember for a lifetime, and we felt more delight than can be easily expressed at even this slight gleam of success. But better things were in store... at half-past two the clouds began to disperse, and the prospect of seeing the sun began to improve... The clouds at length dispersed, and at this time Venus had so completely entered on the sun that the distance from the edge of the planet to the edge of the sun was about twice the diameter of the planet...

In 1892 Ball moved to a position as Lowdean Professor of Astronomy at Cambridge University, where he remained until his death. Four of Ball's siblings were also distinguished scientists. Anne Elizabeth Ball (1808-72) was a botanist who concentrated on cryptogams (non-flowering plants), and some of her work was published *via* William Thompson's *Natural History of Ireland* (1856). Mary Ball (1812-98) was a naturalist, a collector of insects, shells and marine invertebrates. She had a notable collection of dragonflies. Sir Charles Ball Bent (1851-1916) was a surgeon, specializing in diseases of the anus and rectum, and also an amateur naturalist. Valentine Ball (1843-95) was a geologist working on the Geological Survey of India from 1864-81. He held the chair of geology at Trinity College Dublin for two years, resigning in 1883 to become director of the Dublin Science and Art Museum.

Parnell's Funeral
Sunday 11 October 1891

"Berkeley, Swift, Burke, Grattan, Parnell, Augusta Gregory, Synge, Kevin O'Higgins, are the true Irish people, and there is nothing too hard for such as these. If the Catholic names are few, history will soon fill the gap."
W. B. Yeats. *Explorations*

"His funeral was a great affair. The crowd looked so resolute that Sir Garnet Wolseley (the Irish Commander-in-Chief) declared it was 'the only crowd he was ever afraid of.'"
Timothy Michael Healy, *Letters and Leaders of My Day*

"Ah, the sad autumn day,
When the last sad troop came
Swift down the ancient way,
Keening a chieftain's name."
Lionel Johnson, from 'Parnell'

Charles Stewart Parnell (1846-1891), disgraced leader of the Irish parliamentary party, died of pneumonia at his home in Brighton, near midnight on 6 October 1891.

Shortly after Parnell's election to the British parliament as a Home Rule candidate in 1880 he had met Katharine O'Shea, wife of Captain Willie O'Shea, a fellow Home Rule MP. Parnell and Mrs. O'Shea established a covert relationship with the collusion of Captain O'Shea. Katharine O'Shea had three daughters by Parnell and they lived in some degree of domesticity. In 1889 Captain O'Shea decided to sue for a divorce from his wife, citing Parnell as co-respondent. This precipitated Parnell's fall from grace in his party. He was repudiated by the British Prime Minister Gladstone, and by most of his MPs, who feared the influence of the Catholic Church's condemnation on their constituents.

In June 1891 he married Katharine, but his constitution seems to have been weakened by the stress endured in the last stages of his political career. After his death his wife at first rejected the proposal that his body should be returned to the Ireland where he had been spurned, but then she changed her mind.

Parnell's body was transported by boat to Kingstown and was taken to St. Michan's Church in Dublin for a service. The remains were then removed to the City Hall for the lying-in-state. More than 30,000 people came to look at the coffin and pay their respects.

At 2.30 pm the funeral cortege left City Hall, led by members of the Gaelic Athletic Association. The hearse was drawn by six black horses. Behind the hearse, with his master's boots and stirrups reversed, walked the favourite of Parnell's horses, Home Rule. A crowd of 50,000 people joined the procession to Glasnevin cemetery, and the streets were lined with a further 150,000.

The procession took four hours to walk to Glasnevin, and dusk was falling as it approached the cemetery. Roadside lamps were being lit. As the body was being lowered into the grave a shooting star was seen travelling across the evening sky, impressing the sense of grief and powerful atmosphere of the moment on the large crowd present.

The mourners plucked sprigs of ivy from the surrounding shrubs, trees and walls to save as a memento of the day. The ivy leaf subsequently became the symbol of Parnell, and Ivy Day is now commemorated annually on the Sunday closest to Parnell's anniversary, 6 October, when a wreath is laid on his grave.

Seven years after his death, Parnell's mother Delia Stewart, an American, died and was buried beside her son.

The Parnell Memorial Committee was formed in 1937 and in 1939 the committee organized the memorial stone that marks the grave in what is now known as Parnell circle. A granite boulder, brought from a hillside near Poulaphuca in Parnell's native Wicklow, is inscribed with the single word: PARNELL. Many poems were written in memory of Parnell in the years after his death. This is the first verse of Seumas O'Sullivan's "Glasnevin, 9 October, 1904":

They peer about his grave with curious eyes,
And for his sin they pity him, their chief,
With miserable mockery of grief;
Beyond their littleness, serene he lies,
Nor heeds the insult of their sympathies,
This man pre-eminent by strong belief
In his own heat—a little while, for brief
The resting-time is when a hero dies.

Subversion at Victoria's Jubilee Celebrations
Sunday 20 June 1897

> *"Working-class of Ireland: We appeal to you not to allow your opinions to be misrepresented on this occasion. Join your voice with ours in protesting against the base assumption that we owe to this Empire any other debt than that of hatred of all its plundering institutions. Let this year be indeed a memorable one as marking the date when the Irish workers at last flung off that slavish dependence on the lead of "the gentry", which has paralysed the arm of every soldier of freedom in the past.*
>
> *The Irish landlords, now as ever the enemy's garrison, instinctively support every institution which, like monarchy, degrades the manhood of the people and weakens the moral fibre of the oppressed; the middle-class, absorbed in the pursuit of gold, have pawned their souls for the prostitute glories of commercialism and remain openly or secretly hostile to every movement which would imperil the sanctity of their dividends. The working class alone have nothing to hope for save in a revolutionary reconstruction of society; they, and they alone, are capable of that revolutionary initiative which, with all the political and economic development of the time to aid it, can carry us forward into the promised land of perfect Freedom, the reward of the age long travail of the people.*
>
> James Connolly, *Socialism and Nationalism*

The Lawrence Studios opened on Sackville Street in 1865. The firm's founder, William Lawrence, took over the photography business from his brother John, and opened their studios on the premises of his mother's toy shop. Lawrence had a thriving portrait business, but it is the studios' topographical views that are best known today. When it became possible to transport equipment, something that arrived with the development of the dry-plate process, the studio was able to send its best-known and most prolific photographer, Robert French, around Ireland to take images of almost every small village and town in the country. The Lawrence Studios began selling postcards, souvenirs and view-books of French's photographs from the late-1860s onwards.

During the 1880s photographers from the Lawrence Studios took a series of images of evictions in various parts of the country, including those on the estates of Colonel John O'Callaghan in Bodyke and the Vandeleur Estate in Kilrush, both in County Clare. This was one of the first exercises in photojournalism in Ireland. The pictures provide a record of the Plan of Campaign, a tenants' rent protest that subsequently led to hundreds of evictions. The campaign, which was organized by William O'Brien and John Dillon, received widespread coverage in the British and Irish press during the late 1880s. The Plan targeted estates of more economically vulnerable landlords, who were less able to hold out against a rent strike. On some estates, where rents were withheld, the landlords evicted tenants with the active support of members of both the militia and the Royal Irish Constabulary. Many of the eviction photographs depict the use of force against the protesters. Given the slow exposure times at the period, it was necessary for the photographer to gain assistance from both the authorities and the tenants, who had to "pose" even for the action shots.

Lantern slides of these eviction scenes were used as a political propaganda tool against Queen Victoria. During the Queen's Jubilee celebrations in 1897, Maud Gonne orchestrated public displays of images of evictions and deaths from starvation by projecting them on to the exterior of a building in Rutland (Parnell) Square, from the window of the National Club. She had been using the slides for some time in lecture tours to support land agitation. James Connolly arranged with council workers to interrupt power supplies so that the slides would not be competing with festive jubilee lights in the Square.

Other activities were planned to disrupt Jubilee Day. Gonne made black flags embroidered with information about famines and evictions during the reign of Victoria. The committee planning celebrations for the centenary of the United Irishmen's Rebellion of 1798, the following year, called a convention at City Hall as an alternative to the day's celebrations. James Connolly called a socialist meeting in Dame Street, addressed by Gonne. In the evening Connolly led a procession down Dame Street, with the workers' band playing the Dead March, and a handcart carrying a coffin labelled "British Empire". The police arrived and attempted to disperse the crowd with baton charges. Connolly reached O'Connell Bridge with the procession, and realizing that they could go no further, ordered the coffin to be thrown into the Liffey, to shouts of "To Hell with the British Empire". Connolly was arrested and spent the night in Bridewell. Maud Gonne, accompanied that evening by W. B. Yeats, returned to the National Club to see the progress of the slide show.

During the anti-Jubilee demonstrations an elderly woman was beaten to death with batons, and two hundred people had to be treated for their injuries.

In 1943 The National Library of Ireland purchased the William Lawrence Photograph Collection of 40,000 glass plate negatives, and it is held at the National Photographic Archive.

Queen Victoria's Last Visit to Dublin
Wednesday 4 April 1900

"Under all the banners and floral devices and glaring illuminations, was still poor old humdrum Dublin, with its 200,000 dwellers in squalid tenements, its ruined trade, its teeming workhouses, its hopeless poverty—the once-proud capital of a free nation degraded to the level of the biggest city of a decaying and fettered province."
The Irish People

Early in 1900 an announcement came from Dublin Castle that the eighty-year-old Queen Victoria was planning a visit to Ireland. The Castle suggested that this three-week visit would be largely private and informal. Nevertheless the Queen was to undertake some official engagements.

Unionists, royalists and people who felt pride in the British Empire looked forward to the visit, and began preparations for civic festivities. On the other hand, nationalist feeling in the city was strong, and Dublin's Lord Mayor had been elected as a nationalist candidate. There was a widespread belief amongst nationalists that the real reason for the visit was to aid recruitment of Irish soldiers to the flagging British campaign in South Africa.

Local people established committees to decorate the streets, to organize parties, to make formal statements of welcome. The city was transformed for the royal visit, with streets along the royal route, by which Victoria would pass from Kingstown to the city centre, festooned with Union Jacks and red-white-and-blue bunting, Venetian masts, triumphal arches and Royal Standards.

Victoria arrived in Ireland on 3 April 1900, when the royal yacht docked at Victoria pier in Kingstown (Dún Laoghaire), so-named after the visit of George IV in 1821. At night the royal fleet was illuminated and crowds watched as

One after another dazzling devices were lit up by electricity and gas and sprang into notice on the principal buildings so that the town was ablaze with multi-coloured lights—An astonishing wave of loyalty and love seemed to spread over the thousands of spectators who filled the east pier and the roads adjoining, and many persons fluttered mini-union jacks and sang patriotic airs.

The royal party disembarked the next day to be welcomed by a crowd assembled on stands and lining the streets around Victoria Wharf in Kingstown. Wednesday 4 April had been declared a public holiday. Following a formal address of welcome from the Kingstown Town Clerk the parade began. The procession was made up of four carriages carrying various members of the royal party, the Viceroy and his wife, and an array of government figures. This type of parade was the usual currency of royal visits, although perhaps orchestrated with more than usual care when the Queen visited sites of contention or possible dissent. Victoria's route was through the most loyalist parts of the city and crowds that gathered to cheer her along the way were encouraged to feel like participants in the event. Hence, even streets off the main route were decorated and parties organized. Loyalists had come on excursions from all over the country, but particularly from Belfast, to enjoy the celebrations.

The royal cortege passed from the suburbs into the city centre over the Grand Canal at Leeson Street Bridge, where the Queen was formally welcomed into the city and presented with the keys and civic sword. At the bridge a large mock medieval castle gate and tower had been erected in an attempt to echo the more ancient gate to the walled city of Dublin. Austin Clarke recalls how "As a child, I was held up to see Queen Victoria entering Dublin but can remember only the ornamental gateway which had been constructed at the confine of the city." Scarlet-clothed Beefeaters flanked the gate and a stand was erected nearby to seat dignitaries. Thomas Pile, Lord Mayor of Dublin, who had been elected as a nationalist, presented an address of welcome to the Queen on behalf of Dublin Corporation, a gesture which caused offence to nationalists in the city. The Corporation had voted in favour of the address by a narrow majority, and although it refrained from any statement of loyalty to Britain, it was still regarded by some nationalists as treacherous to their cause.

The procession then continued northwards, through the city centre, passing along Merrion Square to College Green, where it received a welcome from the assembled students and fellows of Trinity College. It proceeded along Dame Street and Parliament Street where it crossed the river at Grattan Bridge and made its way along the Liffey quays to the viceregal residence at Phoenix Park. The route missed much of the more nationalist and also more impoverished north side of the city. Sackville Street, Dublin's main thoroughfare, which had been packed for the funerals of O'Connell and Parnell, was not on this itinerary. During the Queen's visit a free party was held in Phoenix Park for 5,000 Dublin schoolchildren. This particular gesture had repercussions outlined below.

Opposition to the visit was vocal and determined. W. B. Yeats suggested that Dubliners should either boycott the visit, or administer a greater rebuke by watching the parade in silence. The nationalist press reported that this was indeed the response along parts of the route. Just as loyalist committees had formed to plan the celebrations for the visit, nationalist groups came together to plan a programme of opposing events, including a torchlight procession on the night of the Queen's arrival. A counter-demonstration by the Transvaal Committee was broken up by the police.

There were nationalists who wanted even the protests against the visit to refrain from insulting Queen Victoria herself since, whatever her history, she was now an old woman. On the other hand, Victoria was reviled in some quarters as "The Famine Queen", and this was the title of an article by Maud Gonne published in the *United Irishman* on 7 April:

Queen, return to your own land; you will find no more Irishmen ready to wear the red shame of your livery. In the past they have done so from ignorance, and because it is hard to die of hunger when one is young and strong and the sun shines, but they shall do so no longer.

This kind of polemical prose was very effective with its intended audience and to Gonne's satisfaction the authorities seized all copies of the journal. Gonne later won a libel action, related to the article, against a society journal, *Figaro*, whose editor's expenses had been paid by Dublin Castle.

Maud Gonne was not in Dublin at the time of the Queen's visit, but when she returned she began to discuss with other women a project to organize an excursion for children who had refused to attend the Queen's breakfast in Phoenix Park. The Patriotic Children's Treat Committee wanted to make a large gesture and by the end of June 1900 they had enrolled the names of 25,000 children eligible and eager to participate in a party at Clonturk Park. Refreshments were donated by sympathetic businesses and on the day the children went to the park in procession, carrying green branches to symbolize the rebirth of nationalist spirit. Many of the children held up cards proclaiming: "Irish Patriotic Children's treat—No Flunkeyism here". Men from the GAA and the Celtic Literary Society acted as marshals, and at the park there were games followed by speeches and refreshments.

One of the direct outcomes of this demonstration was that Maud Gonne and other women involved with the project went on to found a national women's committee, Inghinidhe na hEireann (Daughters of Erin). Founder members included Jenny Wyse-Power, Annie Egan, Anna Johnson, Alice Furlong, Maire Quinn, Dora Hackett, Elizabeth Morgan, Sarah White and Margaret Quinn. Among their objectives they listed "the re-establishment of the complete independence of Ireland" and "to discourage the reading and circulation of low English literature, the singing of English songs, the attending of vulgar English entertainments at the theatres and music hall, and to combat in every way English influence, which is doing so much harm to the artistic taste and refinement of the Irish people."

In 1901 Fanny Parnell, sister of Charles Stewart Parnell, wrote a "forgive and forget" poem on the occasion of Victoria's death:

22nd January 1901
Not four more years have passed to-day
And now the Queen, the Famine Queen
Herself has passed away,
And that dread form will never more be seen,
In pomp of fancied glory and of pride,
Or humbled, scorned, defeated as she died;

For by God's will she was amongst the first to fall
Beneath those mills of His that grind so wondrous small.

James Joyce and Nora Barnacle
Thursday 16 June 1904

"Trieste—Zürich—Paris 1914-1921."
    James Joyce, *Ulysses*

"On June 16 the gloom of the clinic was alleviated by the arrival of
a bouquet of hydrangeas, white and dyed blue, which some friends
sent him in honour of 'Bloomsday', as the day of Ulysses *was already*
called. In his notebook Joyce scrawled, 'Today 16 of June 1924
twenty years after. Will anybody remember this date?'"
    Richard Ellmann, *James Joyce*

James Joyce, graduate of University College Dublin, sometime music
student, and sometime schoolmaster, and an aspiring writer (with a few
published poems and essays to his name), lived in a first-floor room at
60 Shelbourne Road as a boarder with the McKernan family. He was
heavily in debt and could pay neither his rent nor the rental on the
piano he had leased from Piggott's. On Wednesday 15 June the
McKernans suggested to Joyce that he might leave their house until he
could pay his rent, and he took himself to the home of his friends James
and Gretta Cousins, who lived in a small house by the sea at
Ballsbridge.

Five days before his temporary eviction from Shelbourne Road,
Joyce had been walking down Nassau Street when he was moved by the
appearance of a beautiful young woman with auburn hair. He had
struck up a conversation with her. "Are you Swedish?" she had asked
him, with an inspired recognition that he was foreign in his native city.
He arranged to meet her on the evening of 14 June, outside the home
of Sir William Wilde, in Merrion Square. She did not turn up. He
wrote to her and they made a second assignation, for the afternoon of
16 June.

Nora Barnacle, from Galway city, was twenty. She was one of seven
children of Thomas and Annie Barnacle, a baker and seamstress
respectively. During her childhood her family lived in a series of small

houses in the city, but in her early childhood Nora went to live near her parents, with her maternal grandmother, Catherine Healy. She left school at twelve, the usual leaving age, and worked as a porter at a convent. Her grandmother died when Nora was thirteen. Her parents separated. It seems to have been the discipline of her maternal uncle, Tom Healy, who allegedly beat her for going out with a Protestant lad, that led Nora to run away from Galway to Dublin. She worked in Finn's Hotel on Leinster Street, a small twelve-bedroom establishment backing on to Trinity College. Her hours were long and the pay was poor, but she had room and board in the city centre, and every other evening free. She probably missed her first appointment with Joyce because she had to work unexpectedly. The major evidence that the assignation was rearranged to 16 June comes from Joyce's decision to set the action of *Ulysses* on that date.

They met at the corner of Merrion Square and then walked out to the east, past the docks and towards the harbour at Ringsend, where they experienced their first sexual intimacy.

Their courtship proceeded through the summer of 1904, and on 4 October they left Ireland together for Zürich and later Trieste. They had two children, Giorgio and Lucia, and married in 1931. They remained together for life.

Between 1914 and 1921 Joyce, already the author of *Chamber Music* (1907), *Dubliners* (1914) and *A Portrait of the Artist as a Young Man* (1916), composed *Ulysses*, first serialized in the *Little Review*, 1918-20 and then published in Paris by Shakespeare and Company in 1922. Set in Dublin on 16 June 1904, the novel recreates an extraordinary tapestry of Dublin life on that day, as the chief protagonists, Leopold Bloom and Stephen Dedalus walk about the city. Stephen sets out from the Martello Tower at Sandycove, which he shares with Buck Mulligan, while Bloom departs from his home at 7 Eccles Street. The novel is structurally and thematically modelled on Homer's *Odyssey*.

The novel is characterized by its deployment of many different styles, particularly Joyce's technique of the stream of consciousness, which goes further than previous forms of free indirect discourse to give readers access to the inner thoughts of the major characters. This is the style of Molly Bloom's famous soliloquy, on which the novel closes. Joyce also parodies and/or pays homage to literary styles including popular romance and newspaper journalism.

Dublin in 1904 is recreated in meticulous detail. Joyce spent years studying street maps and directories and collecting information from friends and relatives about certain streets and buildings. He famously claimed that if Dublin were to be destroyed it could be rebuilt using *Ulysses* as a guide. This profusion of detail can be misleading, suggesting that somehow everything and everyone from the city in 1904 is referenced in the novel. Between 1914 and 1921, when Joyce was writing *Ulysses*, much of Dublin was being destroyed in the War of Independence, and *Ulysses* is as much about these losses as about the construction of a virtual folk museum of the city. Precisely because Stephen and Bloom see and register so much on their promenades, the things they miss reverberate with significance. In the final words of *Ulysses* the writer signalled his own absence from the city as he created it.

The *Playboy* Riots
Tuesday 29 January 1907

"Audience broke up in disorder at the word shift."
Augusta Gregory

By the time the curtain rose at 8.15pm in the Abbey Theatre on Marlborough Street for the third performance of John Millington Synge's double bill, *Riders to the Sea* and *The Playboy of the Western World*, the producers, the performers, the police and the audience were all expecting trouble.

The first night, the previous Saturday, had been sold out. *Riders to the Sea*, which had premiered three years earlier, was one of the great success stories of the Irish National Theatre Society (originally the Irish Literary Theatre), founded in 1899 by Augusta Gregory, Edward Martyn and W. B. Yeats, and formed a regular part of the group's repertoire. *The Playboy of the Western World*, however, was a new production, and Gregory had anticipated trouble as soon as it went into rehearsal. She objected to the violent oaths and "did not think it was fit to be put on the stage without cutting." Rehearsals for the play had been closed and the first night audience did not know quite what to expect. *Riders to the Sea* was well received, but as the audience sat through *The Playboy* the atmosphere became increasingly uncomfortable.

The play reworks a story that Synge had heard on a visit to the Aran Islands. A young man, Christy Mahon (played by Willie Fay) appears in a remote community in Mayo, in the west of Ireland. Christy has run away after a fight with his father, in which the son fears he has killed the father with the blow of a spade. To his surprise, the recounting of this desperate deed wins him acclaim among the Mayo villagers. The sole set is that of the village pub, run by Michael James Flaherty, where Christy tells his story and woos Pegeen Mike, the landlord's daughter, disenchanting her with her prospective husband, Shawn Keogh. When the play opened, Pegeen was played by Synge's fiancée, Máire O'Neill, also known as Molly Allgood. On that opening night the first act went well enough for Gregory to send a telegram in the interval to W. B. Yeats (lecturing in Aberdeen), claiming: "Play great success."

During Act Two, however, the audience's discomfort at the adulation heaped on the self-proclaimed murderer grew more vocal, and with the appearance of Old Mahon (who has not been murdered), the mood of the audience darkened with that of the play itself. Christy chases his father, promising to finish him off, and returns to pledge his devotion to Pegeen. At this point on the first night Willie Fay famously fluffed his line, and instead of preferring Pegeen to a "drift of chosen females standing in their shifts itself", he mentioned a "drift of Mayo girls", aggravating the insult to the west by naming Mayo. Heroic conflict is debunked and degraded until Christy is lying on the ground, biting the leg of Shawn Keogh, "the like of a mad dog". Pegeen reflects that "there's a great gap between a gallous story and a dirty deed" and Christy, the debunked hero, flies his father once again. Boos and hisses from the audience almost drowned the final ten minutes of the performance, and at the play's conclusion Lady Gregory sent Yeats a second telegram: "Audience broke up in disorder at the word shift."

On Sunday night there was no performance.

Monday evening was the second night, and the audience was small. There were fewer than eighty people in an auditorium capable of seating five hundred. Once again, *Riders to the Sea* went off without disturbance, but from the start of *The Playboy* about half the audience began to boo and hiss. Yeats was back in Dublin and present at the performance. The protests continued until Willie Fay stopped the performance, threatening to call the police. This increased the crowd's ire, and when half a dozen policemen did arrive they were largely ineffectual. Synge and Gregory asked them to leave. Lord Walter Fitzgerald stood up in the stalls and made a speech pleading for the play to be heard, but he was shouted down. The performance continued to be disrupted by noise and protest until the final curtain, when the stage and house lights were turned off and the protesters left in darkness.

On the Tuesday morning, 29 January, Yeats and Synge went to the Metropole Hotel in Dublin where they gave an interview to the *Freeman's Journal*, during which Yeats made several contemptuous references to the class and religious background of the protesters, describing them as "commonplace and ignorant people".

At around seven in the evening a crowd of young men began to gather outside the theatre. Before the doors opened to the public the crowd saw a group of policemen admitted. At 7.50 the house doors opened and the crowd moved towards the sixpenny seats in the pit. A little later a group of students from Trinity College, about twenty in number, arrived at the theatre and were given free seats in the stalls. Earlier that day Gregory had suggested to one of her nephews that he might bring along some fellow students to help in case of a brawl. Presumably she imagined that the Trinity students might act like bouncers, intimidating the rougher elements of the crowd. In fact, they followed the traditional student role of turning up drunk and looking for a fight. In the midst of the students was a Galwayman in a greatcoat, who began to challenge loudly for a fight even before the performance had commenced. "I'm a little bit drunk and don't know what I'm saying," he declaimed from his chair, before making his way onto the stage and playing a tune on the piano. He was escorted back to his seat and the curtain went up on time, with the theatre half full. *Riders to the Sea* was watched quietly and well-applauded.

In the interval Yeats announced that on the following Monday evening there would be a public debate on *The Playboy of the Western World* and the freedom of the theatre. He also threw out a challenge to the audience, insisting that the play would be performed until it was heard "and our patience will last longer than your patience." A few Irish airs from the orchestra filled the remaining interval, and at three minutes past nine the curtain went up on *The Playboy of the Western World*. The first scene went quietly, but from the appearance of Willie Fay as Christy Mahon the audience in the pit began to hiss and stomp while the Trinity students in the stall cheered and clapped as noisily. The management brought up the house lights and the actors left the stage. The Galwayman tried to start a fight, but was restrained. Yeats came onto the stage and pleaded with the audience to listen to the play by "a distinguished fellow-countryman". The audience was unimpressed and the heckling continued. The noisy Galwayman was evicted by Synge himself and by Ambrose Power, the actor playing Old Mahon. The police had been backstage throughout, and they were now summoned by Yeats, Gregory and Synge to evict the noisier members of the pit, who were pointed out by Gregory's nephew, Hugh Lane.

With the wave of evictions complete, the lights went down again and the play recommenced, but so did the uproar, with the pits and the stalls baiting one another, and cries of "That's not the west" punctuating the performance. In the best tradition of theatrical riot, much of the heckling was witty and pertinent, with suggestions that the police would be better employed arresting Christy for his father's murder. Nevertheless, the actors struggled on, with the curtain lowered from time to time as the police picked out more suspects for arrest or simple eviction. The Galwayman reappeared towards the end of the play, and resumed his offers to fight. The scene in the auditorium concluded with the students in the stalls singing "God Save the King" and the audience in the pits responding with "God Save Ireland". It was the Catholic nationalist lower middle-class audience of the pits who had been offended at the supposed slander on the west of Ireland, which in the imaginative geography of nationalism represented an innocent Irish-speaking world relatively uncontaminated by English influence. It was an upper middle-class, predominantly unionist audience from the Protestant Trinity College which saluted the King from the three shilling stalls.

Outside the theatre the fracas continued, with the opposing groups taunting one another as they crossed the Liffey and made their way back in the direction of Trinity. Passers-by joined the growing conflict, which finally degenerated into a brawl in Westmoreland Street, outside the college walls. There was a police station nearby and there were further arrests.

When those arrested were brought to trial it emerged that there was more at issue than the merits of this particular play. The first charged appeared before a Justice Mahony, who fined them all forty shillings, the maximum penalty for disturbing the peace. Later in the week, however, Justice Wall came to a different conclusion. For Wall the fact that the disturbance had begun in a theatre sent him back to legal precedents on theatre riots, and in his judgement he made a distinction between the rights of an audience to "cry down a play which they disliked, or hiss and boo the actors who depended for their position on the good-will of audiences" and other types of disturbance. Premeditation would have made it a criminal act, but disrupting a performance was not in itself a crime. Newspaper commentaries on the trial criticized the Abbey for having involved the police in the whole business.

Meanwhile the play continued its run. On the Wednesday night the controversy drew in an audience of 420. There were more protests and again the evening ended with a brawl in the street, and more arrests. But on subsequent evenings things settled down and while protests continued they were more good-humoured. The play saw out its run, finishing on the Saturday night. On the following Monday, 4 February, the debate on freedom of speech was held in the theatre, where hecklers drowned out most of what was said. By this point the hecklers seemed to be enjoying the comedy of the occasion. There were a number of speakers. W. B. Yeats spoke several times, and seemed determined to offend his audience, which groaned and

hissed at his derogatory references to Catholicism. This was the crowd that Yeats later referred to as "Eunuchs running through Hell" in his poem, "On Those That Hated 'The Playboy of the Western World'" (1914). His father, John B. Yeats, made a speech about Irish piety, also described by the son thirty years later in the poem, "Beautiful Lofty Things":

> *My father upon the Abbey stage, before him a raging crowd:*
> *"This Land of Saints," and then as the applause died out,*
> *"Of plaster Saints"; his beautiful mischievous head thrown back.*

The younger Yeats remembers this as an heroic moment, but on the night the audience was having quite a lot of fun calling out "Where's the loy?" and "Kill your father!"

The Abbey Theatre went on to court controversy over the years, identifying that this role was part of its mission. In 1908 Lady Gregory went to visit George Bernard Shaw in Hertfordshire, and Shaw gave her a copy of *The Shewing-Up of Blanco Posnet*, explaining that it had been rejected by the British censor. The objection was to the play's (mild) blasphemy. Shaw offered the play to the Abbey, since the censor had no jurisdiction in Ireland. Gregory put it into production, eventually taking over the direction herself. In the summer of 1909, while the play was in rehearsal, Gregory was advised that the Lord Lieutenant objected to the production and might revoke the theatre's patent. In *Our Irish Theatre*, Gregory describes a conversation she had with a Castle official:

> He said, "Will you not give it up?" "What will you do if we go on?" "Either take no notice or take the Patent from you at once." I said, "If you decide to forfeit our Patent, we will not give a public performance; but if we give no performance to be judged by, we shall rest under the slur of having tried to produce something bad and injurious." "We must not provoke Public opinion." "We provoked Nationalist public opinion in The Playboy, and you did not interfere." "Aye," said he, "exactly so, that was quite different; that had not been banned by the Censor." I said, "Time has justified us, for we have since produced The Playboy in Dublin and on tour with success, and it will justify us in the case of this play."

Yeats and Lady Gregory decided to make the most of the public relations opportunity and they released a public statement on 22 August, three days before the play was due to open.

> If our Patent is in danger, it is because the decisions of the English Censor are being brought into Ireland, and because the Lord Lieutenant is about to revive, on what we consider a frivolous pretext, a right not exercised for a hundred and fifty years to forbid at the Lord Chamberlain's pleasure, any play produced in a Dublin theatre... We are not concerned with the question of the English censorship now being fought out in London, but we are very certain that the conditions of the two countries are different, and that we must not, by accepting the English Censor's ruling, give away anything of the liberty of the Irish Theatre of the future.

This statement cleverly recruited Irish nationalists behind the Abbey's stance. Meanwhile, the directors of the Theatre raised ticket prices to four shillings for the performance, ensuring a more middle-class and tamer audience. The play was well received and the Castle backed down.

The Abbey Theatre was once again the scene of riots in 1926 when Sean O'Casey's *The Plough and the Stars* was produced in what had recently become the English-speaking world's first State-sponsored theatre. The first act of the play is set in a Dublin tenement in the period leading up to the Easter Rising. The second act in a pub involves a prostitute and a barman as well as some of the tenement characters debating patriotism as a voice from outside the pub is heard delivering a speech by Patrick Pearse. In the third act volunteers and looters return to the tenement reporting on the action at the GPO, and in the final act the characters huddle together in a single room as the world outside seems to be collapsing into violence and horror.

The Abbey directors were aware from the start that the play might cause trouble firstly on account of its low characters and language, and secondly because it would give offence to republicans. During rehearsals the actors themselves protested to O'Casey about aspects of the characterization and dialogue and he reluctantly agreed to some changes. O'Casey was in any case unpopular with most of the company because he had been publicly critical of their abilities in Shaw's *Man and Superman*.

The first night went well, partly because so many seats had been reserved by friends of the government, which was enjoying its new relationship as patron of the Abbey. Trouble began on the second night when Sighle Humphreys, vice-president of Cumann na mBan, the women's auxiliary corps to the Irish Volunteers, began to hiss from the back row of the pit. Cumann na mBan were happy to act as cultural police for the republican movement, but this gesture seems to have been individual rather than premeditated.

On the Thursday night, however, a large number of republican women and members of Sinn Féin attended the packed performance of *The Plough and the Stars* with protest in mind. Many of the women in the auditorium had close links with the executed leaders of 1916: Kathleen Clarke, Maud Gonne and Hanna Sheehy Skeffington were widows, Fiona Plunket a sister and Sighle Humphreys a niece; and to cap it all the mother of Patrick and Willie Pearse, Margaret Pearse, was in the audience. (Kathleen Clarke, widow of Thomas Clarke, was later to be the first elected woman Lord Mayor Dublin). The noise began with the appearance of the actor Ria Mooney as prostitute Rosie

Redmond in Act Two. There were not only verbal assaults, but missiles (coins and lumps of coal) fired at the stage. Women stood on their seats to make speeches. Some male republicans rushed the stage and fought with the actors. W. B Yeats was summoned from his home in Merrion Square, and the police were called. Yeats had a speech prepared and before he even delivered it to the audience he had dispatched a copy to *The Irish Times*.

I thought you had tired of this, which commenced fifteen years ago. But you have disgraced yourselves again. Is this going to be a recurring celebration of Irish genius?

The audience was singularly unchastened, and someone threw a shoe at him. Hanna Sheehy Skeffington made a speech towards the end of the evening, when things were a bit quieter:

I am one of the widows of Easter Week. It is no wonder that you do not remember Easter Week because none of you fought on either side. The play is going to London soon to be advertised there because it belies Ireland. We have no quarrel with the players—we realise that they, at least, have to earn their bread; but I say that if they were men they would refuse to play the parts.

It is unclear whether this call to be a man was specifically directed at Ria Mooney, since it was her role that most offended the protesters. Certainly the sense that the company was prostituting itself to the Free State government and heading off to do more of the same in England inflected subsequent newspaper commentary.

As with *The Playboy of the Western World*, the controversy over O'Casey's play was a signal of a faultline in Ireland's self-imagining. After the initial wave of hostility from the audience *The Plough and the Stars* went on to be one of the most frequently and successfully performed plays in the history of the Abbey Theatre.

The Suffragettes Go to Prison
Thursday 13 June 1912

The Policeman who grabbed my arm instinctively seized the right,
and as I am left handed, that gave me a chance to get in a few more
panes before the military arrived and my escort led me off.
Hanna Sheehy Skeffington, *Reminiscences of an Irish*
Suffragette

When the decision was taken to exclude women from the vote in the
Irish Home Rule Bill in 1912, the Irish Women's Franchise League
(IWFL) decided that it was time to make a gesture of protest in Dublin.
Early in the morning of 12 June a group of activists armed with sticks
went along to a number of government buildings, including the
General Post Office, the Custom House, and Dublin Castle, where they
smashed windows. The two women who attacked the Custom House
were cheered on by a group of dockers who kept a look-out for the
police. They made such good progress that they were able to proceed on
to the GPO.

Hanna Sheehy Skeffington (1877-1946) then aged thirty-five,
was a teacher at Rathmines School of Commerce. She was one of the
founder members of the IWFL (founded in 1908) and a member of
the Socialist Party of Ireland. Her husband Francis Sheehy Skeffington
was also a feminist and they were both pacifists. Hanna was able to
reconcile this with her feminist activism because "The women's
violence was largely symbolic and directed only against property." On
the Thursday morning Hanna went to the Ship Street Barracks,
property of the War Office, near the Castle gates, where she broke
nineteen panes of glass, before she was taken away. She was one of
eight women arrested on the morning and taken to Mountjoy Jail. She
recalled that "we got excellent publicity from an enraged press and
mixed feelings from the general public, but on the whole, naturally,
condemnation. Not only were we enemies of the Home Rule, but
rebels as women."

The eight women arrested in this militant foray received prison
sentences of between two and six months. Hanna Sheehy Skeffington
conducted her own defence, and used the court case, which was widely
reported, to make arguments in favour of female suffrage.

The women were prepared to go to prison. Once there they petitioned for and were granted political status. They were well-supported by feminists who came to visit them; even those who did not agree with their tactics felt sympathy.

Mrs. Haslam came, with a difference: "Don't think I approve—but here's a pot of verbena I brought you. I am not here in my official capacity, of course—the Irish Women's Suffrage and Local Government Association strongly disapprove of violence as pulling back the cause. But here's some loganberry jam—I made it myself." This well summed up the attitude of many of our visitors.

Hanna later observed that their prison experiences left a deep impression on some of the suffragettes. "When prison followed, and later hunger strike, a deeper note was struck; many hitherto protected comfortable women got glimpses of the lives of those less fortunate, and became social rebels."

As Sheehy Skeffington was reaching the end of her sentence, events were moving outside the prison. The Liberal Prime Minister, Herbert Asquith, came to visit Dublin to consult on Home Rule. While he was there he was attacked by Mary Leigh and Gladys Evans, British members of the Women's Suffrage and Political Union, who had followed him to Dublin. Leigh threw a hatchet at the prime Minister, and administered a slight graze to John Redmond. The women were arrested and a strong anti-feminist wave of emotion was generated. Sheehy Skeffington wrote:

We were all put in the same boat as the hatchet-thrower. The Irish Women's Franchise League did not repudiate, whatever our private opinion of the timeliness and manner of the act, because we naturally considered the women strictly within their rights. We lost members (the usual "up-to-this" friends that shook off the tree each time anything fresh was done).

The treatment meted out to the English suffragettes Leigh and Evans (Leigh was sentenced to three years penal servitude) provoked Hanna and a number of other suffragettes to go on hunger strike. She left prison after thirty days, having spent a week on hunger strike. This tactic was one she was to employ in all her future prison episodes. From 1912 to 1914 there were 35 convictions for women engaged in militant activity in Ireland. Hanna Sheehy Skeffington was dismissed from her teaching post at the Rathmines School of Commerce in 1913 for her feminist activities.

The Dublin Lock-Out
Sunday 31 August 1913

"The breathing of the suffocating crowd sounded like the thick, steamy breathing of a herd of frightened cattle in a cattle-boat tossed about in a storm; and over all, as he tried to struggle, he heard the voices of the police shouting, Give it to the bastards! Drive the rats home to their holes! Let them have it, the Larkin bousys!"
Sean O'Casey, *Drums Under the Windows*

The Dublin Lockout was, among other things, a war of wills between two powerful personalities.

Jim Larkin (1876-1947) was born of Irish parents in Liverpool. He left school at the age of eleven to work at the docks. Eventually he became a member of the National Union of Dock Labourers, and in 1907 he came to Ireland as an agent of the union. He worked with Belfast dockers, whose employers responded with a lockout, causing a long and bitter strike in the summer of 1907. In 1909 Larkin founded the Irish Transport and General Workers' Union, which led a revival of Irish trade unionism.

William Martin Murphy (1844-1919) was born in Bantry, County Cork. Originally a building contractor, he built up a network of businesses. He owned transport systems in Ireland, Britain and Africa. He was a Home Rule MP in the British parliament from 1885 to 1892. In 1904 he bought the *Irish Catholic* and *Irish Independent* newspapers. In Dublin he owned the tramlines, and on the city's main thoroughfare, Sackville Street, he owned Clery's department store and the Imperial Hotel.

Both men entered the battle with victories under their belts. In the first six months of 1913 Larkin's union had won a series of industrial disputes with the tactic of sympathetic strikes, and in the process increased wage rates for unskilled Dublin workers by over twenty per cent. In 1911, just two years before the lockout, Murphy had comprehensively defeated the unions in the Great Southern Western Railway with the lockout tactic.

Murphy was not a completely bad employer. Wages on the trams, for example, were relatively high, but working conditions were poor, with long hours and the threat of instant dismissal for misdemeanours.

A month before the lockout, the Mayor of Dublin, Lorcan Sherlock, had appealed to the city's Chamber of Commerce and its Trades Council to agree to the establishment of a conciliation board to settle future industrial disputes. It was Larkin's ambition to gain union recognition from Murphy's Dublin United Tramway Company before the conciliation process was in place. Murphy was determined to stop him. His workers were compelled to withdraw from the union, or face dismissal.

The strike began at 9.40 am on Tuesday 26 August when Dublin tramcar drivers and conductors pinned the red hand badge of the ITGWU to their lapels and abandoned their vehicles. Within forty minutes the trams were moving again, driven by the company's inspectors and office staff. Although night-time services were intimidated out of operation the day-time service was more or less functional as the strike got into its stride. The ITGWU responded by calling out other workers. Frustration at the failure of the strike to stop the trams contributed to the outbreaks of rioting in Ringsend on the evening of Saturday 30 August. Overnight the disturbances spread to several working-class areas of the city. The Dublin magistrates had proscribed a meeting planned due to take place on the Sunday outside Murphy's own Imperial Hotel in Sackville Street, but nevertheless crowds gathered. Jim Larkin entered the hotel in disguise and appeared at a window. The meeting was then baton-charged by members of the Dublin Metropolitan Constabulary and the Royal Irish Constabulary. Two men were killed and between 400 and 600 people injured. "Bloody Sunday" became Ireland's Peterloo. Before the baton charge the strike might have petered out when the employers held firm. Instead, a bitter class war developed, which itself caused divisions within Irish nationalism, much of which was socially conservative and hostile to syndicalism.

By 4 September 1913 William Martin Murphy had persuaded over 400 of Dublin's employers to lock out any employee who would not sign a declaration repudiating the ITGWU. Within a few weeks 15,000 workers were locked out and dependent on unions for food and subsistence. The Trades Unions Congress in Britain raised £106,000 for the strikers' relief fund. Other help to the strikers came from Dublin charities, mainly controlled by the Catholic Church and selective in their assistance, and the female suffrage movement.

Larkin antagonized the Catholic Church in October 1913, when he promoted a scheme devised by Dora Montefiore, member of a prominent liberal Jewish family, to take the children of strikers to temporary homes in Britain. This caused local outrage, with the Church suggesting that the children's faith would be undermined. Murphy used his papers to print the names and addresses of parents who joined the scheme, and families were put under pressure by Catholic vigilance committees, so that only a small number of children actually participated.

As the strike progressed Jim Larkin alienated much of the British trade union movement, castigating its lack of support, and demanding secondary strikes in Britain. He was eventually disowned at a TUC conference in December. Meanwhile, the British Shipping Federation, which ignored the strike to begin with, began to assist the Dublin employers with money and strike-breakers. Lord Iveagh, head of the Guinness family business, donated £5,000 to help smaller Dublin employers. When the TUC fund ran out in January 1914 the Dublin workers had no choice but to return to work on the best terms they could achieve. Although church leaders, British trade unionists and even government agencies suggested some compromise, Murphy held out for a total victory.

Within a year Britain was at war, and the consequent severe labour shortages returned an unexpected advantage to the workers. By 1920 the ITGWU had 120,000 members and was Ireland's largest union.

In 1914 Larkin left Ireland for the United States where he was involved in founding the Communist Party in 1919. He was imprisoned for "criminal anarchy" in 1920. He returned to Dublin on his release in 1923 and in a dispute with William O'Brien, who had succeeded James Connolly and Larkin at the head of the ITWGU, Larkin founded the pro-communist Irish Workers' League. In the 1930s his revolutionary impulses moderated sufficiently for him to become a member of Dublin City Council, and of the Dáil. His critics accused him of a dictatorial love of power and of splitting the labour movement rather than loosening his own authority. For his admirers, Larkin, despite all his faults, made labour into a substantial political force in Ireland. During the Dublin lock-out many constitutional nationalists, most notably Patrick Pearse, turned to the opinion that separatism was the only solution to Ireland's problems. James Connolly wrote, after the strike:

> *All others merely reject one part or other of the British Conquest— the Labour movement alone rejects it in its entirety and sets itself to the reconquest of Ireland.*

Not least of Larkin's claims to fame is that he was the brother of Delia Larkin (1878-1949), a trade union activist who worked along side him in Dublin. She became first general-secretary of the Irish Women Workers' Union.

A statue of James Larkin, his arms raised in defiance, stands in O'Connell Street.

The Easter Rising
Monday 24 April 1916

> *"Sometimes now when I consider the pitiful mess of rebuilt O'Connell Street from the Bridge to Nelson's Pillar I smile back sadly to that other time, when this present stretch of absolutely comical commercial vulgarity was a huge, swept-away arena of tragedy, in black and white."*
> Kate O'Brien, *My Ireland*

There are probably more extant accounts of the events of this day than of any other day in Irish history. The plan by the insurgents was to take a number of key buildings in the capital and hold them under siege from the British, while insurrection took off around the country. Rising leader Patrick Pearse believed that the British would hold back from destroying government buildings to unseat the rebels. But by the morning of 24 April 1916 plans for the nationwide rebellion were already in chaos.

On Easter Monday morning 1,600 volunteers led by Pearse and

200 members of the Irish Citizen Army led by James Connolly took over a number of sites around Dublin, establishing headquarters at the General Post Office in Sackville Street (O'Connell Street). The leaders had met in the morning at Liberty Hall. Just before noon they stepped out to survey their troops and lead off the march. There was a sudden unexpected interruption when Pearse's sister, Mary Brigid, appeared and remonstrated with him to come home.

The GPO, designed by Francis Johnston and built 1814-18, was the architectural focus of Sackville Street, and had recently been refurbished. When Pearse and Connolly led their troops into the post office, staff and customers were allowed to flee, apart from a policeman and a soldier identified by their uniforms. Pearse ordered men to search the upper floors where they found a guard of seven soldiers with guns but no ammunition. These were also taken prisoner. Connolly realized that in the excitement of leaving Liberty Hall they had forgotten their flags, and he sent Seán T. O'Kelly to retrieve them. When O'Kelly returned two flags were raised over the GPO, one a green flag with a harp in the centre and the words Irish Republic in gold and white lettering; the other the green, white and orange tricolor, later to become the flag of independent Ireland. From the portico of the GPO Pearse read the proclamation of the Irish Republic:

THE PROVISIONAL GOVERNMENT OF THE IRISH REPUBLIC TO THE PEOPLE OF IRELAND.
IRISHMEN AND IRISHWOMEN: In the name of God and of the dead generations from which she receives her old tradition of nation-hood, Ireland, through us, summons her children to her flag and strikes for her freedom.

Having organised and trained her manhood through her secret revolutionary organisation, the Irish Republican Brotherhood, and through her open military organisations, the Irish Volunteers and the Irish Citizen Army, having patiently perfected her discipline, having resolutely waited for the right moment to reveal itself, she now seizes that moment, and, supported by her exiled children in America and by gallant allies in Europe, but relying in the first on her own strength, she strikes in full confidence of victory.

We declare the rights of the people of Ireland to the ownership of Ireland, and to the unfettered control of Irish destinies, to be sovereign and indefeasible. The long usurpation of that right by a foreign people and government has not extinguished the right, nor can it ever be extinguished except by the destruction of the Irish people. In every generation the Irish people have asserted their right to national freedom and sovereignty: six times during the past three hundred years they have asserted it in arms. Standing on that fundamental right and again asserting it in arms in the face of the world, we hereby proclaim the Irish republic as a Sovereign Independent State, and we pledge our lives and the lives of our comrades-in-arms to the cause of its freedom, of its welfare, and of its exaltation among the nations.

The Irish Republic is entitled to, and hereby claims, the allegiance of every Irishman and Irishwoman. The Republic guarantees religious and civil liberty, equal rights and equal opportunities to all its citizens, and declares its resolve to pursue the happiness and prosperity of the whole nation equally, and oblivious of the differences carefully fostered by an alien government, which have divided a minority from the majority in the past.

Until our arms have brought the opportune moment for the establishment of a permanent National Government, representative of the whole people of Ireland, and elected by the suffrages of all her men and women, the Provisional Government, hereby constituted, will administer the civil and military affairs of the Republic in trust for the people.

We place the cause of the Irish Republic under the Most High God, Whose blessing we invoke upon our arms, and we pray that no one who serves that cause will dishonour it by cowardice, inhumanity, or rapine. In this supreme hour the Irish nation must, by its valour and discipline and by the readiness of its children to sacrifice themselves for the common good, prove itself worthy of he august destiny to which it is called.

Signed on Behalf of the Provisional Government,
THOMAS J. CLARKE.
SEAN Mac DIARMADA.
THOMAS MacDONAGH.
P. H. PEARSE.
EAMONN CEANT.
JAMES CONNOLLY.
JOSEPH PLUNKETT.

A thousand copies of the proclamation, chiefly drafted by Pearse and Connolly, had been printed the previous afternoon on a flatbed press in Liberty Hall, and the first copy was taken from the press and read aloud to a small crowd on the steps of Liberty Hall by Constance Markievicz. When Pearse had finished reading James Connolly clasped his hand and said "Thanks be to God, Pearse, that we have lived to see this day." There was little enthusiasm from the few spectators, however. Stephen McKenna wrote that "for once his [Pearse's] magnetism had left him; the response was chilling; a few thin, perfunctory cheers, no direct hostility just then; but no enthusiasm whatever; the people were evidently quite unprepared, quite unwilling to see in the uniformed figure, whose burning words had thrilled them again and again elsewhere, a person of significance to the country."

Shortly afterwards, a company of Lancers from Marlborough Barracks rode on horseback from the north end of Sackville Street. Just as they approached the GPO, at Nelson's Pillar, the volunteers opened fire and four of the soldiers were killed.

While the Lancers retreated, and while the rebels waited for a heavier onslaught, foraging parties went out to local hotels and businesses to commandeer bedding, food and medical supplies. Inside the GPO the leaders had plenty of time to discuss the morality of their actions. One of the men in the GPO, Joseph Plunkett, was so seriously ill that he spent most of his time lying down on a mattress while others came to talk and keep him company. Pearse sent to the nearby Catholic Pro-Cathedral for a curate to hear the confessions of the volunteers.

By the middle of the afternoon a crowd had gathered outside in

Sackville Street, and in the absence of any police force, the windows of shops were broken and looting began. The only move by the British authorities that day was to deliver a printed proclamation enjoining law-abiding citizens to stay away from public places. The military response from the British was yet to come.

On the day of the rising Constance Markievicz watched the companies march off from Liberty Hall, then joined Dr. Kathleen Lynn in a car packed with medical supplies. She was at the City Hall about noon, where Lynn stopped with some of the supplies. Markievicz drove on to St. Stephen's Green with the rest of the medical supplies. When she arrived she was asked by Michael Mallin to stay and help. There were about 110 volunteers in the park at the Green, digging trenches and barricading railings. While she was at there it has been alleged (and contested) that Markievicz shot an unarmed policeman, PC Lahiff. As the afternoon progressed she took part in a small raid to secure the College of Surgeons, overlooking the north end of the Green, for the rebels. A doorman attempted to defend the building, and there was some discussion about shooting him, but Markievicz ordered him to be locked in a room with his family.

(There is a bust of Markievicz in St. Stephen's Green and several others of her around the city, including one in Townshend Street which shows her walking her little dog.)

From the grandeur of the Shelbourne Hotel, overlooking the Green, some off-duty soldiers took pot-shots at the rebels, and Markievicz was one of those who began to shoot back. Among the other women rebels at the Green were Madeleine ffrench-Mullen and Nellie Gifford. The writer, James Stephens, who lived nearby, walked down to see what was going on and saw a man shot dead as he approached the barricades.

As evening fell the weather turned chilly, and Markievicz spent the night sleeping in Dr. Lynn's car, reproaching herself the next morning for having missed her watch. Markievicz's role in the rising was very different to that of the women of Cumann na mBan, including Louise Gavan Duffy, who had joined Pearse in the Post Office. There women were relegated to roles as cooks and nurses.

The rebels failed to capture Dublin Castle or other sites of strategic importance. In the six days until Saturday 29 April there was street fighting between the volunteers and the better armed British forces, who drew reinforcements from elsewhere in Ireland. Approximately 500 people died in the fighting, with a further 2,500 wounded, and more than 100 building were destroyed.

On the Saturday Pearse surrendered "to prevent the further slaughter of Dublin citizens." The leaders of the rising were court-martialled by secret military tribunal, and between 3 and 12 May fifteen were shot by firing squad. These included all the signatories of the proclamation and Con Colbert, Edward Daly, Sean Heuston, John MacBride, Michael Mallin, Michael O'Hanrahan, William Pearse, and Thomas Kent. Other death sentences, including those of Constance Markievicz and Éamon de Valera were commuted, but the executions had galvanized Irish public opinion in favour of the rebellion. Maud Gonne was in France with her children when she heard news of the rising and of the death of her former husband.

Personal testimonies published for many years after the rising describe the terrible fear and suffering endured by people on all sides of the conflict. An anonymous woman working as a volunteer nurse at Dublin Castle described the arrival of the badly wounded James Connolly:

The nurses in charge of him acknowledged, without exception, that he was entirely different from their expectations: no one could have been more considerate or given less trouble. About a week after his arrival he had an operation on the leg. He was strongly opposed to this himself, but until he had been tried, he had to be treated entirely from a medical point of view. When he was brought round after the ether, the sentry changed, and he turned to the nurse who was minding him and asked, "Have they come to take me away? Must I really die so soon?" All through, his behaviour was that of an idealist. He was calm and composed during the court-martial and said, "You can shoot me if you like, but I am dying for my country." He showed no

*sign of weakness until his wife was brought to say goodbye to him, the
night he was to be shot.*

Nora, Connolly's daughter, later described that meeting:

> *He turned to me then and said, "I heard poor Skeffington was shot."
> I said, "Yes," and then told him that all his staff, the best men in
> Ireland, were gone. He was silent for a while. I think he thought
> that he was the first to be executed.*

The death of Francis Sheehy Skeffington did great damage to the
reputation of the British Army. Owen Sheehy Skeffington, his son, later
recalled:

> *My father, who was a pacifist as well as a feminist, and a socialist,
> published an open letter to Thomas MacDonagh, in which he said
> that he had been on a platform lately with MacDonagh—whom he
> greatly admired—but was shocked to hear him looking forward to
> bloodshed, to military feat of arms. If you resort to arms you are in
> a sense failing to think beforehand of your aims. Also if you resort to
> arms you tend to find yourself at the end with the gunmen, the mili-
> tary men in charge, who don't know anything about running the
> social and economic matters. All the men that my father admired—
> the Connollys and the MacDonaghs, and the Pearses, were doing
> something by means which he disapproved, though he approved of the
> ultimate aims. What could he do? Well, what he did do seems
> quixotic and foolish, but he just couldn't sit still and do nothing.
> What he did do was to go down town and try to organize a Citizens'
> Defence Force to prevent looting. It seems odd because he was not
> concerned with private property; he was a socialist, and something
> indeed of an anarchist, but what he was concerned with was that the
> name of the Irish revolutionary should not be blackened. And so he
> successfully organized a little band of a kind of Citizens' Defence
> Force. Tuesday evening my mother came home as usual but my father
> didn't. We didn't know what had happened to him. He had, in fact,
> been arrested at Portobello Bridge walking up the middle of the street,
> had been arrested and taken to Portobello Barracks. He had later that
> night been taken out by Bowen-Colthurst, who was I think then a*

Captain, and used as a hostage. He was brought back to barracks, and the following morning Bowen-Colthurst, first consulting his Bible— he was a very religious man—read, somewhere in the Bible, something that seemed to indicate that he should take out my father and two other journalists who were in the cell at that time and have them shot. This he did; he formed a firing squad and had them shot on the Wednesday morning. My father had been shot and buried in quicklime.

Bowen-Colthurst was court-martialled and judged to have been insane at the time of the killings, but not before he had been posted to Newry in charge of a regiment. On the night before Sheehy Skeffington's death, when he had been taken out as a hostage, he had witnessed Bowen-Colthurst order the shooting of a young boy named Coade. The verdict was not immediately revealed, since it would call into question the Captain's subsequent promotion. Bowen-Colthurst was, indeed, only arrested after his senior officer, Sir Francis Vane, went to London to report the incident in person. Bowen-Colthurst went to Broadmoor, and was released in less than two years, going on to a new life in Canada. Following the murder of Sheehy Skeffington his widow was granted a judicial inquiry. She travelled to the United States to publicize the case and met President Woodrow Wilson.

John Bowen-Colthurst was a cousin of the future novelist, Elizabeth Bowen, who wrote of the changes wrought on Dublin by the rising. In *The Shelbourne* she wrote:

Battles were associated with battlefields, not yet cities. To that extent, in spite of the Great War, the Edwardian concept of civilisation still stood unshaken. It was held still that things should know where to stop—and also where not to begin. But also, Dublin had by now become a modern city—as such, she was destined to be the first to see the modern illusion crack… more than cracked, it shivered across; not again to be mended in our time.

Chapter Seven
PARNELL SQUARE

"Dublin is brown and weather beaten and old fashioned, and it looks like a place in which history has been made for ages. The stamp of the alien is upon much of its architecture, but undoubtedly its street statuary has something to tell of a national past. In its libraries and museums and public places there is much that is truly metropolitan—much to convince you that you are in touch with the core of the nation's intellectual life.
William Bulfin, *Rambles in Eirinn* (1907)

Parnell Square was the second Georgian square to be laid out in Dublin after St. Stephen's Green. It was originally named Rutland Square, and the northern terrace was laid out in 1755. At that point it was already envisaged that the south side of the square would be occupied by a new maternity hospital, now the Rotunda. As you approach from O'Connell Street to the south you can see 5 Parnell Square East, the home of Oliver St. John Gogarty, doctor and writer, and one-time friend of James Joyce, whose memoirs provide a source of information about early twentieth-century Dublin.

The Gate Theatre
On the opposite side of the street from Gogarty's house is the Gate Theatre, founded in 1928 by Hilton Edwards (1903-82) and Mícheál Mac Liammóir (1899-1978), and located since 1930 in Bartholomew Mosse's new Assembly Rooms (1786). Edwards and Mac Liammóir, both actors and theatre managers, were Dublin's most prominent gay partnership for much of the twentieth century. Both were English, but an early friendship with an Irish student at the Slade School of Fine Art encouraged Mac Liammóir to reinvent himself as Irish. Mac Liammóir was also a writer of plays in Irish and English, and produced seven volumes of autobiography. He became most famous for his sympathetic one-man show about Oscar Wilde, *The Importance of Being Oscar* (1960). Edwards appeared in Orson Welles' film, *Othello* (1951).

The Garden of Remembrance

The Garden of Remembrance is a memorial garden for those who died in the Easter Rising, and was opened in 1966 on its fiftieth anniversary. The design of the garden itself, although typical of its era, now seems uninspired. Most of the garden is taken up with a shallow rectangular pool of water beneath which one can see Celtic-inspired mosaic tiles. The dominant feature of the garden is a large sculpture by Oisín Kelly (1915-81) of The Children of Lir, figures in an Irish folktale. Lir is a mythical king of Ireland. When his first wife dies, he marries the wicked Aoife, who, jealous of her four stepchildren, turns them into swans, in which form they live for 900 years. At the end of this period they go to the island of Inis Gluaire, where they meet a holy man. They resume their human forms as very elderly people, and the holy man baptizes them before they die. This was once a popular lunchtime spot for office workers and tourists, and locals still eat sandwiches on the steps in the heat of the day, but the atmosphere has become distinctly seedy. The space is too rigid and unadaptable, and it has become a place more associated with drink and drugs than a useful public space.

The Municipal Gallery of Modern Art

Even in big cities there are certain art galleries and museums—the Frick collection in New York is one, the Isabella Stewart Gardiner Museum in Boston is another, and examples include the Wallace Collection and John Soane museums in London and the Borghese Gallery in Rome—that feel like sanctuaries, no matter how many visitors pass through on a given day. These are places where all the visitors seem to share a love of art as well as a love of tourism and a desire for peace as well as for stimulation.

The Municipal Gallery of Modern Art in Parnell Square, at the top of O'Connell Street, is such a gallery. It is old-fashioned, its dimensions are stately and sombre, and the decoration gives the impression of shabbiness. It is always a cool space and it has a kind of cold light, as if the vibrancy of the paintings had sucked all the life from the surrounding atmosphere, so that the walls and furniture seem faded. The very word "municipal" has lost its respectability in other places, and I dread turning up one day to find that the gallery has called in management consultants and replaced a name full of historical resonances to re-brand itself with an acronym or some vacuous piece of nonsense like "Purple" or "The Square".

Charlemont House, which houses the Hugh Lane collection, was commissioned by James Caulfield (1728-1799), 4th Viscount Charlemont and later 1st Earl of Charlemont. It is one of those great eighteenth-century town houses built by a nobleman who had taken the Grand Tour in his youth and returned inspired with a vision of continental grandeur and elegance. In 1763 Charlemont commissioned the young Scottish-born architect William Chambers (1723-96), whom he had met in Rome, to design his new town house at the top of Rutland Square. Set back from the street, the stone-clad house is designed on strict classical lines. The original gardens have been built over, and the square itself has lost its former elegance and proportions,

but the building remains imposing. Inside, the hall and staircase remind one that this was a house before it was a gallery, and the upstairs rooms retain many of their original features. A house from the 1760s might seems an odd home for a collection of modern art, but what particularly works here is the relationship between the paintings, which are rarely crowded, and the small gallery rooms with their high ceilings. Caulfield also built the lovely Casino at Marino (1759), a neo-classical Doric temple which was designed to sit on an elevated site in his demesne overlooking Dublin Bay.

Hugh Lane (1875-1915) was the nephew of Augusta Gregory, one of the founders of the Irish Literary revival. He had a fine art business in London. In 1901 Lady Gregory introduced him to W. B. Yeats, Douglas Hyde and Edward Martyn, founders of the revival, and they inspired in him a desire to see some equivalent movement for the visual arts in Ireland. In 1908 he helped Dublin Corporation to establish a Municipal Gallery of Modern Art in Harcourt Street, and organized a Franco-Irish exhibition there. John Millington Synge wrote an article about the exhibition for the *Manchester Guardian* in January 1908:

Although the Irish popular classes have sympathy with what is expressed in the arts they are necessarily unfamiliar with artistic matters, so that for many years to come artistic movements in Ireland will be the work of individuals whose enthusiasm or skill can be felt by the less-trained instincts of the people. These individuals, a few here and there like the political leaders of the nineteenth century, will be drawn from the classes that have still some trace or tradition of the older culture, and yet for various reasons have lost all hold on direct political life. The history of the founding of this new gallery and the work done for it by Mr. Hugh Lane and a few others since 1902 is a good instance of these new courses in Irish affairs... This gallery will impress everyone who visits it, but for those who live in Dublin it is peculiarly valuable. Perhaps no one but Dublin men who have lived abroad also can quite realise the strange thrill it gave me to turn in from Harcourt-street—where I passed by the school long ago—to find myself among Monets, and Manets and Renoirs, things I connect so directly with life in Paris.

Lane gave to the Corporation a conditional gift of 39 French impressionist paintings. He had a vision of a gallery for modern art, linked with the National Gallery of Ireland and spanning the Liffey in the place of the Ha'penny Bridge. In 1912 he commissioned Sir Edward Lutyens to design such a gallery, but the plans ran into all kinds of controversy and Dublin Corporation was in any case unwilling to bear the cost. W. B. Yeats wrote a poem on the affair, "To a Wealthy Man Who Promised a Second Subscription to the Dublin Municipal Gallery if it were Proved the People Wanted Pictures". In 1913, in protest at the failure of these plans to materialize, Lane removed his collection to the

National Gallery in London. The following year he was appointed Director of the National Gallery of Ireland. Unsurprisingly, his sympathies returned to Ireland and he wrote a codicil to his 1913 will, returning his French bequest to Ireland:

> *This is a codicil to my last will to the effect that the group of pictures now at the London National Gallery, which I had bequeathed to that Institution, I now bequeath to the City of Dublin, providing that a suitable building is provided for them within five years of my death. The group of pictures I have lent to Belfast I give to the Municipal Gallery in Harcourt Street. If a building is provided within five years, the whole collection will be housed together. The sole Trustee in this matter will be my aunt, Lady Gregory. She is to appoint any additional Trustees she may think fit. I also wish that the pictures now on loan at this [National Gallery of Ireland] Gallery remain as my gift.*
>
> *I would like my friend Tom Bodkin to be asked to help in the obtaining of this new Gallery of Modern Art for Dublin.*
>
> *If within five years a Gallery is not forthcoming, then the group of pictures (at the London National Gallery) are to be sold, and the proceeds go to fulfil the purpose of my will.*
>
> *Hugh Lane.*
> *3rd February, 1915*

But the codicil was not witnessed. When the Cunard passenger liner, the Lusitania, en route from New York to Liverpool, was torpedoed by a German submarine off the coast of Ireland in 1915, Hugh Lane was among the 1,198 passengers and crew who died. Dublin and London disputed the will, a dispute which became more bitter as it coincided with the Irish War of Independence. In 1933 Charlemont House opened as the permanent location of the Hugh Lane Municipal Gallery of Modern Art, funded by Dublin Corporation. Eventually (in 1959) an interim agreement was reached whereby the paintings are shared between the two countries on a five-year rotation. In 1994 a revised (short-term) agreement allowed 27 of the pictures to remain on loan in Dublin, while the remaining eight continue in rotation with London.

Among the best-known works in the Lane bequest are Renoir's *Les Parapluies*, and two paintings by Manet, *Le Concert aux Tuileries* and

Eva Gonzales. When they are in Dublin, these great paintings lift the collection, and one can see Lane's influence on early twentieth-century Irish collectors, and make sense of the themes in their donations to the gallery.

Eva Gonzales is a portrait of one of Manet's pupils at her easel, and nicely connects Hugh Lane's work in Ireland to that of the artist and patron Sarah Purser (1848-1943), who trained in Paris, was instrumental in bringing French ideas to Dublin, supported Lane's activities to establish the municipal gallery and led moves to recover the Lane bequest. *Le Concert aux Tuileries* also has a special resonance in the Lane Gallery. This group portrait shows a number of Manet's family, friends and associates gathered in the Tuileries Gardens in Paris for an afternoon concert. Manet himself appears at the extreme left, half obscured by the figure of Albert de Balleroy, another painter with whom Manet shared a studio. Elsewhere in the painting are portraits of Baudelaire, Offenbach, Henri Fantin-Latour, Gautier, Monginot and other prominent figures of the Second Empire. This pantheon of luminaries assembled on an informal occasion where friendship mediates and contributes to intellectual and political debates chimes with the famous poem by W. B. Yeats about the Hugh Lane Gallery—"The Municipal Gallery Revisited"—in which Yeats, viewing the portraits of Roger Casement, Arthur Griffith, Kevin O'Higgins, Augusta Gregory, Hazel Lavery, John Millington Synge and Hugh Lane himself, affirms that artists and writers along with politicians and revolutionaries were the makers of modern Ireland:

You that would judge me, do not judge alone
This book or that, come to this hallowed place
Where my friends' portraits hang and look thereon;
Ireland's history in their lineaments trace;
Think where man's glory most begins and ends,
And say my glory was I had such friends.

The portraits referred to by Yeats are not on permanent display, but some or all are to be seen from time to time, and a recent exhibition was devoted to the poem itself.

The Hugh Lane Gallery is as well known to Dubliners for its temporary exhibitions and its encouragement of contemporary art as for its permanent collection, and it has a strong community outreach programme.

In 2001 Francis Bacon's reconstructed studio, from 71 Reece Mews, South Kensington, London, was opened in a special gallery at the Hugh Lane. Bacon was born in Dublin to English parents, and his family remained in Ireland through his childhood. Bacon's heir, John Edwards, donated the studio and Bacon's archive to the Hugh Lane, and it provides a remarkable contrast to the rest of the gallery space.

One might single out a number of notable works in the Municipal Gallery. My own favourite pieces are by artists with Irish origins. Seán Scully was born in Dublin but has lived most of his life in Britain and America. His work is well-represented in Irish collections, and he is best known for his commitment to forms of abstract painting. His early works were dominated by a striped motif, and he later developed paintings of chequer-boards. One of these is *Sanda* (1992), with nine rich red squares of oil on canvas, in which a striped metal plate is inset. Some of the luminosity usually associated with Scully is muted by the light in this gallery, but the reward is the extraordinary depth, intensity and movement within the shadowy red boxes. It is an emotional painting, in the tradition of Rothko, one of Scully's major influences. Although Scully is so interested in geometry, his shapes have imprecise edges that both suggest and resist perfect forms. He has talked about this in terms of a resistance to closure, because the closure of certain abstract forms leaves us with nothing to think about. Scully has described in interviews the shock he experienced in childhood when his parents moved him from a Roman Catholic convent school to an English state school full of violence. He yearns for a spiritual dimension to everyday life. He talks about his form of abstraction being a "figurative form" with a story-telling dimension.

Kathy Prendergast was born in Dublin in 1958 and studied at the National College of Art and Design, and at the Royal College of Art in London. She makes sculptures in many media—bronze, stone, cloth and chalk, for example—and she also creates work on paper. She is perhaps best known for her work on mapping, where she adopts conventions of cartography to make two- and three-dimensional maps of the human body and other forms. Her works on mapping the female body with landscape conventions reinvigorate rather tired images of Mother Ireland.

Prendergast is represented in the Municipal Gallery by a piece called *Waiting*, a mixed media sculpture which uses dress patterns as a background to three seated, more or less life-size female figures in long gowns of neutral shades. The women are incomplete, with heads and some of their upper torsos missing. It is one of the artist's early works, for which she won the Carroll's Award in 1980. To sit alone in the gallery with these figures is like sitting in the presence of ghosts.

Dublin Writers Museum

The idea of a Dublin Writers Museum started with the journalist and author Maurice Gorham (1902-75), who proposed it to Dublin Tourism. The project was in gestation for several years before a suitable building was found. The museum at 18 Parnell Square, close to the Hugh Lane Gallery, opened in November 1991. It occupies what was originally an eighteenth-century house, which accommodates the museum rooms, library, gallery and administration area. The annexe behind it has a coffee shop and bookshop on the ground floor and exhibition and lecture rooms on the floors above. The Irish Writers' Centre, next door in no. 19, contains the meeting rooms and offices of the Irish Writers' Union, the Society of Irish Playwrights, the Irish Children's Book Trust and the Translators' Association of Ireland. The basement beneath both houses is occupied by a restaurant.

The museum was established to promote interest in Irish literature as a whole and in the lives and works of individual Irish writers. The organizers decided that initially it would commemorate only the lives and works of dead writers. The adjacent Irish Writers' Centre has frequent readings by living writers and promotes their work in various ways.

The writers featured in the museum are those whom the curators judge to have made an important contribution to Irish or international literature or, on a local level, to the literature of Dublin. This Dublin focus means that important literary figures from the north or the west of the country, for example, get short shrift unless they came to ply their wares in Dublin.

Two rooms present a history of Irish literature from its beginnings up to recent times. The panels describe the various phases, movements and notable names, while the showcases and pictures illustrate the lives and works of individual writers. It is a pleasantly old-fashioned and wordy display, dependent on cases of rare books and on photographs. There are relatively few literary manuscripts, as such, but quite a few notes from famous writers and inscribed books. Room 1 takes the story through to the end of the nineteenth century and the beginning of the Literary Revival, while Room 2 is entirely devoted to the great writers of the twentieth century. Many of us would quibble at this sense of proportion. The displays often claim to be authoritative on matters of literary judgement where there is no real critical consensus.

At the top of the grand staircase is the Gorham Library with its Stapleton ceiling. The museum has a small library, including some rare editions and critical works. Next to the library is a salon, known as The Gallery of Writers. This room, decorated as a nineteenth-century drawing room, has portraits and busts of Irish writers around the walls, and is used for receptions, exhibitions and special occasions. Upstairs is an exhibition room on the first floor, and a room devoted to children's literature. There are also lecture rooms and meeting rooms available for various sized events.

Dublin Tourism made a decision in the 1990s that "literary Dublin" would be one of the central themes according to which a narrative of the city would be presented to visitors. The museum addresses an implied audience that is literate and discriminating, but it does not challenge the idea that there is a single coherent narrative of Irish literature. The collection has relied on donations and in its publicity it tries to be tactfully charming about some of the idiosyncrasies of its collection (which, needless to say, are its best features):

The Museum Collection is as fascinating as it is various. As might be expected, there are plenty of books, representing the milestones in the progress of Irish literature from Gulliver's Travels *to* Dracula, The Importance of Being Earnest, Ulysses *and* Waiting for Godot. *Most of these are first or early editions, recapturing the moment when they first surprised the world. There are books inscribed to Oliver Gogarty by W. B. Yeats and to Brinsley MacNamara by James Joyce, while a first edition of Patrick Kavanagh's "The Great Hunger" includes in the poet's own hand a stanza which the prudish publisher declined to print.*

Portraits of Irish writers are everywhere, including fine originals by artists such as Edward McGuire, Harry Kernoff, Patrick Swift and Micheal Farrell. Among the many letters are an abject note from Sheridan to a creditor, a signed refusal from Bernard Shaw to provide an autograph, a letter from Yeats to Frank O'Connor, a typically concise card from Samuel Beckett and Brendan Behan's postcard from Los Angeles ("Great spot for a quiet piss-up").

Among the pens, pipes and typewriters there are some particularly curious personal possessions—Lady Gregory's lorgnette, Austin Clarke's desk, Samuel Beckett's telephone, Mary Lavin's teddy bear, Oliver Gogarty's laurels and Brendan Behan's union card, complete with fingerprints—and such exotic intrusions as Handel's chair and a silver tazza decorated with scenes from the work of Burns.

It would take a heart of stone not to enjoy Samuel Beckett's telephone and Mary Lavin's hair slides (there along with her teddy). When I last visited the museum in September 2003, it also had on display a pair of John F. Kennedy's boxer shorts, recently purchased by an Irish businessman and briefly on display in a Dublin shop window. I hope this is a permanent addition to the Writers Museum.

The James Joyce Centre

Many visitors to the Dublin Writers Museum will walk round the corner into North Great George Street to visit the James Joyce Centre at no. 35. The residents of North Great George Street have been campaigning for several years to have this beautiful Georgian street restored. The houses are large and the restoration work very expensive. In the twentieth century the area went into marked decline and by 1982 twelve houses on the street had been demolished as dangerous buildings. One of the residents is the Irish senator, David Norris, a Joycean scholar, former lecturer at Trinity College Dublin, and campaigner for gay rights, who is chairman of the James Joyce Centre and who did much of the campaigning and fund-raising to make its existence possible. The centre has a library and exhibition space. A room from the Paris apartment of Joyce's friend Paul Leon is recreated in the centre. There are numerous photographs from the various places in Joyce's life and of his family and friends. The original door of 7 Eccles Street (home of Leopold Bloom), which was for a

long time in The Bailey pub, is now kept here. One can listen to recordings of Joyce reading his works and view short films about the writer and the city.

The house itself was built in 1784 by Francis Ryan as a townhouse for Valentine Brown, the Earl of Kenmare. The plasterwork is by Michael Stapleton, responsible for many of Dublin's finest interiors. Despite its auspicious beginnings, however, the area was already in decline when Joyce was living in Dublin. The back room on the ground floor was leased to Dennis Maginni, a colourful figure who ran a dancing academy on the premises, and who appears at several brief moments in *Ulysses*. This tenuous connection is the only link between Joyce and the house, but few people would begrudge the inventiveness of the restorers who were able to save such a fine building by giving it a marketable use.

The Rotunda

Dr. Bartholomew Mosse (1712-1759), surgeon and philanthropist, served his apprenticeship in Dublin and received his licence as a barber-surgeon in 1733. He travelled abroad, first as a British Army surgeon, and later to study midwifery, and in 1745 he founded The Dublin Lying-In Hospital in George's Lane (South Great George Street), the first maternity hospital in Ireland and the first practical school for obstetrics in the world. The hospital, opened thanks to his munificence, could only cater for ten women at any one time. Mosse wrote that "every woman is to have a decent bed to herself and to be provided with all manner of necessities and the greatest imaginable care will be taken of her and her new-born infant from the time she is admitted and until well able to leave the hospital, and all without the least expense to her." The hospital was a huge success, and Mosse very soon wanted to expand. He leased lands and began to raise money towards a new hospital. Work began in 1751, and the Rotunda Hospital received a charter in 1756, in which its aims were defined:

That such Hospital, when established will be a means not only of preserving the lives and relieving the Miseries of numberless Lying-in Women, but also of preventing that most unnatural (though too frequent) Practice of abandoning, or perhaps murdering, new born Infants. And that it may prevent such Gentlemen as intend to prac-

tice Midwifery in our said Kingdom, from going Abroad for Instruction.

That by admitting and instructing in such Hospital, Women, who after some time spent there, being duly qualified, may settle in such Parts of our said Kingdom as most stand in need of such persons, it will be a means of preventing the unhappy Effects owing to the Ignorance of the generality of Country Midwives. That by preserving the Lives of so many Infants, who in all probability must otherwise perish, it will increase the number of our Subjects, in our said Kingdom.

The Rotunda was designed by Richard Castle, the German Huguenot who came to Ireland in 1728 and became one of the country's most distinguished architects, building Newman House, Leinster House and the Printing House at Trinity, as well as numerous private dwellings, and many of Ireland's most important country houses. Attached to the hospital was the circular entertainment complex which gave it its name, and in which charity concerts were held to raise money for the hospital. In the grounds of the hospital the Rotunda gardens became an elegant pleasure garden, the scene of concerts, garden parties and masquerades. The garden included a coffee house, and an orchestra sometimes played there. It was, however, plagued by vandalism, perpetrated particularly by local children, and rewards for information on those responsible were repeatedly offered. The Rotunda chapel, open only to residents and their visitors, has a fine rococo interior. In the 1760s the chapel was opened and funds were increased by the practice of charging for seats, with the inducement of hearing fashionable charity sermons.

Visitors to Parnell Square will see an information board reproducing James Malton's view of the Rotunda in 1795. There were many additions to the building and the square through the second half of the eighteenth century when Dublin was, as it is now, constantly in the midst of redevelopment and transformation, so it is worth remembering that Malton's view does not show the original building, but one of its many incarnations.

Chapter Eight
THE CAPITAL SINCE INDEPENDENCE

The Civil War and Reconstruction

The 1916 Easter Rising came at a period of low self-confidence and civic pride for the city. Belfast was growing in population and prosperity and seemed much more the type of the twentieth-century industrial capital than Dublin with its slums, poverty and class divisions. In Belfast the businessmen and factory owners shared religious and political affiliations with much of their workforce. In Dublin there was a sectarian schism.

The War of Independence and the subsequent civil war between pro- and anti- treat forces wreaked havoc on much of the city centre. One of the accomplishments of the new government was to reconstruct much of the damaged architecture of the city and remake many of the symbols of colonial authority into central emblems of a new national pride. The new parliament was dignified with a certain amount of eighteenth-century grandeur by being situated in Leinster House, once the home of a great political grandee and later owned by the Royal Dublin Society, which had done so much to preserve the city's cultural heritage. The General Post Office was filled with pictures and sculpture to commemorate the Rising. And in the most quixotic re-imagining of the city many of the street names were changed to honour the pantheon of nationalist heroes. Suddenly, too, the Irish language was made visible on signs all over the city, but this gesture did less to reinvigorate language usage than might have been hoped.

The government of the Free State had a strong centralizing impulse which indirectly fostered the growth of Dublin. There was no attempt to spread the work of state bodies or cultural institutions around the country. The legal system, the civil service and most of the media were concentrated in Dublin. There was recognition of the terrible public health and morale problems caused by inner-city slums, and the new government, with its limited resources—for independent Ireland was not a wealthy country—attempted to reform Dublin housing by creating new low-density suburbs. A good bus service and the increased ownership of private cars from the 1940s meant that many of the city's workers commuted in from the suburbs. These suburbs themselves were not well designed in terms of becoming community centres or providing amenities, so that by the 1970s and 1980s, as alcohol and drug abuse became an ever greater social problem, the suburban housing estate became one version of the quintessential dystopia.

On the other hand, Dublin also had the more utopian version of the suburbs, particularly in the southern part of the city, developed in many cases around older villages. The ease of commuting along the route of the DART from places such as Sandymount and Killiney raised house prices, and the views of Dublin Bay and the Wicklow Mountains eased the sense of containment and claustrophobia often associated with urban development.

In the city centre there was almost none of the high-rise expansion in commercial or living spaces found in other European cities. Many of Dublin's most interesting historic buildings were left to fall into decay, until they were destroyed by vandalism and bulldozed by developers.

Dublin experienced a deep sense of isolation during the Second World War, when Ireland was neutral. The immediate origins of Irish neutrality lay in the collapse of collective security agreements with Britain and other western countries in the 1930s. Economic hardships were accompanied by feelings of guilt and shame among many people aware of Nazi atrocities, or emotionally linked to the allied powers. Many Irish citizens volunteered for the British forces during the war, but their gesture went largely unrecognized at home. Anti-British feeling in Ireland made neutrality even more popular with those nationalists who thought of Germany rather than Britain as Ireland's natural ally. Elizabeth Bowen was one of many who felt loyalties divided between Britain and Ireland. In 1940 she began reporting secretly to the British Ministry of Information about Irish attitudes to the war. Her best-selling novel, *The Heat of the Day* (1949), reflects on the links between personal and political treacheries.

Two British films of the 1940s reflect on Irish ambivalence, if not hostility, to Britain and on Ireland's potential pro-German sympathies: in *I See a Dark Stranger* (dir, Frank Launder, 1946) Deborah Kerr gives a comic rendition of a passionate Irish nationalist who becomes a German spy, but is "saved" by her friendship with a British officer (Trevor Howard), while Thorold Dickinson's Ministry of Information propaganda film, *The Next of Kin* (1942), has a "neutral seaman" (Irish) as one of a chain of people who betray a British mission and cause the deaths of hundreds of troops. A great deal has been written about Bohemian Dublin in the 1950s and 1960s—an era dominated in literary terms by Flann O'Brien, Brendan Behan and Patrick Kavanagh—but this was far from the Bohemia of London or Paris. It was all about men getting drunk in pubs, and very little about sex and drugs and rock 'n' roll. Edna O'Brien's vibrant *Country Girl Trilogy* describes a city which promises promiscuity and glamour, but was very short on delivery, where the ambitious and the wayward longed to get away to London, Paris or New York. V. S. Pritchett wrote a profile of Dublin in 1967 in which he described its strange, and appealing, provincialism:

> *The fact is that it is still very much a city caught by anxieties, for it is half way between an old way of life and a new one. It is crowded with country people who bring with them the obduracy, the gossipy pleasures of small town-life. Shop assistants gather in corners excitedly whispering, and if an impatient customer calls to them, they turn with offended astonishment at him, wondering who "the stranger" is, as all country girls do, and then turn round and go on whispering. Shops, in the country, are meeting places. Before anything else Dublin is dedicated to gregariousness, to meeting people, to welcome, to the longing to hear who they are and what they will say. As you walk down St. Stephen's Green past the Shelbourne or the clubs, indeed as you walk down any street, in the wealthy quarters or the poor, you see the man or woman who is coming towards you pause for a second. They gaze at you perplexedly, search your face, even smile to convey that they wished they knew you, and not knowing you, are puzzled by this break in the natural order. They ache for acquaintance; and if they don't find out who you are, they will invent it.*

In 1991 Dublin became the European City of Culture. The consequent publicity provoked a media examination into the role of the city in national life and questioned the absence of policy-led planning for Dublin's future development. Dubliners were obliged to hear what other people thought of their city, and it was a painful experience. The British architectural historian Dan Cruikshank told them that "no

European city has done more in recent years to destroy its architectural heritage" and an architect from the Finnish Ministry of the Environment wrote to the *Irish Times* after a visit to Dublin:

> *It is difficult to express my disappointment and sad feelings as I saw the horrifying state of buildings and the streetscape. I have been travelling around a lot, but I don't think I have anywhere else seen so many beautiful buildings—and right in the centre—left empty, left in the hands of vandals and weather. It looked like Dublin's historic core was left to rot.*

Dublin's year as City of Culture became, then, a year of soul-searching rather than of celebration. There were some positive responses by policy-makers, who at least began to ask questions about the city even if they did not yet come forward with coherent plans. And among the most significant developments of the 1990s was the greater audience that emerged for those individuals who had worked for years to salvage objects and stories from the vanishing city. Environmental campaigners and local historians including Vivien Igoe, Peter Pearson, Frieda Kelly and Deirdre O'Brien, who feature largely in the bibliography of this book, attracted more attentive audiences. The O'Brien Press and others have made notable contributions to publishing books on the city.

Another, but related, form of civic pride emerged in the 1970s and 1980s in the campaigns to redress social injustice, expressed in the journalism of Nell McCafferty and Mary Holland, and less explicitly in the fiction of Roddy Doyle. What these very different writers have in common is an attention to the local and the particular. In her column from the law courts McCafferty made readers rethink Dublin from the perspective of the prisoner in the dock, and ask whether modern Ireland had got the society it wanted and deserved. Doyle's novels sit within the long tradition of creating the city through listening to its sound, particularly its dialogues, and Alan Parker's film of *The Commitments* (1991) drew attention to the ways in which popular music is also a soundtrack to the city

And then along came the economic boom caused by the emergence of the Celtic Tiger, and the script flew out of the window. In the last ten years the city has been flooded with the money for new building and development projects that have totally transformed its atmosphere and meaning. This prosperity has, of course, created problems, as well as solutions. Everyone you meet in Dublin will be talking about house prices and traffic. The sudden access of wealth has put a home in Dublin, a city where there is a long tradition of living as owner-occupier, well beyond the reach of many in the middle classes, never mind the working classes. People now commute extraordinary distances into work in the city, but in spite of all the new road building and the modernization of public transport the infrastructure can barely support the population and traffic. Stand at either end of O'Connell Bridge and you can barely hear yourself think for the noise of the traffic. In 2004 the government announced plans to relocate several government departments, and hence jobs, to other parts of the country.

The Celtic Tiger developed a new aesthetics both celebratory and critical, expressed in the work of novelists like Anne Enright and Keith Ridgway.

Meanwhile prosperity attracts immigrants and for the first time Dublin feels like a cosmopolitan city. In the last decade the court services have dealt with people speaking over 200 native languages. Radio stations are now broadcasting programmes in Mandarin to the city. There is a monthly multi-cultural newspaper, *Metro Eireann,* founded by Nigerian journalists, Chinedu Onyejelem and Abel Ugba, produced by and for Dublin's new ethnic-minority citizens and immigrant communities.

However one might choose to characterize Dublin today, the key word is no longer that chosen by James Joyce in *Dubliners.* Dublin may be in the grip of many forces, but not of *paralysis.*

Germany Bombs Dublin
Saturday 31 May 1941

"Although a complete survey has not yet been possible, the latest report which I have received is that 27 persons were killed outright or subsequently died; 45 were wounded or received other serious bodily injury and are still in hospital; 25 houses were completely destroyed and 300 so damaged as to be unfit for habitation, leaving many hundreds of our people homeless. It has been for all our citizens an occasion of profound sorrow in which the members of this House have fully

shared. (Members rose in their places.) *The Dáil will also desire to be associated with the expression of sincere thanks which has gone out from the Government and from our whole community to the several voluntary organisations the devoted exertions of whose members helped to confine the extent of the disaster and have mitigated the sufferings of those affected by it.*

Éamon de Valera, Statement to the Dáil, 5 June 1941.

May 1941 marked the height of the German airforce's bombing blitz on Britain. The north of Ireland had also been targeted. In the course of four Luftwaffe attacks on Belfast on the nights of 7-8 April, 15-16 April, 4-5 May and 5-6 May 1941, lasting ten hours in total, 1,100 people died, over 56,000 houses in the city were damaged (53 per cent of its entire housing stock), roughly 100,000 made temporarily homeless and £20 million of damage was caused to property at wartime values.

The people of Dublin often heard the sound of German planes, and were aware of explosions out to sea. The city was protected by an anti-aircraft battalion, with responsibility to fire on any unidentified planes flying above the city. Before May 1941 there had been four incidents of apparently stray German bombs falling in Éire, in Wexford, Monaghan, Meath and in South Dublin at Sandycove and Dún Laoghaire.

In the early hours of Saturday 31 May army searchlights went into operation, responding to reports of aircraft flying over Ireland's eastern seaboard. At half past midnight the anti-aircraft battalion opened fire.

At 1.30 am the first bombs dropped on North Richmond Street and Rutland Place. Another bomb fell near the Dog Pond pumping station in Phoenix Park, damaging some of the Dublin Zoo buildings but causing no injuries. Also damaged by this bomb were the windows of Áras an Uactaráin, the residence of the Irish President, Douglas Hyde.

At 2.05 am a German landmine landed on the North Strand Road between the Five Lamps and Newcomen Bridge. Among the rescue services at the scene were members of the Dublin Auxiliary Fire Service, which had been established in 1939/1940, at the onset of war, to augment the full-time brigade in times of greater need. The AFS expanded quickly to over 700 officers and men. During the Belfast Blitz on 15 April, the AFS and the Dublin Fire Brigade had, in defiance of Irish neutrality, crossed the border to help their colleagues and the Belfast victims. At the end of the war the AFS was disbanded.

The Dublin bombing killed 34 people, with 90 injured and 300 houses destroyed or damaged. Twelve of those killed were buried by Dublin Corporation at a public funeral on 5 June, attended by the Taoiseach and government ministers. On 5 June de Valera made a statement in the Dáil about the incident, indicating that "a protest has been made to the German Government."

Eduard Hempel, the German Minister to Ireland, had called on de Valera immediately after the bombing. His first suggestion was that the bombing had actually been carried out by the British, using captured German planes, in an attempt to bring Ireland into the war on the Allied side. In due course the Germans investigated the matter, agreed that the Luftwaffe was responsible, blamed high winds for knocking them off course from their intended target (Liverpool), and apologized. In 1958 the post-war German government paid Ireland £327,000 compensation for the raid. British security sources later offered another theory to account for the German mistake. The bombers were following two radio beacons which were designed to form an x over the target. The British transmitted a third beam which moved the cross hairs to a different location, sending the planes off target.

De Valera Defends Irish Neutrality
Wednesday 16 May 1945

"That Mr Churchill should be irritated when our neutrality stood in the way of what he thought he vitally needed, I understand; but that he or any thinking person in Britain or elsewhere should fail to see the reason for our neutrality I find it hard to conceive."

Éamon de Valera

On 16 May 1945, Éamon de Valera, the 63-year-old Taoiseach of Éire, travelled to the Radio Éireann studio in Henry Street to make a broadcast to the nation, in reply to Winston Churchill's victory speech of 13 May. The city came to a standstill as people gathered in their homes, in pubs and in dance halls fitted with loudspeakers to listen to the broadcast.

Churchill had taken the opportunity in his broadcast to condemn roundly Ireland's neutrality during the war, and to praise the loyalty of Northern Ireland in terms that would commit the British government to unionism for decades to come:

Owing to the action of Mr. de Valera, so much at variance with the temper and instinct of thousands of southern Irishmen who hastened to the battle-front to prove their ancient valour, the approaches which the southern Irish ports and airfields could so easily have guarded were closed by the hostile aircraft and U-boats.

This was indeed a deadly moment in our life, and if it had not been for the loyalty and friendship of Northern Ireland we should have been forced to come to close quarters with Mr. de Valera or perish for ever from the earth.

However, with a restraint and poise to which, I venture to say, history will find few parallels, His Majesty's government never laid a violent hand upon them, though at times it would have been quite easy and quite natural, and we left the de Valera Government to frolic with the Germans and later with the Japanese representatives to their heart's content.

Neutrality has been a feature of Irish foreign policy more or less since independence. Before the Second World War Ireland's positions at the League of Nations had been in favour of neutrality. During the war, while Ireland was formally neutral, it was a neutrality that leaned heavily towards the Allies, especially after America's entry into the war. This was, naturally, not good enough for the Allies, and de Valera had a particularly troubled relationship with David Gray, the American Minister in Ireland during the conflict.

The Allies professed particular shock and displeasure when de Valera gave his condolences to the German Ambassador, Edouard Hempel, on the death of Adolf Hitler, on 2 May 1945. The shock was by then, of course, mainly rhetorical, since the war was ending in an Allied victory. Yet for many Irish citizens de Valera's gesture that day was disgraceful, while for others it was puzzling. Ireland had operated a heavy censorship during the emergency, but by the time of Hitler's death his awful war crimes were known. Moreover, no Irish interest could be served by courtesy to the Germans. De Valera represented the gesture to his friends precisely as an act of courtesy, specifically towards Germany's representative in Dublin, Dr. Edouard Hempel:

> *During the whole of the war, Dr. Hempel's conduct was irreproachable. He was always friendly and inevitably correct*—in marked contrast to Gray. *I was certainly not going to add to his humiliation in the hour of defeat.*

There might be greater cause for pride in Ireland's neutrality at this period had more been done to assist refugees. The number of Jewish people to find asylum in Ireland before and during the war was tiny. On the other hand, the 1937 Constitution had formally acknowledged the rights of Jewish citizens. The Irish government was not as vigorously anti-fascist as it might have been, but neither did fascism gain a significant hold on mainstream public opinion in the 1930s and 1940s.

Writing in *The Bell* in June 1945 on "What It Means To Be a Jew", A. J. Leventhal described growing up in Dublin:

> *It was at about the age of seven that I became aware... of the boundary between certain Dublin Streets. The cul-de-sac known as Oakfield Place, where I lived with my parents and co-religionists in the natural gregariousness of my people, was invisibly lined off from the lower end of Lombard Street West where non-Jews lived. Between them there might as well have been a ghetto wall, so well drawn into their own loyalties were the young denizens of each locality. Perhaps, at first, it was merely regional "gang" rivalry, the battle of stones between neighbouring groups of ebullient boyhood—the young idea that had learned to shoot with a catapult with no further thought than the assertion of the physical superiority of one district over another. Later, however, it became clear to me, that we of Oakfield Place were regarded as strangers who, as such, ought to be liquidated.*

When Ireland joined the United Nations, in 1955, Irish neutrality once again became allied with a defence of the interests of small nations, and of refugees and minorities. In spite of the strongly anti-communist ideological bent of the Republic of Ireland, its non-aligned status often saw the country take positions that were against western interests and in favour of dialogue between the superpowers.

When Éamon de Valera went to Henry Street to defend Irish neutrality on 16 May 1945, he addressed the point of principle, but more effective for his first audience was the quivering nationalist rhetoric about plucky little Ireland standing alone against tyranny:

Could he not find in his heart the generosity to acknowledge that there is a small nation that stood alone, not for one year or two, but for several hundred years against aggression; that endured spoliations, famines, massacres in endless succession; that was clubbed many times into insensibility, but that each time on returning consciousness took up the fight anew; a small nation that could never be got to accept defeat and has never surrendered her soul?

The broadcast was greeted by cheering all over the city, and when de Valera left the radio station a crowd had gathered to congratulate and applaud him. The immediate sense of vindication covered up but could not permanently obscure the divisions produced by the war. In recent years Irish people who served with the Allies have begun to speak out about the ways in which they were made to feel that their war experiences were at worst disloyal, at best irrelevant in post-war Ireland.

When Ireland entered the European Union debates over neutrality featured largely in the national debate. Neutrality survived that challenge but in the so-called "war on terror" Ireland's pro-American stance seems to call into question how far it can be described as a neutral state.

Kavanagh's Weekly
Saturday 5 July 1952

"An audience makes a writer as much as a writer makes an audience."
Patrick Kavanagh, *Kavanagh's Weekly*, Volume 1, No 13

"Kavanagh's Weekly,
62 Pembroke Road, Dublin
EDITED BY PATRICK KAVANAGH
Publisher: Peter Kavanagh, M.A., Ph.D.
7 July 1952
Dear Mr —————,

Enc. No 13. We are returning all monies—which we received as token of interest and all 20 copies available to public have been posted today.

Patrick Kavanagh"

The thirteenth and final issue of *Kavanagh's Weekly* was published on 5 July 1952. Early in 1952 Patrick Kavanagh's younger brother Peter had returned from America with some savings which the writer persuaded him to invest in a weekly newspaper. The two brothers shared a flat at 62 Pembroke Road. Patrick Kavanagh (1904-67) was 48 years old, unmarried and living in poverty. Most of the copy for *Kavanagh's Weekly* was produced on the typewriter in his flat. The paper was printed in Dublin by the Fleet Printing Company. Each issue was eight pages long and cost sixpence. In April 1952 Peter Kavanagh wrote to friends and writers whom Patrick hoped might be sympathetic, asking them to contribute articles (for which the paper could not offer payment). The most distinguished of the few writers who did contribute on this basis was Myles na gCopaleen, who appears in four issues. The Devon-Adair Publishing Company in New York placed one advertisement for *1,000 Years of Irish Prose*, and over the next few weeks a couple of other advertisements for Dublin businesses appeared.

From the first article, "Victory of Mediocrity", in the first issue, *Kavanagh's Weekly* was scathing in its denunciation of the ways in which contemporary Irish society betrayed the struggle for independence in its pursuit of materialism. Favoured themes in the arts reviews include attacks on the Gaelicization of Irish culture, condemnation of censorship, and the repeated complaint that what passed for an arts establishment in Dublin was deeply hostile to truth and creativity. The following comments on *The Irish Times* from Issue 2 are not untypical of Kavanagh's style and preoccupation:

Without ourselves claiming infallibility we can say that The Irish Times *has been for a few years now on the side of the dullest, deadest elements in the country.*

Because it is dull many people are inclined to imagine it sound. This doesn't happen. Truth is the gayest of things and since Myles na gCopaleen left there has been no laughter at The Irish Times. *Its Saturday Book-page is a square of flooring timber that would if usable advance any building scheme. Strip the mask of dullness from the other contributors and you find a vacuity.*

But we don't want to be derogatory of The Irish Times *or of any newspaper per se. If you choose to patronise the tenants of the intellectual graveyard it is in the end your misfortune.*

It was only too easy for people to sneer at *Kavanagh's Weekly* and to find more than a hint of sour grapes in Kavanagh's attack on an establishment that did not hold him at his own estimation. In fact, Kavanagh was greatly admired by his peers, and many people tolerated his abusiveness out of respect for his abilities; but he also met with a great deal of snobbery and mediocrity. There is a lot of nonsense in *Kavanagh's Weekly*, as in Kavanagh's rant about women writers: "The body with its feelings, its instincts, provides women with a source of wisdom, but they lack the analytic detachment to exploit it in literature." At fifty years' distance, though, it is more striking how the very amateurishness of the endeavour produces a rawness and edge in the questions Kavanagh asks about truth and art and how they can be produced in Irish society. Kavanagh was aware himself that his newspaper had the capacity to embarrass its audience, and that the very resistance to a poet addressing questions of political economy and foreign affairs, for example, violated the decorum that was hedging the arts in the 1950s.

On the front page of issue 12 there was an announcement:

The next issue of this paper will be the final one; it will be a limited edition, autographed by the Editor, and will be sold only as part of the complete file. The price of the complete file will be £1 and it will be available only from P. Kavanagh, 62, Pembroke Road, Dublin. If, however, we receive in the meantime a sum of £1,000 or upwards we will distribute next week's issue in the ordinary way and continue publishing KAVANAGH'S WEEKLY.

Twenty people sent a pound. Kavanagh opened the four-page article, "The Story Of An Editor Who Was Corrupted By Love", which constitutes the whole of Issue 13 , by writing: "The first thing that we must emphasise is that we are not closing down primarily for lack of money or because our circulation was too small. Our circulation was

remarkably large and was rising; last week we sold out." For Kavanagh the revelation of working on the newspaper was that it exposed him as friendless in ways he had not fully anticipated or realized.

It would not be completely appropriate to term *Kavanagh's Weekly* a failure, but the isolation of Kavanagh in Dublin's intellectual community in 1952, if such a thing existed, does seem to have been a prelude to the trauma he suffered during his 1954 libel case. In October 1952 an anonymous article appeared in a weekly paper, *The Leader*, under the title "Profile: Mr Patrick Kavanagh". The article, over 2,000 words in length, begins by describing Kavanagh as a bar-room bully, humiliating his acolytes, and goes on to describe Kavanagh's critique of Dublin in terms that suggest the poet is slavishly infatuated with other metropolitan centres where he fantasizes himself as the centre of attention. *Kavanagh's Weekly* is singled out for criticism:

> *Afraid of the magazine becoming a commercial success (though this seemed to imply an unwarranted lack of faith in his own integrity) and afraid, too, it may be assumed, of its Revelations sweeping the Government from power and, with thousands of refugees streaming from the city, of being left with the country on his hands, Mr Kavanagh closed down after twelve issues. His brother, resplendent in a white bawneen jacket, green pants and a yellow tie, departed for America, there to denounce, not Hollywood films, nor spivvie ties, not American manners, not the American way of life, but the harmless little gatherings of Irish exiles in the United States. One cannot be other than touched and amazed at the strength of the umbilical cords that bind both Mr Kavanagh and his brother to Mucker.*

The profile is very snobbish, a bit vicious and quite funny. Kavanagh was too sensitive to laugh it off and sued the newspaper and its printer for libel. In February 1954 the action was heard in the High Court in Dublin. *The Leader's* defence was led by John Costello, who had been Taoiseach in the inter-party government of 1948-51, and was to become Taoiseach again later in 1954. On each day of the trial the court was crowded with members of the public anxious to hear Kavanagh give evidence. *The Leader's* legal team called no witnesses, and the chief action of the trial was the thirteen hours spent by Kavanagh in the witness box, mainly in cross-examination by Costello.

Kavanagh lost the case, but as sometimes happens in libel cases, this mobilized public sympathy on his behalf. With costs likely to be very heavy a fund was started for his appeal, with distinguished contributors including T. S. Eliot. The appeal court found in Kavanagh's favour and ordered a retrial. At that point, however, Kavanagh was in hospital suffering from lung cancer, and in May 1955 the action was settled out of court.

Fiftieth Anniversary of Bloomsday
Wednesday 16 June 1954

> *"James Joyce was an artist. He has said so himself. His was a case of Ars gratia Artist".*
> Brian O'Nolan, *Envoy* 5: 17 (April 1951)

On the fiftieth anniversary of Leopold Bloom's fictional wanderings through Dublin, a group of literati met the architect Michael Scott, at "Geragh", the home he had designed, in Sandycove, near to the Martello Tower where the opening scene of *Ulysses* is set. Anthony Cronin (poet and editor), Tom Joyce (dentist and cousin of the author), Patrick Kavanagh (poet), A. J. (Con) Leventhal (Registrar of Trinity College), Brian O'Nolan (a.k.a. Myles na gCopaleen and Flann O'Brien, novelist and newspaper columnist) and John Ryan (painter and owner of the literary magazine, *Envoy*) were in the group. They planned to travel round the city through the day, visiting in turn the scenes of the novel, ending at night in what had once been the brothel quarter of the city, the area which Joyce had called Nighttown. The members of the party had been assigned roles from the book: Leventhal, who was Jewish, represented Bloom; Cronin was Stephen; O'Nolan was to combine Martin Cunningham and Simon Dedalus; John Ryan was Myles Crawford. According to Ryan (in his book, *Remembering How We Stood*), Kavanagh was the muse, "and Tom Joyce the Family; for he was a cousin of James—a dentist, who had, in fact, never read *Ulysses*!"

Scott had provided the party with a tray of drinks, which may have been more kind than wise. Kavanagh and O'Nolan began the day with an attempt to climb the steep wall backing from Scott's garden onto the Martello Tower, causing some anxiety to their friends, especially when O'Nolan grabbed the foot of Kavanagh, who was above him, and

Kavanagh began to kick out in panic. John Ryan had hired two horse-drawn cabs, or "growlers", of the kind Bloom travels in when he goes to Paddy Dignam's funeral, and the two writers were dragged into the cabs. Then they were off, along the seafront of Dublin Bay, and into the city. They stopped in pubs along the way and more drink was taken. Tom Joyce and Anthony Cronin sang some of the songs of Thomas Moore which Joyce had loved, such as "Silent O Moyle". In a betting shop in Irishtown they listened to the running of the Ascot Gold Cup on a radio. While they were retracing the route of the funeral party, O'Nolan chastised them for a lack of proper dignity.

The best anecdote of the day involves an incident on the funeral route, in a pub near Blackrock , and is told by John Ryan. The publican mistook the party for genuine mourners:

> *He took Myles' hand to offer condolence.*
> *"Nobody too close, I trust?" he queried hopefully.*
> *"Just a friend," replied Myles quietly, "fellow by the name of Joyce—James Joyce..." meanwhile ordering another hurler of malt.*
> *"James Joyce..." murmured the publican thoughtfully, setting the glass on the counter, "not the plastering contractor from Wolfe Tone Square?"*
> *"Naaahh..." grunted Myles impatiently, "the writer."*
> *"Ah! the sign writer," cried the publican cheerfully, glad and relieved to have gotten to the bottom of this mystery so quickly, "little Jimmy Joyce from Newton Park Avenue, the sign writer, sure wasn't he only sitting on that stool there on Wednesday last week—wait, no, I'm a liar, it was on a Tuesday."*
> *"No!" Myles thundered, "the writer. The wan that wrut the famous buke—'Useless'." "Ah, I see," said the bewildered publican, and then more resignedly, "I suppose we all have to go one day," and resumed the drawing of my pint.*

Eventually the party arrived at the Bailey public house in Duke Street, gave themselves over to drinking, and went no further. For Cronin, as O'Nolan's biographer, one of the most striking features of the day lay in O'Nolan's desire to make it a genuine act of piety. O'Nolan, like Kavanagh, was celebrated for his scepticism towards Joyce. Under the name "Brian Nolan" he had, three years earlier, edited a special issue of

Envoy devoted to Joyce. His editorial note, "A Bash in the Tunnel", was full of barbs, while the first of Kavanagh's contributions, the poem "Who Killed James Joyce?" had a go at one of the things the Dublin crew most hated, namely the American critical industry on Joyce. But for Cronin the Bloomsday celebration revealed something different:

> *What was noticeable about the rest of the day, however, was how structured and, in a way, humourless an event Brian wanted it to be. While we were retracing the route of the funeral party he wanted us to preserve a decorum proper to the occasion and to behave at all other times with the outward respectability of the characters in the book. It struck me then that he had a deep imaginative sympathy with them, that he was still part of their world, a world in which the appearances of respectability had to be kept up, even as a life collapsed.*

The centenary of Bloomsday in 2004 was celebrated by Ireland's largest cultural event of the year, a festival named *ReJoyce Dublin*, running from April to August with more than fifty events, including street theatre, Joyce look-alike contests, guided tours of landmarks, concerts, and exhibitions of his manuscripts and of art influenced by Joyce, and including the four-day International James Joyce Symposium. US cities with Bloomsday events included San Francisco, Philadelphia, and New York City, where the community-based arts organization Symphony Space presented the 23rd annual Bloomsday on Broadway, a twelve-hour reading of *Ulysses* by 100 actors, broadcast on radio station WBAI.

Who killed James Joyce?

Dublin hosts the Eurovision Song Contest
Saturday 3 April 1971

"The whole map of Europe has been changed."
Winston Churchill, 1922

"How are things in Glocamarra?"
Finian's Rainbow

When Dublin hosted the Eurovision Song Contest at the Gaiety Theatre in 1971, it was RTÉ's first indoor colour transmission and brought an estimated viewing audience of 400 million people. In 1970 the contest had been won by Dana (Rosemary Brown, later Scallon) singing "All Kinds of Everything". Because Dana was a Catholic from Derry who made her appearance at the start of the Troubles, she had won particular sympathy with her innocent act.

Ireland's next victory occurred in 1980 when Johnny Logan sang "What's Another Year?" Logan triumphed again in 1987 with "Hold Me". In 1980 Logan was merely dreadful, but by 1987 he emerged— along with the contest itself, and its folksy Irish presenter, Terry Wogan—as camp. Ireland won the Eurovision Song Contest four times in the 1990s in what came to be seen as a joke at the expense of Irish musical taste—literally at the expense of the Irish, in fact, since each year the previous year's winner is obliged to host the ghastly event and it soon became an albatross around the neck of RTÉ.

Ireland snatched triumph from the jaws of disaster (or *vice versa*) in 1994, with "Riverdance", a seven-minute long interval entertainment for the contest, directed by Moya Doherty, performed by Jean Butler, Michael Flatley and others. "Riverdance", based on traditional Irish dancing, was so successful that it was developed into a two-hour show which has since toured the world, remorselessly. Butler, an articulate spokesperson for theories of dance and performance, went on to the more adventurous *Dancing on Dangerous Ground*, which earned some critical acclaim but lost a great deal of money over runs in London and New York in 1999 and 2000.

In the 1950s Flann O'Brien had managed to annoy quite a lot of people with his relentless war on Irish kitsch, while at the same time he celebrated the campness of figures like Jimmy O'Dea. From the 1980s there has been a growing recognition that a certain image of Ireland itself is kitsch, and a willingness to pander to old stereotypes. At the same time, the success of Irish comedians abroad and at home indicates a profound change in sensibility. Honourable mention in this respect would have to go to *Father Ted* written by Arthur Matthews and Graham Linehan, and to Graham Norton who had a breakthrough in that series. The singer Sinéad O'Connor, novelist Patrick McCabe and film director Neil Jordan have all exploited versions of Irish kitsch

Dana brought a little bit of bible-belt kitsch to Ireland when she returned in the late 1990s, after some years in the American south, to enter Irish politics promoting "family values".

The Dublin Bombings
Friday 17 May 1974

> *"The bodies and the maimed had been rushed off in ambulances by 5.45 pm but the terrible smell of death could not be so easily erased."*
> *The Irish Times,* 18 May 1974

There was a bus strike in Dublin. Coming up to 5.30pm many workers were on the streets, walking home, although many more had left early because of the strike. In Talbot Street pedestrians were making their way to Connolly railway station. In Parnell Street 29-year-old Eddie O'Neill had just left Liam O'Sullivan's barber shop with his two sons, Edward aged four and Billy aged six. They had had haircuts in preparation for Billy's first communion the next day. Edward later recalled the moment, at 5.28, when the bomb went off: "It was just a big ball of flame coming straight towards us, like a great nuclear mushroom cloud whooshing up everything in its path." The next thing of which the little boy was aware was the sight of the bones sticking out of his legs and the feeling of the huge piece of metal (part of a car) protruding from his face and head. As a strange man lifted him and carried him to the hospital, Edward did not yet know that his father was dead, pierced through the heart by shrapnel. Ten other people were killed in Parnell Street.

A couple of minutes later a second bomb exploded outside Guiney's department store in Talbot Street, in the very area to which many people were fleeing from Parnell Street. The scene in Talbot Street was nightmarish. Bodies were dismembered and the gutters ran with blood from the dead and wounded. Mary McKenna aged 55, who lived in Talbot Street, died as she opened the door to her flat. She was one of fourteen people who died in this second explosion. The third bomb went off at 5.32pm in South Leinster Street. Two people were killed.

Twenty-five people were killed outright or fatally injured in the three bombs, including Edward O'Neill; a family of four, Joseph and Anna O'Brien with their baby daughters Jacqueline (17 months) and Anne Marie (5 months); Colette O'Doherty, a 21-year-old woman due to go into hospital that evening for the birth of her second child; and Simone Chetrit, a 31-year-old Parisian in Dublin to learn English. Over 250 people were injured. The other fatalities were Josephine (Josie) Bradley, Marie Butler, Anne Byrne, John Dargle, Concepta Dempsey (died 11 June 1974), Patrick Fay, Elizabeth Fitzgerald, Bernadette (Breda) Grace, Antonio Magliocco, Anne Marren, Anna Massey, Mary McKenna, Dorothy Morris, Christina O'Loughlin, Marie Phelan, Siobhán Rice, Maureen Shields, Breda Turner, and John Walsh. Colette O'Doherty's unborn baby also died, and three months after the bombings Edward O'Neill's widow, Martha, gave birth to a stillborn daughter, also named Martha, whose death was attributed to the shock suffered by her mother.

Ninety minutes later another car bomb went off in Monaghan, killing six people and fatally injuring a seventh. The Monaghan victims were Patrick Askin, Thomas Campbell, Thomas Croarkin (died July 24th), Archie Harper (died May 21st), Jack Travers, Peggy White and George Williamson.

The following day descriptions of "Bloody Friday" filled the Irish newspapers.

> *Parnell Street with small shops and working class folk had pathetic heartbreaking reminders; the bodies and the maimed had been rushed off in ambulances by 5.45 pm but the terrible smell of death could not be so easily erased.*
>
> *There littering the roadway with the debris of smashed cars and the broken glass were the paraphernalia of the dead and injured, shoes, scarfs, coats, shopping bags, even a bag of chips.*
>
> *Women were crying because they heard that one of their children or a relative had been taken away to hospital. Some were demented with grief and I heard one woman say in a sobbing voice "He'll never be back."*
>
> (*The Irish Times*, Saturday 18 May 1974)

The bombings took place on the third day of the Ulster Workers' Council Strike in Northern Ireland. Responsibility for the attack has been laid at the door of an Ulster loyalist paramilitary group, the UVF, and a number of men have been repeatedly named by journalists in connection with the atrocity: Billy Hanna, Robin Jackson, Robert

McConnell and Harris Boyle, all of whom are now dead. No one was ever arrested and tried for the bombings, and the Government of the Republic of Ireland seemed to place its emphasis on a crackdown on republican activists in the period immediately succeeding Bloody Friday. Over a decade later, relatives of the victims formed a pressure group, "Justice for the Forgotten", to campaign for a proper inquiry into the bombings. A Yorkshire Television investigative documentary in July 1993 implied that the Northern Ireland security forces colluded with loyalists in the planning and execution of the attack, and obstructed subsequent investigations by Garda Síochána. Nine days after the broadcast the UVF issued a statement claiming sole responsibility. On Friday 26 September 1997 a memorial to the people who were killed in the Dublin and Monaghan bombing was unveiled in Talbot Street in Dublin, and in 2002 a memorial garden was opened at Glasnevin cemetery. In 2003 the Barron Inquiry into the bombings criticized the British and Irish governments for failures in their justice systems after the event. The families continue to call for a full public inquiry.

The Dublin bombings involved the greatest loss of life in a single incident during the Troubles.

There were many other occasions on which the Troubles came to Dublin. In 1970, Richard Fallon, a member of Garda Síochána was shot dead by republicans during a bank raid at Arran Quay. In October 1971 Peter Graham, a member of the small left-wing republican group, Saor Eire, was shot dead in Dublin, apparently by former colleagues in the group. Two months later Jack McCabe, a republican activist, was killed in a premature explosion in the Santry area.

The British Embassy in Merrion Square, Dublin, was burned down by demonstrators on 2 February 1972. They were protesting against the killing of 13 people in Derry by British paratroopers on "Bloody Sunday" two days earlier.

On 1 December 1972 two people were killed and 127 injured when two car bombs planted by loyalists exploded in the centre of Dublin. At 7.58pm a car bomb detonated in Eden Quay, close to Liberty Hall, Dublin. At 8.16pm the second car bomb exploded in Sackville Place (near O'Connell Street). Two men, George Bradshaw and Thomas Duff, both bus conductors, were killed in the second explosion.

In January 1973 a car bomb exploded in Sackville Place, killing Thomas Douglas and injuring 17 others. No organization claimed responsibility but the bomb was believed to have been planted by one of the loyalist paramilitary organizations. The car had been hijacked in Belfast and the explosion was very close to the site of the December 1972 bomb.

In August 1973 James Farrell was shot dead in an armed payroll robbery. On St. Patrick's Day, 1975, Thomas Smith, an IRA prisoner, was killed when 140 prisoners attempted to escape from Portlaoise Prison. Michael Reynolds, an off duty policeman, was shot dead when he gave chase to a car involved in a bank raid in Raheny in September 1975. Billy Wright, a member of the official IRA, was shot dead at his brother's hair salon on the Cabra Road. John Hayes, an airport worker, was killed by a loyalist bomb in the arrivals terminal at Dublin airport.

On 21 July 1976 the newly appointed British Ambassador to Ireland, Christopher Ewart-Biggs, and a civil servant, Judith Cook, were killed in an IRA landmine ambush 200 yards from the gates of his official residence at Sandyfort, Dublin. In September 1977 John William Lawlor was shot dead by the IRA in a Dublin pub. A major Irish National Liberation Army (INLA) leader, Seamus Costello, was killed in his car at North Strand road in an internal republican dispute. The death of Arthur Lockett in January 1979 was also attributed to the IRA.Patrick Reynolds of the Garda Síochána, was shot dead while searching a flat in Tallaght after an armed robbery.

Five years after the killing of Seamus Costello his alleged assassin, James Flynn, was shot in the back outside Cusack's pub on the North Strand, a short distance from the spot where the earlier killing had happened. In 1985 building contractor Seamus McAvoy was shot and killed at his bungalow in Donnybrook. The IRA claimed he had been supplying materials to the security forces, while friends claimed he had repeatedly refused to pay the paramilitaries protection money. On 21 May 1994, just four days after the twentieth anniversary of the Dublin bombings, Martin Doherty was shot dead by members of the UVF attempting to plant a bomb in the Widow Scallan's pub, in Pearse Street.

On 18 August 1994 Martin Cahill, a powerful figure in Dublin's criminal underworld, known as "The General", was shot dead by the IRA close to his home in Ranelagh. Cahill was the IRA's last victim before the 1994 cease-fire, but it is unclear to what extent his death should be linked to the Northern Ireland conflict.

Pope John Paul II Visits Ireland
Saturday 29 September 1979

"From the moment it was announced that the highlight of Pope John Paul II's itinerary in this country would be a visit to Knock, most of us had a shrewd suspicion that the Virgin Mary was about to make a comeback into Irish politics.

Few of us could have foreseen just how strongly the emotions would be stirred as the Pope drew on some of the deepest hidden wells of the Irish psyche, reaching a crescendo at Limerick with his appeal to Irish women and young girls to embrace the vocation of mother-hood, and to ignore the siren voices telling them that there might just be more to life than rearing children. Finally, inevitably he entrusted us to 'Mary, Bright Sun of the Irish Race'."
Mary Holland.

John Paul II made the first ever papal visit to Ireland in September 1979. Over three days approximately 2,500,000 people attended the different venues where he appeared. On his first day he held mass for a huge congregation in Phoenix Park.

At the time the national interest in and excitement over the visit seemed to confirm Ireland's self-imagined role as the most devout Catholic country in Europe. With hindsight it looks like the last moment when there was some assured consensus that the majority of Irish people were cleaving to the faith of our fathers. In fact, one might read into the mass media coverage and television audiences for the papal visit the start of something different and perhaps opposite to religious devotion—the birth of celebrity culture.

The secularization of middle-class Dublin is almost complete, but there are occasional signs of religious revival elsewhere In spring and summer 2001 the coffined body of St. Thérèse of Lisieux was brought to Ireland and exhibited all over the country, causing an outpouring of enthusiasm for the Little Flower and attracting up to three million visitors, according to Church estimates reported in the Irish press. Many of these pilgrims came from the streets of Dublin, Belfast,

Monaghan and Cork. Is this the kind of faith that will carry into the future?

The Election of Mary Robinson
Friday 9 November 1990

"I was elected by men and women of all parties and none, by many with great moral courage who stepped out from the faded flags of the Civil War and voted for a new Ireland. And above all by the women of Ireland—Mná na hÉireann—who instead of rocking the cradle rocked the system, and who came out massively to make their mark on the ballot paper, and on a new Ireland."
Mary Robinson, Inauguration Speech, 3 December 1990

On the second day of the count in the election to succeed Patrick Hillery and choose the seventh President of Ireland, the three candidates and their supporters were gathered in Ballsbridge at the RDS (Royal Dublin Society). Austin Currie, the Fine Gael candidate, had grown up in Northern Ireland and been first a civil rights activist and then a member of the Stormont parliament before moving south to a political career in the Irish Republic. The Fianna Fáil candidate was Brian Lenihan, a popular minister who had been serving as Tánaiste in the government led by Taoiseach Charles Haughey, until he was forced to resign after a scandal which emerged during his presidential campaign. The Labour Party candidate was Mary Robinson, formerly a member of the Labour Party, but now an independent running under the party's nomination.

Mary Robinson (née Bourke) was born in Ballina, County Mayo, in 1944. She was educated at Trinity College Dublin, the Honourable Society of the King's Inns, Dublin, and Harvard University, USA. At the early age of twenty-five she became Reid Professor of Law at Trinity. She also became the first Catholic returned by Trinity to Seanad Éireann and the youngest women ever elected to the Senate. She became a member of the Labour Party in 1977 but left after a disagreement within the party over the Anglo-Irish agreement. Robinson's career in the Senate was controversial. She was a committed radical and feminist, when it was neither popular nor profitable. She introduced legislation to legalize contraception (defeated) and spoke out against the British government's use of internment in Northern Ireland. As a constitutional lawyer she was at the forefront in promoting human rights in Ireland, and in the 1970s and 1980s this often meant becoming an advocate for women's rights. She attacked all-male juries, unequal pay and pensions provision, fought for the decriminalization of homosexuality, campaigned to save Dublin's architectural heritage from developers, and participated in Ireland's anti-apartheid movement. When her candidacy for president was announced, popular wisdom suggested that with this record she could not possibly win.

Until the Robinson campaign the presidency had been defined primarily as an honorary post awarded to an elder statesman, which, even though it was decided by direct election, was largely in the gift of the party in power. On several previous occasions, including the two terms of Patrick Hillery, there had been no contest. Dick Spring, the leader of the Labour Party, had a vision that the presidency could be transformed into a more representative and effective role, with a younger candidate willing to campaign hard and start a debate over constitutional issues. He saw Mary Robinson's potential as a candidate who might unify forces across party politics and also felt that there was strong symbolic value for the left in fielding a younger woman as a candidate.

During the campaign Robinson came under sustained attack, particularly as the other parties saw that her policy of travelling all over the country and speaking to as many constituencies as possible was beginning to bear fruit in the opinion polls. Fianna Fáil, in particular, relied on Ireland's traditionally conservative attitudes towards sexual morality and repeatedly tried to associate Robinson with controversial issues such as divorce, contraception, abortion, even implying that she had communist sympathies. Robinson managed to put across her message effectively in media interviews, and particularly in public appearances. Her candidacy came along at a time when the Irish electorate was becoming disillusioned with alleged corruption in the major political parties, and although her political beliefs were more radical than those of most of the electorate, she communicated an idealism that appealed to people, and promised to take Ireland into a more tolerant, liberal future. Whether or not individual Irish electors were self-conscious about sending a message to the world, it was clear that if Ireland was to choose a woman president, it would in itself indicate a country ready and willing to change. A few days before the election, Padraig Flynn, Minister for the Environment, appeared on a radio programme attacking Robinson. With an extraordinary lack of judgement he suggested that the image she projected in her campaign was a hypocritical façade:

> *Of course it doesn't always suit if you get labelled a socialist, because that's a very narrow focus in this country—so she has to try and have it both ways. She has to have new clothes and her new look and her new hairdo and she has the new interest in family, being a mother and all that kind of thing. But none of us, you know, none of us who knew Mary Robinson very well in previous incarnations ever heard her claiming to be a great wife and mother.*

Women all over Ireland seem to have felt that in this speech there was a contempt for women—and an attempt to traduce any woman active in public life—that summed up the ways in which the Irish Republic had betrayed the legacy of founding activists such as Constance Markievicz and Hanna Sheehy Skeffington to become a narrow, oppressive, misogynist society.

On the day 64.1% of voters turned out to take part in the election. At the first count 44.1% (694,484) voted for Lenihan, 38.9% (612,265) voted for Robinson, and 17% (267,902) for Currie. On the second round, with Currie eliminated, Lenihan achieved 47.2% (731,273) and Robinson 52.8% (817,830). When Robinson's victory was announced Lenihan and Currie came forward to congratulate her and to acknowledge that the election of Ireland's first woman president was a day of historic significance.

The Robinson team went on that evening to hold a celebratory news conference at Jury's Hotel, where the international interest in the election was striking. At her inauguration in Dublin Castle on 3 December 1990 Robinson set the tone for her term of office:

> *The Ireland I will be representing is a new Ireland, open, tolerant, inclusive. Many of you who voted for me did so without sharing all my views. This, I believe, is a significant signal of change, a sign, however modest, that we have already passed the threshold to a new, pluralist Ireland.*

Just over six years later, when Robinson announced her decision not to run for a second term of office, the broad consensus of opinion was that her presidency had been an almost unqualified success, although some critics from the left felt that there had been more show than substance to her presidency. It had coincided with the arrival of the economic boom that turned Ireland into the so-called Celtic Tiger, and she profited from the resulting feel-good factor. She also presided over the country when there was a dramatic widening between rich and poor. In the early 1990s there was also widespread debate in Ireland over a series of issues traditionally associated with women's politics: contraception, rape, divorce, domestic violence and child abuse. In some of these areas women's rights were advanced and in the realm of individual morality and sexual expression Ireland became a notably more liberal country, at least in terms of public policy. With the decriminalization of homosexuality, gay social spaces in Dublin began to be more openly acknowledged. The relaxation of the prohibition on divorce meant that it was possible to elect a Taoiseach separated from his wife and openly living with another woman. At the point at which the internet made it practically impossible to control information about sexuality, Ireland became a country willing to relax censorship. Until the 1990s Ireland had seemed resistant to the secularization which had been spreading across Europe since the end of the Second World War, but Mary Robinson's presidency saw a collapse in clerical authority, with scandals involving Bishop Eamonn Casey (exposed as the father of an illegitimate child) and Father Brendan Smyth, a child-abuser sheltered by the Catholic Church and the Irish state.

Robinson promised in her campaign to welcome a reconnection between Ireland and its diaspora communities, and to be a voice for the dispossessed. In symbolic terms these ambitions were strikingly fulfilled, but an Irish president cannot introduce or promote legislation, and there have been those on the left who question whether Robinson did much to further a redistribution of wealth during Ireland's period of strongest economic growth. An answer to that criticism has been that she removed the taboo of voting for leftist candidates and opened a space which may be subsequently developed.

In terms of women's politics Robinson was a figurehead for changes in society, but the male grip on political power in the Republic of Ireland remains strong. Yet such was the resonance from her election that in 1997 all but one of the presidential candidates were female. That year Mary McAleese, a Belfast-born academic lawyer from Queen's University Belfast, was elected president as the Fianna Fáil candidate. Women's representation in the Dáil, however, remains low by European standards. After her presidency Mary Robinson served as United Nations Commissioner for Human Rights (1997-2002) and became a high-profile advocate for refugees around the world.

Chapter Nine
NEVER GET OLD: CULTURE AND COUNTER-CULTURE

"Anybody can be good in the country."
Oscar Wilde, "The Critic as Artist"

The culture this book has looked at has mainly been literary and visual, so I decided to end not with any overview or summation of the state of the arts in the city today, but rather with a look at four specific aspects of culture that I have neglected elsewhere. Cinema, music and sport are all forms of popular culture and have something to say about collective imaginings and types of energy on the loose in the life of the city. I conclude with discussion of Irish Travellers, Dublin's largest minority population, whose language and cultural practices strike an important note of dissent, particularly on the important question as to who owns public spaces and who feels entitled to inhabit them. The defining Traveller experience is to be harassed off the streets and out of the parks, asked to "move on". The leisurely promenade which some "respectable" Travellers are invited to enjoy might, it seems, be disturbed by the people who are not allowed on the streets. One of the most haunting stories by the nineteenth-century gothic writer, Sheridan Le Fanu, is about a man who hears footsteps following him wherever he goes through the streets of Dublin. Of course, these are the footsteps of a man he has wronged.

Cinema
The first moving pictures of Dublin were of O'Connell Bridge in a short sequence shot by the Lumière brothers in 1897. A Canadian screenwriter and director of Irish parentage named Sidney Olcott was the first person to make narrative films about Ireland in Ireland. In the silent film era he became one of the first directors to specialize in making films on location. He came to Ireland for several trips during 1910-14, collaborating with the actor and screenwriter Gene Gauntier

on adaptations of Dion Boucicault's *The Colleen Bawn* (1911), *Arrah-na-Pogue* (1911) and *The Shaughran* (1912). Olcott also directed original screenplays on the topic of emigration, and historical dramas such as *Rory O'Moore* (1911) and *Bold Emmet: Ireland's Martyr* (1914). Ireland's first cinema was the Volta Picture Palace in Mary Street, which opened in December 1909, established by James Joyce, who returned briefly to Dublin from Trieste to supervise the venture. The funding came from Trieste business people and the early shows were mainly Italian. The venture folded after a year. In 1916 the Film Company of Ireland, which ran until 1920, began to produce indigenous films, notably adaptations of popular literary texts. In the Irish Free State films were subject to the Censorship of Films Act (1923), which operated, like the contemporaneous censorship of books, as if Ireland was under siege from foreign culture intent on smuggling immorality into the minds of the naturally innocent and healthy Irish population.

In the 1920s and 1930s filmmakers were preoccupied with the events of the War of Independence, and Dublin made its first significant appearances as a cinematic location in films about revolution and internecine warfare. John Ford's version of Liam O'Flaherty's *The Informer* (1935) constructs an expressionist vision of the city, where Gyppo Nolan becomes an outcast pursued by the lurid shadows of his guilty imagination. Ford's version of Sean O'Casey's *The Plough and the Stars* (1936) brings out the angry, satiric and embittered voices of the urban poor.

In so far as Dublin appears in films of the mid-twentieth century it suffers a broad stereotyping of the kind also applied to the more frequently represented Irish countryside. The ideas of experience and innocence suggested in the urban/rural contrast are reinforced by a representation of the city as noisy and decaying. Ardmore Studios were established at Bray in 1958 with a view to adapting Abbey Theatre productions for cinema, and Abbey actors dominated representations of the Irish in cinema at home and abroad for most of the twentieth century. Sara Allgood and Barry Fitzgerald settled in Hollywood, thereafter generally playing Irish character roles; Dan O'Herlihy, another emigrant to the US, was less confined to the Irish stereotype; and Cyril Cusack migrated between character acting and a classical repertoire on stage, television and in cinema, in which he escaped the confines of the stage Irishman. Ardmore's mission lent itself to the idealization, or the related debunking of idealization, of rural Ireland as the location of authentic Irish identities.

Some of the earliest films to embrace and celebrate Dublin as a site of modernity were *The Girl With Green Eyes* (dir. Desmond Davis, 1963), an early adaptation of the Edna O'Brien novel, and *Ulysses* (dir. Joseph Strick, 1967). In the late 1970s the city as dystopia begins to appear in the work of more socially critical filmmakers including Joe Comerford, whose work deals with the working classes, drug addicts, disaffected youth, and Travellers. Kieran Hickey has a different take on metropolitan identities in films that explore and adumbrate crises of middle-class identity. If the city forms an alienating backdrop for the drama of independent filmmakers in the 1970s and 1980s, in the 1990s Dublin finally emerges as a character, if a somewhat dubious one, in a number of films shot on location and/or interrogated as a theme. Neil Jordan's *Michael Collins* (1996), Pat Murphy's *Nora* (2000) and Seán Walsh's *Bloom* (2003) are all set in early twentieth-century Dublin and all attempt to think about the meanings of the city's history. John Huston's adaptation of Joyce's story from *Dubliners*, *The Dead* (1987), examines interiority as it spends an evening inside a single comfortable middle-class house, only leaving that house in the final sequence when Gabriel returns to his hotel, where his wife tells him a story that opens his mind and the film's imaginary to a vision of the west of Ireland.

Neil Jordan's recreation of the city under assault in *Michael Collins* is extraordinarily effective. Cinema-goers in the last decade have found that the previous neglect of Dublin in films has been replaced with two dominant modes of narrating the city. In one, exemplified by *Circle of Friends* (dir. Pat O'Connor, 1995) and *About Adam* (dir. Gerard Stembridge, 2001) Dublin is at first glance largely incidental; these films could have been set anywhere but they took advantage of financial inducements to set them in Dublin. A second mode of narration is one in which Dublin is normalized in terms of the urban crises that are the staples of films about other cities—poverty and crime. *The Commitments* (dir. Alan Parker, 1991) and *Into the West* (dir. Mike Newell, 1992) represent different (non-naturalist) techniques for translating the poverty of the under-classes into a marketable story, one through comedy and music, the other via magical realism. *The General* (dir. John Boorman, 1998), *Ordinary Decent Criminal* (dir. Thaddeus

O'Sullivan, 2000) and *Veronica Guerin* (dir. Joel Schumaker, 2003) trade on the excitement of organized crime which allows them to import the thriller as a new genre for thinking through the city. Paddy Breathnach's gangster film *I Went Down* (1997) was a comedy-crime hybrid, indebted to American genres. *Intermission* (dir. John Crowley, 2003) is high-energy urban drama with a feel for Ireland's new youth culture. While it starts as a certain kind of genre piece—petty criminal Colin Farrell is planning a bank robbery on the proceeds of which he will retire into domesticity—the clever script by Dublin playwright Mark Rowe weaves together a tangle of narratives that illuminate the city in quirky, unexpected ways. Against a trend in filmmaking which stresses the smallness of Dublin society, in *Intermission* Dublin has something of the quality of London or Los Angeles. There is an emphasis on the ways in which urban experience relies on the possibility of coincidence rather than on the narratives of community. It does not, however, depart from genre sufficiently to interrogate the misogynistic objectification of women in the narrative.

Popular Music: From Blues to Boy Bands
From the period of the Irish Literary Revival through most of the twentieth century literature, and particularly poetry, dominated popular perceptions of the arts in Ireland. This is not to say that there were not significant achievements in the other arts, but the associations between Ireland and writing, confirmed by the Nobel Prizes and international acclaim collected by Yeats (Nobel Prize 1923), Shaw (1925), Joyce, Beckett (1969) and Seamus Heaney (1995) drew youthful talent towards writing, and gave writers a certain amount of authority and prestige in the public sphere.

The 1960s, the decade of youth culture in much of Europe and North America, could not really be described in such terms in Dublin. The novels of Edna O'Brien reveal the huge resistance in Irish life to transformations taking effect elsewhere. Things began to change in the 1980s, though it would take another book to explain why. These were not changes that involved an abrupt dismissal of the past, but rather a kind of swerve whose most distinctive feature is probably the delayed impact of feminism and the not unrelated secularization of Irish culture. The troubles in Northern Ireland, Ireland's entry into the European Union, the influence of easier, cheaper travel, particularly between Ireland and the US, the impact of television and cinema all contributed to a change in the way that Dublin conceived itself. In the face of the increasing dominance of global corporate brands, the small-scale, local attachments to be observed in Dublin made it seem cool and alternative.

It was first in music, and then in literature, that a poetics of the suburbs began to emerge. One of the Irish artists most closely associated with this emergence, and who came into his own in the 1980s was Roddy Doyle. Doyle worked as a schoolteacher for many years in the north Dublin suburb of Kilbarrack, which became the setting for his Barrytown trilogy of novels: *The Commitments*, *The Snapper* and *The Van*.

The Barrytown trilogy begins with *The Commitments*, which Doyle published himself in 1987. It describes a group of Dublin teenagers intent on forming a band that will be more influenced by American music than by traditional Irish culture. A film version of *The Commitments* directed by Alan Parker came out in 1991. A moment in the film when the teenagers decide to adopt the blues seemed to articulate a new kind of attitude coming out of working-class suburbs, for they perceive that "The Irish are the blacks of Europe. Dubliners are the blacks of Ireland. North Dubliners are the blacks of Dublin." By 1991 the packaging of that attitude in a sentimental Hollywood musical defused its radical potential, if such potential had ever existed.

There are many different stories to be told about the evolution of popular music in Ireland from the 1960s onwards, but the one that strikes me now concerns my own sense as a teenager that Celtic rock, as performed for example by Horslips (formed in 1971), was deeply embarrassing, and the subsequent realization of how wrong I was. Celtic rock combined Irish traditional musical instruments like the fiddle, mandolin and concertina with electric guitars, keyboards and drums. When Horslips cast *O'Neill's March* in a rock setting it seemed like a terrible sell-out of "authentic" traditional music values. Horslips was part of a wider folk-rock movement, but it seems more interesting now to observe that even though it was an image-conscious group anxious to bring a sense of glamour and modernity to a youth scene that seemed hopelessly old-fashioned, its chosen route was via a reinvention of the past rather than by moving wholesale into rock or pop. Horslips took on the showbands that had dominated rural Ireland

and, unlike some of their talented contemporaries, they stayed with an Irish base, even at their most successful, becoming a prototype for later Irish musicians.

Another kind of fusion was offered by Andy Irvine, Christy Moore, Dónal Lunny, and Liam O'Flynn, who were all involved with the traditional music group, Planxty, in the 1970s. They inflected their interpretations of traditional tunes with a variety of influences from other musical traditions, and Moore, Irvine and Irvine's later collaborator, Paul Brady, were all songwriters, intent on introducing new material to the tradition. Although there were popular groups in the 1970s who specialized in a republican repertoire—notably the Wolfe Tones—one can also detect in Planxty, The Bothy Band, and even Dé Danann, a more fundamentalist traditional group, an intersection between the preservation of musical traditions and an engagement with contemporary politics. What separated Irish folk rock from its English equivalent was not so much an unbroken line of transmission as the shadow of the Northern troubles. It was U2 who pushed this line into a meshing of music and politics which suggested the shock tactics whereby Ireland could be recognized as both American and Vietnam.

U2, formed in Dublin in 1976, is Ireland's most successful ever rock band. Through the 1980s the group had a remarkable worldwide dominance. The musicians' wealth and celebrity influenced the transformation of Dublin into a more hip place to live and inspired hundreds of young Dubliners to get involved in music. It would be possible to say a lot of things about the ideas in their albums and about their engagement with politics that could make them sound interesting—and the phenomenon of their success is interesting—but musically they are fairly one-dimensional. Their success has brought them opportunities to play with some great musicians, and some tracks are very effective, but when they have posed as critics it has not seemed much more than a pose. As celebrities they have fronted a lot of philanthropic projects, and like the English-based Bob Geldof of the Boomtown Rats, they have been active in raising awareness about development issues and AIDS. U2 have remained based in Ireland in spite of the temptations of their huge international standing and should be given credit for the ways in which they have championed Dublin as a cultural centre.

Thin Lizzy had already popularized Irish music on the British rock scene in the 1970s with high energy performances, although Phil Lynott *et al* did not have the long-term influence of blues guitarist Rory Gallagher and singer-songwriter Van Morrison, or the interest of Skid Row.

The sense that Irish music was leading rather than following international trends began to emerge during the punk period, with the success of the Undertones, the Radiators, and, on the coat-tails of punk, the inferior Boomtown Rats. The Pogues, founded in the early 1980s, blended traditional music with punk in a gritty combination. They aggravated traditionalists in a way that folk rock did not, and the hostility expressed towards them was a tribute to their energy. They engaged with the emerging idea of an Irish diaspora in a way that exposed the rawness of the relationship between homeland and exile. Their singer-songwriter Shane MacGowan was an incredible talent, capable of distilling traditional themes into new melodies of great simplicity and poignancy, and of performing his songs in a way that was at one and the same time deeply sentimental and anti-sentimental. His hit single with Kirsty McColl, *Fairy Tale of New York* (1987) is raw, poignant, and terribly compelling. Like many other talented musicians, MacGowan often seems to draw on a visibly damaged life for his emotional punches. His heavy drinking gave an edge to The Pogues, but was also inevitably self-destructive at a creative and personal level. He left the band in the 1990s to work with a new group, The Popes.

I have mentioned elsewhere the kitsch glories of Ireland's Eurovision history, and a complementary phenomenon was Ireland's dazzling success in the manufacture of boy bands in the 1990s. Boyzone blazed a trail and Westlife followed. They are so lovely they would make you weep. During the era of the Celtic Tiger, wealthy musicians, their love lives, their fashions, their properties and their interior décor have become the staple of Ireland's lifestyle magazines.

The contrast in the strategies of two very successful female singers draw attention to the ways in which music can intersect with conceptual and performance art. Enya was briefly a member of the Donegal group Clannad, a family group, before she went on to a successful solo career. Her work is all studio-based and she never performs live, thus presenting a highly controlled image and product with her music. Sinéad O'Connor also began a singing career in the mid-1980s and her first two albums were highly praised by critics and well-received by audiences. She shattered taboos associated with female performance in Ireland by her attacks on the Catholic Church and her disclosures of an abused childhood, and in the US she provoked huge hostility by refusing to have the American national anthem played before one of her shows and by tearing up a picture of the Pope on TV. She is a mistress of embarrassment and shock tactics, playing the Virgin Mary in Neil Jordan's film *The Butcher Boy* and announcing that she has been ordained as a Catholic priest. In this sense, she disrupts a progressive narrative about Irish women coming into their own in the 1990s by reminding her audiences of unreconciled tensions.

While popular music has tapped the resources of the traditional music canon and skills in the last thirty years, undiluted traditional music itself is also thriving. Musicians are still primarily learning their tunes from one another, but the increased access to electronic media means that regional distinctions may well be lost. The Chieftains are the most internationally recognized group performing traditional music. They formed in the early 1960s under the influence of Seán Ó Riada (1931-71) who was, in spite of an early death, one of the most influential thinkers in twentieth-century Irish music. Dozens of traditional groups and individual artists emerged to release recordings in the 1980s and 1990s, and in the early twenty-first century there is still significant interest among the young in learning and playing the music.

Sport

In the 1880s, as Gaelicism spread though all aspects of Irish culture, Michael Cusack led the movement to found the Gaelic Athletic Association (GAA), "for the preservation and cultivation of the national pastimes of Ireland". The GAA was heavily involved in politics and in wider forms of cultural nationalism, and sport has tended to be a highly politicized realm in Ireland, particularly since partition, when many, but not all sports, have been separately organized in the north.

Chief among the pastimes the GAA wished to encourage was hurling, which is of ancient provenance in Ireland. The English authorities in the Middle Ages objected to hurling and attempts were made to ban it, but it survived right down until the nineteenth century. It nearly disappeared after the Famine, but was revived by the GAA and codified in the 1880s. The modern game is played between two teams of fifteen players each. The ball is similar in size to a hockey ball and is struck with a stick (the *camán* or hurley). The game is fast, skilful and hugely exciting for players and spectators. Gaelic football was also promoted by the GAA, which in its early days banned its members from playing "foreign" or "garrison" games. This ban was only rescinded in 1971, and GAA hostility to soccer re-emerged a few years ago when Ireland and Scotland put forward a joint bid to host the European soccer championships in 2008. The bid's credibility depended on Ireland being able to promise use of some GAA grounds for the tournament, but this proposal was resisted.

The GAA is a very successful community-based organization with an integrated approach to sport, culture and community relations. Without the significant television revenue and sponsorship available to soccer and rugby, the GAA was able to raise funds for the renovation of Croke Park stadium by the architects Gilroy McMahon (1997-2002). Croke Park, seating 80,000, is now the fourth largest sports stadium in Europe.

Gaelic football dates at least to the sixteenth century and also met with English disapproval. Today it is more popular than hurling, and Dublin is second only to Kerry in the number of all-Ireland titles it has secured. Camogie is a form of hurling played by women, and Dublin has had great success over the decades in which it has been played competitively.

At the time of the foundation of the GAA athletics was the most popular sporting activity. The first formal athletics meeting in Ireland was held in 1857 at Trinity College Dublin. For a small nation Ireland has had significant international success in athletics, and today Sonia O'Sullivan, several times world champion in long-distance running events, is among the country's most celebrated sports people ever. This national success has not been without its problems, notably in the strained relationship in the past between the sport's governing bodies in Northern Ireland and the Republic. It was the Champion Athletic Club, founded in 1872, which first leased land for a track at Lansdowne Road, a name now associated with some of Ireland's greatest international sporting successes. It is to Lansdowne Road that Dubliners and Irish fans from elsewhere go to cheer on Ireland in Six-Nations Rugby Union, another game claimed to have ancient Irish origins. Lansdowne Road was the location of Ireland's first international rugby victory over England on 5 February 1887. When Union went professional in 1995, the Irish club game suffered as several talented players left for clubs in Britain. The defeat of the victorious World Cup English team at Twickenham in 2004 was particularly sweet for Ireland fans, whose team seems to be on the rise again.

Lansdowne Road is also home to Ireland's international soccer team. Walking the streets of Dublin ten years ago, you might have gained the impression that most children were more likely to support Manchester United, Liverpool, Arsenal or Celtic than any local club: Bohemians, Dublin City, St. Patrick's Athletic, Shamrock Rovers and Shelbourne, for example. Nevertheless, a certain disillusion with the English premiership in the last couple of years, and a rise in local attachments, or perhaps just a change in fashion, has seen more visible support for Dublin sides. There has also been a significant rise in the status value of GAA shirts.

Since its introduction in 1878 soccer has captured the hearts and allegiances of the working classes in particular, but Ireland has never had a strong enough league to keep her best players playing at home. Soccer in Ireland had a neo-colonial dimension, with Irish league clubs serving largely as incubators for big English clubs, and youth programmes judged more successful when they exported players overseas than if they retained them in Ireland. In 1986 Jack Charlton, former England World Cup winner, became manager of the Irish international team. "Big Jack" recruited a number of players from second- and third-generation Irish emigrants to Britain to play for the Irish national team, bypassing Irish league football. Although he had some talented creative players at his disposal over the years, notably Arsenal and Juventus' Liam Brady, Manchester United and Aston Villa's Paul McGrath Manchester United's Roy Keane, Charlton encouraged his team into a defensive tactics that smothered the opposition and a counter-attack based on hoofing the ball up the pitch. It was not necessarily a pleasure to watch the team, but Ireland did begin to win games and make modest progress in international tournaments. The policy of introducing second- and third-generation Irish brought more players of mixed ethnic origins into the team and made visible more multi-ethnic forms of Irishness. Famous victories under Charlton included a 1-0 defeat of England at Stuttgart in 1988, reaching the quarter finals of the 1990 World Cup in Italy and the 1-0 defeat of Italy in Giants' Stadium, New York during the 1994 World Cup. In 1990 and 1994 the Irish teams were welcomed home to Dublin with huge festivities and civic receptions. During his management tenure Charlton was a major celebrity and national hero, and Ireland's international success, along with the arrival in Ireland of satellite television, contributed to the cultural phenomenon of the new Sunday worship, where families spend an afternoon at the pub in front of a wide-screen TV.

Since Charlton's retirement more sceptical accounts of his tenure have emerged, and dissension within the camp are revealed in players' autobiographies, the most readable of which are *Full Time: The Secret Life of Tony Cascarino* as told to Paul Kimmage and *Keane: The Autobiography* by Roy Keane with Eamon Dunphy. The status of football in the national imagination became clear during the 2002 World Cup when Roy Keane left the squad after a row with manager, Mick McCarthy. The controversy obsessed the country for weeks and there was even speculation that the Taoiseach, Bertie Ahern, would intervene. The Keane-McCarthy conflict was even turned into a play, *I-Keano*, premiered at Dublin's Olympia Theatre in February 2005. One source of information on current events in Irish football is *www.soccercentral.ie.*

If soccer is the favourite sport of the working class (and of the middle classes who love to identify with working-class culture), then rugby and golf are *par excellence* the game of the business classes and gentry. Golf seems to have been spread through Ireland by Scots military regiments in the nineteenth century, with the first club in Belfast dating from 1891. Over a quarter of the world's premier link golf courses are in Ireland—a statistic to make any lover of the countryside shudder. Golf enthusiasts, of course, will claim that their courses preserve the countryside, and contribute to surrounding the city with green belts of clean air, and the two courses on North Bull Island do not seem to interfere with its role as a UNESCO world biosphere centre and a bird sanctuary. North Bull Island was the birthplace of Michael Moran, one of Ireland's earliest successful golfers, who died in the First World War. Male and female Irish golfers have achieved well over the years. Dubliner Padraig Harrington was a member of the European Ryder Cup winning teams in 2002 and 2004 and winner of the Linde German Masters, and the Omega Hong Kong Open in 2004.

An evening at the dogs is another chance to see working people at their leisure. There has been a recent revival in greyhound racing, which takes place at Shelbourne Park. The Irish Derby is the richest greyhound event in the world. The two most famous Irish dogs are Master McGrath from Lurgan, who won the Waterloo Cup in 1868, 1869 and 1871, and is celebrated in song and image, particularly in his native town, and Spanish Battleship, who won the Derby three times in the 1950s. The cruel sport of live hare coursing continues, with other blood sports, in Ireland.

Dublin is the birthplace of show-jumping, with the first ever event having taken place at a Royal Dublin Society show on the lawn in front of Leinster House in 1868. The original object was to foster horse breeding in Ireland. It became clear in the 1860s and 1870s that the Kildare Street premises of the RDS were too restricted for the annual spring and winter agricultural shows, and in 1881 the RDS moved to Ballsbridge. The annual horse show became an increasingly important means of raising funds for the society, and a new social season developed around the racing calendar and the RDS horse show.

I cannot resist offering you the piece of trivia, that Bridget Dowling met her future husband, Aloïs Hitler (brother of the more famous Adolf) at the Dublin Horse Show in 1909. The show continues to be a major event in Dublin life, and the Aga Khan Cup is a prestigious trophy attracting international teams to the competition.

Ireland's biggest horse-racing venue is outside Dublin, at the Curragh in Co. Kildare. Racing is administered by Horse Racing Ireland, a government-backed body set up in 2001, and by the Turf Club, and is heavily subsidized by the state. Betting is a huge component of horse racing and the betting shop a locus of social activity in working-class areas of Dublin. Leopardstown Racecourse, in the southern suburb of Foxrock, was built by Captain George Quin in 1888, having been modelled on Sandown Racecourse in England. It now belongs to The Racing Board and is one of the best racecourses in Europe. Racing followers straddle class boundaries.

Travellers

One of the symptoms of an unresolved problem over national identity in Ireland is to be found in the emotional and often angry responses generated by the presence of Irish Travellers. There is no consensus of opinion as to the origins of Irish Travellers, an indigenous minority group, with its own languages and culture, long established in Ireland, but they are probably not related to the European Roma. There are 26,500 Travellers in Ireland, the majority living in the greater Dublin area. According to Nan Joyce's controversial *Traveller: An Autobiography* (1985):

> *The original Travellers were tinsmiths and musicians and they were great carpenters, they made all their own musical instruments and the wagons and carts. Over the years they mixed in with Travellers from other countries, like the Spanish who came to Ireland four or five hundred years ago... then there were settled people who took to the roads for various reasons and mixed in with the Travellers. One of my great-grandfathers going back six or seven grannies, was a Protestant minister. His son married in with the Joyces, a tribe from Galway... the various tribes have different beliefs and ways of going on. Some of them are strong fighting people because for hundreds of years they had to fight to survive, it wasn't that they were bad.*

There are some old Romany families established in Ireland that move, like other Traveller families, back and forth across the Irish Sea. It is likely that they have been here since the sixteenth century when the first references to "Egyptians" appeared in Ireland, Scotland, Wales and England. Gypsies, like Irish Travellers, have no standard theory of their own origins, eschewing the forms of racialized histories dominant in Western Europe. Which is not to say that individual spokespeople and groups do not offer such theories—it is rather that they have not garnered widespread acceptance among Travellers themselves or among academics. Since the early 1990s there has been a new immigration of Eastern European Roma, fleeing violence and discrimination in countries such as Albania and Romania, but often meeting with hostility and prejudice in Ireland. In the early nineteenth century Ireland's small Jewish population had a large proportion of pedlars, whose occupation, foreign language and mobility allied them with Travellers in popular perceptions.

Irish Travellers speak a language known as Shelta, with two distinct dialects, Gammon and Cant. The origins of Shelta and its status as a language are matters of dispute. Travellers speak a distinctive dialect of

English in their dealings with settlers (or Country people, as they call the settled), incorporating many words and phrases from their own language; Cant or Gammon is the language of the home. Settled communities find Traveller mobility deeply unsettling and it seems likely that this hostility goes back several centuries, although it is not always possible to distinguish when early records on vagrancy are referring to Travellers. Eighteenth- and early nineteenth-century novels certainly record prejudice against Travellers and a tendency to associate them with criminality. Official hostility to Travellers in this period was also connected to a suspicion that pedlars were instrumental in spreading through rural areas secret messages to organize insurgency.

Mobility is highly valued by Travellers themselves, and although the Irish state has brought pressure on them to settle in fixed accommodation, a large proportion continue to travel. Travellers construe ideas of community through kinship patterns rather than on the basis of geographical proximity. They organize time around grand gatherings at fairs and patterns (traditional religious festivals), while weddings and funerals are major family gathering at which marriages are arranged and family bonds reaffirmed. Most Irish Travellers are Catholics, but in traditional Irish folk belief they are also often associated with fairies and with healing. Some Travellers campaign for an increase in the number of sites and an improvement in facilities. They want their children settled in school for much of the year, and the right to travel during holidays. Travellers have protested that planning laws discriminate against them and prevent them from building their own sites.

In theory, the idea of the Traveller life is appreciated in Irish society, being associated with traditional values and occupations. Their musical and story-telling cultural forms are rich and vibrant and in many ways they seem to represent a connection with the past that has been lost to much mainstream Irish life outside the rural Gaeltachts. Artists and intellectuals often appear to cast Travellers as symbols of authenticity, and they have been celebrated with various degrees of credibility and caricature in films including Joe Comerford's *Traveller* (1981), *Into the West* and *Snatch* (dir. Guy Ritchie, 2000). Until the prosperity of the 1990s drew in more immigrants Ireland had very small populations of ethnic minorities and so anyone who wished to demonstrate in practical terms a commitment to anti-racism was likely to advocate Travellers' rights.

In practice, Travellers' culture and identity came under sustained assault in Ireland through the twentieth century. In the 1970s and 1980s Nell McCafferty wrote court reports for the *Irish Times* which exposed the miseries of Dublin life for members of those under-classes created by poverty, and also exposed the systematic injustices of the legal system. Travellers figure largely in her accounts. Historically, Travellers tended to withdraw from confrontation with non-Travellers and move on. This culture may have contributed to their relative slowness to adopt political activism and self-advocacy. A notable exception is Nan Joyce, quoted above. Her autobiography was in the vanguard of voices from Travellers choosing to represent themselves, and inspired the writing projects that have flourished in the last twenty years. Here is how Bridget Gaffey describes her childhood in Dublin:

> *When I was living in Dublin we lived on a site which was miles away from all houses but as time went on, houses gradually was built beside them and the children of the houses got first priority to the school. When they all got in we were given two classrooms for ourselves, all of different ages, mixed. But the other children were all in classrooms to suit their age group. I will never forget those classrooms which had showers in—only the two we were in. So my mother took me out of it because she said that she doesn't have to send me to school to learn to get washed because she could do the washing. So then the showers were taken out when the mothers protested against it and I went back to school.*

In the 1960s the more socialist-oriented members of the Women's Liberation Movement in Dublin tried to argue that the poverty and discrimination suffered by Travellers was an important feminist issue, but they failed to win this argument with other feminists. In many ways the 1960s was the low point in attitudes towards Travellers from the settled majority. The state attempted to impose a system of settlement and assimilation (*The Report of the Committee on Itinerancy*, 1963), and many traditional Traveller sites were denied to them. This coincided with the move from horse-drawn caravans into motorized mobile homes, and restriction on Traveller movement led to health problems and a poverty trap.

Irish society tolerates an extraordinarily vile use of hate language against Travellers. In recent years there have been proposals to tag electronically all Travellers, and to allow publicans the discretion to bar them *en masse* from public houses. These and similar attitudes are routinely condemned in the Irish media, but also routinely gather support. Dublin Travellers tend to live out in the suburbs, and city-centre beggars are as likely to be recent immigrants as indigenous Travellers. A visitor to the city may be most likely to see Travellers in and around markets where many of them work as traders. Travellers have a cultural and heritage centre in Dublin, at Pavee Point, Great Charles Street.

One of the most prominent spokespeople for Travellers in the 1980s was Nan Joyce, who was a founder member of the Travellers' Rights Committee and stood as an independent candidate in the 1982 general election. Her autobiography offers a haunting description of social exclusion followed by a growing political awareness.

> *When I was a child we were hunted from place to place and we never could have friends always to be going to school with. The little settled children would run past our camps—they were afeared of the Travellers. Other people had sort of romantic ideas about us, because of the horses and the colourful wagons. They would ask us did we come from some place special like the gypsies you see on the films. They thought that the Travellers had no worries and that we didn't feel pain, or hunger or cold. The truth is that we're people like everybody else but we're a different speaking people with our own traditions and our own way of life and this is the way we should be treated, like the Gaeltachts, not like dirt or drop-outs from the settled community.*

It is obviously important to pay attention to Travellers themselves as the authorities on their community, but even quotations from Traveller writings must be approached with care. The motive for much of this writing has been the need to combat racism among the settled Irish, and such accounts have often emphasized the oppression suffered by Travellers rather than celebrating their way of life. Travellers should not be construed primarily as victims. The extraordinary fact is that settled Irish know so little about the fullness and variety of Traveller life in spite of centuries of shared existence on this island.

Epilogue
An Abcdarium

In the end, cities remain intriguing and pleasurable places to explore because they resist the stories we impose on them, and constantly surprise us with the arbitrary and inconsequential. Their meanings are generated out of juxtapositions and collisions. I find it hard not to approach Dublin, and books about Dublin, like a magpie picking up scraps to hoard. I decided to conclude this book with a little abcdarium, in which I have collected some things that interest me in Dublin, places people and events that might have been folded into a historical event, or encountered on a promenade, but might also be thought of as the scraps of information and anecdote one carries through the city.

A writer with some respect for the arbitrary and felicitous connections of the English and Irish languages was Flann O'Brien, whose novel *At-Swim-Two-Birds* (1939) is one of the great literary works in which the role of Dubliner overwrites that of Irisher. An unnamed University College Dublin student is narrating a story about a novelist named Trellis, who lives in a seedy environment, writing a novel about sin, in which the major characters have been recruited (or plagiarized) from the annals of Irish literature. When Trellis falls asleep, his characters take on a life of their own, and one of them determines to write a book about Trellis himself.

The **Bewley** family were Quakers who came from England to Ireland in the early eighteenth century in flight from religious intolerance. In the 1830s the Bewley family begin to import tea to Ireland directly from China. In 1894 the first *Bewley's Oriental Café* was opened at Great George Street, and two years later Bewley's opened the café at 10 Westmoreland Street, frequented by James Joyce. In 1927 the flagship Grafton Street store was purchased and fitted out at great expense. Art Nouveau features are incorporated into all aspects of the design, and its mosaic front remains one of the most striking features of Grafton Street. Among the shop/café's decorative features are a set of six of Harry Clarke's exquisitely designed and coloured windows on the ground floor. These are among the few pieces of non-religious stained glass in the city. During the Emergency restrictions on tea (mainly imported from British plantations) caused many of Bewley's customers to switch to coffee. In the 1950s the shops were frequented by writers and artists including Patrick Kavanagh and Mary Lavin, and the short stories of the period often incorporate an encounter in Bewley's. In the 1960s the Grafton Street café tried to increase business by opening a self-service area and also a men's only smoking room. In the 1970s the business opened a chain of shops in the suburbs and diversified to create a catering company. That decade the Westmoreland Street café was destroyed by fire. A clever marketing strategy in the 1990s, which involved a merger with Butler's Irish chocolates, took the brand, which had been special to Dublin, and gave it worldwide recognition. The consequence, of course, is that a cup of coffee with friends in the original cafés no longer seems so special.

There was nevertheless general dismay when Bewley's announced their decision to close the cafés in Grafton Street and Westmoreland Street from 30 November 2004. High rents and overheads, changing fashions in consumption and competition from international "coffee-to-go" brands were all blamed for a decline in profitability. Questions were asked in the Oireachtas, and the Taoiseach spoke about his concern for the loss to Dublin's heritage and for the employees. He also rejected suggestions that the government should intervene to save the cafés. In theory, the buildings themselves are protected, but huge protests at the decision to close the cafés registered a general sense that a significant part of the city's history and ambience was being lost.

In pre-Independence Ireland the "Illustrious Order of St. Patrick", instituted by George III in 1783, was the Irish equivalent of the English "Order of the Garter" and the Scottish "Order of the Thistle". Knights were required to be "descended of three descents of nobleness" on both paternal and maternal sides. Its purpose was to secure the loyalty of senior peers by giving them a marked social advancement. An award of the knighthood was seen as evidence of the high social standing of the recipient and there was considerable competition for the limited places.

The Insignia of the Knights of St. Patrick became known as the "Irish **Crown Jewels**" .These consisted of the Grand Master's diamond badge set in silver with a trefoil in emeralds on a ruby cross, and various other valuable jewels. They were used at the investiture ceremonies of knighthood which took place in St. Patrick's Hall in Dublin Castle,

where stall plates along the walls chronologically record the names and banners show the family crests of the Knights of St. Patrick. As soldiers lined the route, the new knights in elaborate garb, walked in procession to an installation ceremony in St. Patrick's Cathedral.

The "crown jewels" were stored in a bank vault, except when in use. In 1903, they were transferred to a safe, which was to be placed in the newly constructed strong room in Bedford Hall, at Dublin Castle. The steel safe to house the jewels proved to be too large for the doorway, however, and Sir Arthur Vicars, the Officer of Arms, agreed to the jewels being stored in the Library.

Four days before the state visit of King Edward VII and Queen Alexandra it was discovered that the jewels had been stolen. King Edward had intended to invest Lord Castletown as a Knight of the Order, but, furious over the theft, he cancelled the ceremony.

Suspicion fell on Arthur Vicars, but he refused to confess or to resign. Rumours that he was a homosexual began to spread, possibly originating in the Castle and founded in the hope that he would be shamed into leaving quietly. Homosexuality was, of course, illegal. These rumours may have hindered the investigation, since they involved links between Vicars and a London-based network of socially prominent gay men, including politicians and aristocrats. In any case, Vicars accused his second-in-command, Francis Shackleton (brother of Ernest who later became famous as an Antarctic explorer). A Viceregal Commission exonerated Shackleton and found Vicars culpable, although no legal conviction followed.

Later Shackleton was jailed for theft, while Arthur Vicars spent his remaining years as a recluse in Co. Kerry. On 14 April 1921, in the period between the War of Independence and the Civil War, an armed IRA contingent brought him out of his home at Kilmorna Castle and shot him dead, before burning the building.

The Irish Crown Jewels were never found.

Evelyn Gleeson founded the **Dun Emer Guild** with the help of Elizabeth and Lily Yeats in 1902. Emer was the wife of the mythic medieval warrior Cú Chulainn, and was celebrated for her needlework. The Dun Emer Guild was partly inspired by William Morris' arts and crafts movement. It was a quintessential revival project that aimed both to create beautiful objects of Irish craftsmanship and also to educate and train workers and provide jobs. Lily Yeats ran an embroidery workshop, and Dun Emer produced embroidered banners and furnishings of high quality design and execution. In 1908 the Yeats sisters split away to found Cuala Industries, specializing in embroidery and in hand-printed books. In 1912 Gleeson moved her workers from the house at Dundrum which was their first base, to Hardwicke Street, and later to Harcourt Street. Dun Emer went on producing rugs, tapestry, furnishings, fabric as well as some printing and bookbinding until the late 1950s.

The Roman Catholic Church's thirty-first **Eucharistic Congress** for the promotion of devotion to the sacrament was held in Dublin in 1932. Over a million people attended a mass in Phoenix Park, celebrated by the Papal Legate Cardinal Lauri. Count John McCormack, believed by many to be the greatest lyric tenor of his generation, sang *Panis Angelicus* at the mass. The Congress was seen as a triumph for the Irish Free State, although such a marked identification of the new state with the Roman Catholic Church inevitably alienated religious minorities and secular opinion.

Ireland in the 1920s and 1930s was not merely indifferent to jazz. There was active hostility from the Catholic Church, which feared that "indecent" dancing would advance promiscuity. If only. The Gaelic language preservation society, Conradh na Gaeilge, also promoted notionally "indigenous" language, arts, sports and culture, including an "anti-jazz campaign". The Church's pressure against the evils of all-night dancing led to the Public Dance Halls Act (1935), which was a move to confine dances to licensed halls. In fact, this act bore heavily against traditional house dances in rural Ireland. In the 1940s jazz was included in a self-imposed ban on the playing of dance music on Irish radio. Naturally the effect of such prohibition was to increase the public appetite for dance music, but in Ireland dance bands traditionally had little swing, and almost no improvisation.

Flann O'Brien, in an article on "The Dance Halls" in *The Bell* in February 1941, provided a hilarious collection of quotations from lawyers, clerics and newspaper leader writers on the evils of the dance hall. He went on to describe the scene at a country dance hall.

The band may be good or bad. Bands will vary enormously for this reason—a dance is regarded as successful according to the distance a band has to travel. *For the best possible dance the band would have to come from India. This is the great immutable law that determines the local prestige of every event. A Committee is doing pretty well if they can get a band from a hundred miles away. What is regarded as a good band in the country will have their own "electrical amplification" but may lack a piano. Their tunes will be old and grey and far behind the whistling repertoire of any diligent cinema-goer. "Goodnight Sweetheart" is still a rage in the west.*

Jazz struggled to establish itself as an art form in Ireland, almost as much as it struggled for a purchase in popular culture. From the 1950s the Jazz Society at Trinity College Dublin brought in visiting artists, particularly from Britain. Many Irish jazz musicians emigrated to pursue their interests. One notable figure who stayed in Dublin and played a major role in promoting jazz both as a performer and through presenting radio programmes on the topic, was **Rock Fox** (the stage name of Charles Meredith, otherwise a Dublin solicitor). He adopted his stage name in 1952 because a solicitor's apprentice was prohibited from taking a second job. Fox plays trumpet, clarinet and sax, and is also a composer and arranger. Among the bands for which he has played are the Jazz Heralds, the Butler-Fox Band and Rock Fox and his Famous Orchestra. In the 1970s he wrote *Civil Rights Suite*, inspired by the life and death of Martin Luther King.

Rock Fox played in two of the bands showcased in a celebration of Irish jazz at the Olympia Theatre in Dublin in 1962. Interest in jazz has grown in Dublin since the 1960s, but there has never been a dedicated jazz venue. It has been a small scene dependent on individual enthusiasts, such as George Hodnett, jazz critic for *The Irish Times*, Honor Heffernan, actor, jazz singer and radio presenter, and Ronan Guilfoyle, bass guitarist and director of jazz studies at Newpark Music Centre, Blackrock.

Observatory Lane in Rathmines takes its name from the nineteenth-century works of **Thomas Grubb** (1800-78), which were located there. Grubb founded his business in 1830 and his first premises were on a piece of land behind the gardens of 1-4 Ranelagh Road. His home was at No. 1, and there he built his first observatory. Grubb's business was the building of astronomical telescopes. In 1835 he supplied a 15-inch reflector to the Armagh observatory; the Great Vienna Telescope, which, when it was built, was the largest refracting telescope in the world. This instrument was constructed at Rathmines, as was the great telescope Grubb built for the observatory in Melbourne. Grubb's genius for instruments and instrument-making found other outlets. He built microscopes, and also machines for printing bank notes. His hobby was photography and he was a member of the first committee of the Dublin Photographic Society. His son, Sir Howard Grubb, inherited the business and the other interests, himself becoming President of the Photographic Society of Ireland in 1894. During the First World War the business made military instruments, including periscopes and gun-sights, where optical engineering was central. The Ministry of Munitions transferred the factory to Hertfordshire and Grubb's manufacturing interests were concentrated in England, but Sir Howard kept a home in Ireland and retired to Monkstown. Many Grubb telescopes are still in regular use.

In April 2004 Tony Maguire, the Chairman of Shamrock Rovers, published a statement on behalf of the Club's Board of Directors in response to an article in the *Evening Herald* making allegations about the Ultras supporters group. He praised the Ultras for their contribution to the club and for their behaviour, repudiating any suggestion "that these supporters are hooligans or that they have forged links with Nazi groups on the continent."

Dubliners are pretty keen on their soccer. In the city centre you will see youths wearing international shirts demonstrating their loyalty to Ireland, but also their admiration for Brazil, Portugal and other cool teams. There is also a high level of allegiance to British and Scottish premiership clubs, particularly Celtic, Manchester United, Liverpool, Arsenal, Chelsea and Spurs. The modest Eircom league cannot do much to compete against the glamour of these huge businesses with their internationally famous stars, but local clubs attract an intensity among supporters that can be both comic, and occasionally a bit frightening.

Shamrock Rovers Football Club was formed in the summer of 1901 in Ringsend. They became known as **The Hoops** from their green-and-white horizontal striped shirts. After a couple of years playing friendly matches the club progressed to competitive football when it joined the Dublin County League. The first trophy came in 1904-05 when the league title was won.

The 1921-2 season was the most successful season for Rovers as a junior club, when it progressed to the first ever F.A.I. Cup Final. Rovers lost the final but the following season joined the League of Ireland, where the club has been ever since. In 1924-5 Rovers won the league title, the F.A.I. Cup and the League of Ireland Shield. In the F.A.I. Cup Final they beat their Ringsend rivals Shelbourne before a crowd of 25,000.

In the 1926-7 season the club moved from one part of the Milltown Road to another and officially opened Glenmalure Park. In February 1927 the players wore the famous green-and-white hoops for the first time. They also won the League title for the third time. In March 1926 Ireland had played its very first international game, against Italy in Turin. Four Shamrock Rovers players were in this team: Dinny Doyle, John Joe Flood, Bob Fullam and John "Kruger" Fagan.

Shamrock Rovers became the first club to represent the League of Ireland in Europe when they were drawn against Manchester United in the European Cup in 1957, just months before the Munich air disaster destroyed Matt Busby's first great team. The Busby Babes were too strong for Rovers when the teams met before a crowd of 46,000 at Dalymount Park; the result was 6-0 to United. A different Rovers turned up for the second leg at Old Trafford and put up such a brave fight in the 3-2 defeat that the United fans applauded the Dubliners off the pitch after the game.

In the 1970s the former Manchester United and Leeds midfield general Johnny Giles was brought in as manager, in an attempt to arrest the decline that was widespread in Irish soccer. Giles began to make the club more professional and brought in former professional players such as Eamon Dunphy and Ray Treacy.

Dunphy, a native Dubliner, had spent most of his playing career in English league football before coming to Rovers as a player-coach. He was capped 23 times for Ireland between 1966 and 1977. He went on to a career as a writer, journalist and broadcaster, and is one of the best-known and most controversial figures in Irish sport. To suggest that he is forthright would be an understatement, but to his many critics he is merelyan unabashed self-publicist. His autobiography, *Only a Game* (1976), is a fierce account of football as a business and reveals some of the uglier tactics players and fans enjoy, but are supposed to condemn. He wrote a book about U2 and a biography of Matt Busby (Dunphy served his apprenticeship at United); and his collaboration with United's captain (and ex-Ireland captain) Roy Keane (*Keane: The Autobiography*, 2002) attracted huge publicity, especially after Keane's early exit from Ireland's 2002 World Cup squad, a scandal that divided the nation.

In April 1987 Shamrock Rovers decided to raise money by selling their ground at Glenmalure Park and, despite opposition from fans, the former pitch was soon covered by housing. (The provision of housing also served parts of the community, of course.) Rovers have since played at Tolka Park, Dalymount Park, the Royal Dublin Society, Tolka Park (again) and Morton Stadium, Santry. Following a lengthy battle, the club finally secured planning permission for a new 6,000 all-seater stadium in Tallaght, south-west Dublin, but the project was held up by funding problems and is likely to be taken over by the GAA. Rovers recently merged with Tallaght Town AFC.

Are some of their fans hooligans? That is not a question specific to The Hoops. Soccer has never been more popular or more dominant in the public imagination. It has become the site of debates about national character as well as local allegiances. It is the hobby of what Roy Keane famously described as the "prawn sandwich"-eating middle-class brigade, as well as a reservoir of authentic working-class masculinity (although GAA followers claim that they are the *real* men). Like the novels of Jane Austen, soccer is here to offer a little regulated hatred, as well as some lessons in loyalty.

The Hoops, by the way, have the most successful team in the history of women's football in Ireland.

The **Islamic Cultural Centre** at 19 Roebuck Road, Clonskeagh, was opened by President Mary Robinson in 1996. It is a centre of worship, education and cultural activity for the more than 19,000 Muslims in Ireland, many of whom are recent arrivals. While the occasional individual Muslim traveller or trader may have come to Ireland in earlier generations, the first significant immigration was in the 1950s, when students began to arrive to study, mainly in Dublin. A Dublin Islamic Society was founded by students in 1959. Dublin's first mosque opened in Harrington Street in 1976, and it moved to the South Circular Road in 1983. Numbers of Irish Muslims had increased steadily, but still remained small until the 1990s. The arrival of refugees from Bosnia, Kosovo and Somalia coincided with a growth in Irish prosperity, so that Muslims became part of a sudden increase in immigration and settlement in Ireland. Dublin has two state-funded Muslim schools, and a number of businesses. In 1996 the first Muslim TD, Mr. Moosajee Bhamjee, was elected in County Clare.

The Dublin Islamic Centre is run by the Islamic Foundation of Ireland, the official representative body of Muslims in Ireland, and its membership is open to all Muslims. In 1992 the Maktoum family, the ruling family of Dubai, agreed to fund new facilities for the Islamic community in Dublin. The Islamic Cultural Centre not only offers facilities for daily prayers and religious celebrations, but also resources for education and the general welfare of the community, including a Muslim National School, a library, a shop and restaurant. The mosque, situated on the South Circular Road, also incorporates a library, a shop, a restaurant and a Sunday school for Islamic teachings. Heightened awareness in recent years of Islam and Muslims means that the centre has become a resource for information on Islam and on Islamic countries.

The Chester Beatty Library in Dublin Castle has one of the world's finest collections of Islamic manuscripts and art, and its education and outreach programmes foster awareness in Ireland of Islam's extraordinary cultural heritage. The library was begun by Alfred Chester Beatty (1875-1968) an American mining engineer who established a mining consultancy in London and who began to collect Persian manuscripts and early printed books during the 1910s and

1920s. His interest expanded to other Middle Eastern cultures and to China and Japan, from where he collected art and manuscripts, with a particular emphasis on illustrated material. In 1950 Chester Beatty moved to Ireland and built a library for his collections, which he opened to the public, in Shrewsbury Road, Dublin. In 1957 he became Ireland's first honorary citizen. On his death his collection passed to a trust for the public benefit and it is now supported by the Irish government. The library was moved to the Clock Tower building in Dublin Castle in 1999.

John Jameson arrived in Ireland from Scotland in the 1770s. He had connections in the Scottish whisky industry and had married into the Haig family. His son consolidated those connections by marrying a daughter of John Stein, whose family were among the biggest grain distillers in Scotland and who owned Dublin's Bow Street distillery. John Jameson bought the distillery and opened his business there in 1780. It soon grew to be a large undertaking covering eleven acres north of the River Liffey near Smithfield Market. John Jameson insisted that Irish farmers supply him only with his preferred strain of barley, and the superior quality of his whiskey soon established its reputation.

The word "whiskey" (this is the Irish usage as opposed to the Scottish preference for "whisky") is derived from the Irish term, *uisce beatha*, a translation of the Latin, *aqua vitae*, water of life. It may have been introduced into Ireland by monks, who wrote of its healing properties. By the sixteenth century, however, whiskey was becoming associated with drunkenness in Ireland, and in 1556 the Irish parliament passed an act prohibiting distillation without a licence.

The fermenting of spirits from cereals went on, particularly in remote rural areas. The first levy was imposed on *poitín* in 1661 but was largely ignored. From the late eighteenth century, the increase in taxes and other restrictions on distilling increased the popularity of *poitín*, and nineteenth-century Irish literature is full of examples of the war of wits between the *poitín* makers and the excise men.

Distilling was at first established in Ulster and the midlands, with Bushmills claiming the longest continuous tradition. In the late eighteenth century Jameson, along with Power and Roe, brought large commercial distilleries to Dublin. Irish whiskey was traditionally distilled in large copper vessels called pot stills in which raw beer was condensed and evaporated into spirit. Three successive distillations purified the spirit.

Today, Jameson whiskey, like most other Irish whiskeys, is made by the Irish Distillers Group, which has a Jameson heritage centre at its distillery in Midleton, County Cork. Jameson's whiskey is distilled in Midleton or at Bushmills. Distilling ceased at Bow Street in 1971 and was transferred to Midleton, Co. Cork, and the old Bow Street Distillery is now the home of the Old Jameson Distillery and the head office of the Irish Distillers Group. There is a glazed observatory tower at the top of the Jameson chimney in Smithfield.

If you are having a hot whiskey on a cold winter's day, then it should be a hot Power's, but if you want to drink it straight up, Jameson's will do.

Love and whiskey both,
Rejoice an honest fellow;
Unripe joys of life
Love and whiskey mellow.
Both the head and heart
Set in palpitation;

From both I've often found
A mighty sweet sensation.
Love and whiskey's joys,
Let us gaily twist 'em,
In the thread of life,
Faith, we can't resist 'em.
(from "Love and Whiskey", c. 1778)

In 1811 the government agreed to give financial support to the Society for Promoting the Education of the Poor in Ireland, otherwise known as the **Kildare Place Society**. The society's initial aim was to promote mixed-religion education and to bring some organization and structure to the education system in Ireland. It was founded by a group of philanthropic lawyers and businessmen, with several Quakers prominent in their ranks. They approved of the success of several Sunday and day schools on the English model operating in some Dublin parishes, and wanted to extend these benefits to the rest of the country. At first, the Kildare Place Society was supported by all Christian denominations. It produced a series of reading books, which contributed to its lasting fame. It also offered training for teachers and inspected schools and promoted the monitorial system. In these ways it addressed some of the abuses endemic to the Charter Schools set up in the early years of the eighteenth century and run by the Incorporated Society for Promoting English Protestant Schools in Ireland. At the start of the nineteenth century most Catholic children were educated in hedge-schools, an umbrella term covering a range of privately owned and managed schools, some of which might have involved as little a few families paying a local tutor, others perhaps representing small private academies with several classes and teachers. Although the Kildare Place Society had been initially supported by some leading Catholics, including Daniel O'Connell, by 1820 the Catholic Church was accusing the society of proselytizing, and withdrew its support. The Church found unacceptable the society's key principle that the Bible should be read by all children together "without note or comment". In 1831 a system of national schools was set up, and government grants were withdrawn from the society.

Margaret Plunket Leeson was born at Killough, Co. Westmeath, in 1727, the daughter of a landowner from near Corbetstown. She was one of twenty-two children, of whom eight survived infancy. Two older sisters married prosperous tradesmen in Tullamore and Dublin. While Plunket was in her teens her mother and eldest brother died of fever. Her father was then a bereaved invalid and signed over the whole of his estate to his son Christopher, a violent alcoholic who beat and starved his brother and sisters.

One sister married well, but against Christopher's will, leaving Margaret at home with a younger brother and sister and an ailing, distressed father, as well as Christopher. The sister died, a victim of cruelty and neglect according to Plunket, and she herself tried and failed to elope before she was finally assisted to escape by her father and her younger brother, who were frightened by the beatings she received. She moved to her sister's home in Arran Street, Dublin, and soon after began an affair with a man named Dardis. When she became pregnant he persuaded her to move into lodgings in what subsequently turned out to be a brothel. After the birth of her daughter she separated from her lover, tried and failed to be reconciled with her family, became a "kept woman" and eventually a prostitute and then a brothel-keeper. Her most famous establishment was in Wood Street, Dublin. In her sixties, to pay off her debtors, she published the first two volumes of *The Memoirs of Mrs Margaret Leeson, Written by Herself; in which are given Anecdotes, sketches of the Lives and Bon Mots of some of the Most Celebrated Characters in Great Britain and Ireland, particularly of all the Filles des Joys and men of Gallantry which have usually frequented her Citherean temple for these Thirty Years Past* . She was later attacked by a gang, beaten and raped, and later died of a venereal disease in 1797. The third volume was published posthumously.

In the mid-eighteenth century the Female Penitentiary Movement in England began to open homes for female sex workers, with the aim of converting the women into practising Christians, encouraging repentance of their former sins, and setting them to respectable forms of labour. Lady Arabella Denny (1707-92) was a philanthropist best known for the reforms she initiated at the Dublin Foundling Hospital over the period 1759-78. In 1764 she was publicly thanked for her work by the Irish House of Commons, and in 1765 she was given the Freedom of the City of Dublin. In 1767 Denny founded the Dublin **Magdalen Asylum** in Lower Leeson Street. It was open only to

Protestant women, but Catholic Magdalen homes soon followed. There were also houses of refuge designed to shelter respectable women. The House of Refuge in Ash Street was established in 1809. A leaflet advertising its good works asserted that "A more interesting object cannot be presented to the commiseration of the charitable than a virtuous and unprotected female struggling with distress, and unable to extract herself from it." At first, Magdalen Asylums were intended as short-term refuges, in which women might, for example, develop the skills to enter employment. In 1848 the Catholic homes were transformed by the arrival in Ireland from France of a Catholic religious order, the Good Shepherd Sisters, who developed long-term institutions for women. Inmates were actively discouraged from leaving and sometimes detained illegally for life. Inevitably, such as system was open to many kinds of abuse.

The use of the figure of Mary Magdalen to symbolize these projects indicates the degree to which they were driven by Christian attitudes towards sin and redemption. In Denny's asylum the inmates were referred to as "penitents". In the early years the asylums were not targeted at "professional" or "regular" sex workers, but at women in danger of becoming prostitutes or living on the fringes of prostitution. Among other concerns asylums wanted to be able to demonstrate some success rate from their endeavours, and therefore they concentrated on younger women, who were more easily influenced.

Although asylum regime was strict, women did enter into them voluntarily. Some prostitutes may have gone in for a respite from work and poverty. In Catholic refuges it became increasingly commonplace to assert that only nuns, who were celibate, could influence the behaviour of "hardened" prostitutes.

In the twentieth century more women were entered into the asylums by referral from priest, family members, police or employers, and more emphasis began to be placed on the unmarried mother or the promiscuous woman. The Magdalen Asylums were used by families to shield themselves from the shame attached to having a member's unregulated sexuality exposed. Sometimes this included incest victims, women with learning difficulties, or poor relations. Inmates worked under harsh conditions in laundries attached to the convents. The last of these laundries, in Gloucester Street, Dublin, closed in 1996.

Surviving inmates of the asylums joined those victims of Catholic Ireland anxious to make their voices heard in the 1990s. A television documentary about the asylums caused public scandal and debate. Peter Mullan's film, *The Magdalene Sisters* (2002) brought international attention to this murky history.

In the decade after the Act of Union public projects to cement unification included the erection, in 1808, of a 134-foot column in Sackville Street to honour Horatio, Lord Nelson (1758-1805), who had died at The Battle of Trafalgar, an important British victory in the Napoleonic Wars. The Duke of Richmond, Lord Lieutenant of Ireland, laid the first stone of **Nelson's Pillar**, Dublin, on 15 February 1808. The inscription on a plate placed on the stone read: "By the blessing of Almighty God, to commemorate the transcendent heroic achievements of the Right Hon. Horatio Lord Viscount Nelson, Duke of Bronti, in Sicily, Vice-Admiral of the White Squadron of his Majesty's Fleet, who fell gloriously in the Battle off Cape Trafalgar, on 21st day of October 1805; when he obtained for his Country a victory over the combined Fleets of France and Spain, unparalleled in Naval History; the first stone of this Triumphal Pillar, was laid by his Grace, Charles, Duke of Richmond and Lennox."

Nelson's Pillar was a fluted Doric column, carved from Wicklow granite, and surmounted with a Portland stone figure of Nelson himself. The monument was designed by William Wilkins and Francis Johnston, architect of the Chapel Royal at Dublin Castle, and the General Post Office on Sackville Street. The figure of Nelson was carved by Thomas Kirk, sculptor of the skyline statutory on the GPO and of the Nathaniel Sneyd Monument in Christ Church Cathedral. Nelson's Pillar had an internal spiral staircase that took visitors to a viewing platform.

As the chief monument in the city's main street the pillar became a popular reference point and meeting place. It features in many paintings and photographs of the city, and is mentioned in numerous literary works. "Before Nelson's Pillar trams slowed, shunted, changed trolley, started for Blackrock, Kingstown and Dalkey, Clonskea, Rathgar and Terenure, Palmerston Park and upper Rathmines, Sandymount Green, Rathmines, Ringsend and Sandymount Tower, Harold's Cross." In *Ulysses* Stephen Dedalus indulges in a fantasy about some old Dublin women spitting plum stones from the top of Nelson's Pillar as they gaze up at the "onehandled adulterer".

That Dublin's most notable public monument should commemorate a British military leader naturally grated with many nationalists, and on 7 March 1966, a few weeks before the fiftieth anniversary of the Easter Rising, the Pillar was blown up by an IRA splinter group. The damaged head of the statue was retrieved and is now in the Dublin Civic Museum. The upper half of the column was destroyed and the lower half was subsequently demolished. Oddly enough, the pillar seems to have left a shadowy trace on the skyscape of O'Connell Street—a felt absence—which may finally be erased by the erection of the giant "needle" to celebrate the millennium.

The Spire of Dublin (nicknamed The Spike and victim of many more inventive and lewd soubriquets) is a large, pin-like monument, almost 400 feet in height and lit from the top. Designed by London architect Ian Ritchie, it was originally intended that the spire would be completed by 2000 in honour of the new millennium, but construction was delayed. It was completed on 21 January 2003 on the site of the former Nelson's Pillar.

The spire was commissioned as part of a redesigned street layout in 1999. O'Connell Street had gone into decline from the 1970s, with fast food chains, bargain basements and amusement arcades dominating the streetscape. In the 1990s, plans were launched to re-landscape the thoroughfare and manage traffic to encourage pedestrians to see O'Connell Street as more of a boulevard. The number of trees in the central reservation was reduced; statues were cleaned and in some cases relocated. Shop-owners were required to replace plastic signage and frontage with more attractive designs. The spire was chosen through a public competition. It was very expensive, and many objections were raised on the grounds that the design was "meaningless" and that unlike Nelson's Pillar, the spire would not provide a viewing platform from which to overlook the city.

Jimmy O'Dea (1899-1965) was the archetypal Dublin comedian of his generation. He began his collaboration with Harry O'Donovan in 1928, at the Queen's Royal Theatre, with *We're Here*. Variety emerged in Ireland in the period after the Civil War, and as British visiting acts became less frequent, there was space for a distinctively Irish brand of comedy to develop. O'Dea was most famous for his female impersonation in pantomime and his portrayal of Biddy Mulligan, market trader, the Pride of the Coombe. O'Dea starred in the Royal and Gaiety Theatre pantomimes for nearly forty years. He drew around him an excellent cast of Irish comedians, with whom he toured. His most notable performing collaboration was with the comedian and actor Maureen Potter. O'Dea's films include *Penny Paradise* (1938), *Let's Be Famous* (1939) and *Darby O'Gill and the Little People* (1959), in which he played the king of the fairies. O'Dea was alert to developments in high culture, and in 1955 introduced Godot into his act. Shortly before O'Dea's death RTÉ producer James Plunkett commissioned Myles na gCopaleen to script a series for Dea set in a railway signal box. *Your Man* ran through 1963-4. O'Dea made his last appearance at the Gaiety in *Finian's Rainbow* in 1964, his final line being "We will meet in Gloccamorra some fine day."

Bridge House on Baggot Street was built in 1916. Any fan of post-war Dublin writers will have come across references to May **Parson's Bookshop**, which operated in Bridge House until 31 May 1989. In the 1950s Parson's Bookshop was frequented by Brendan Behan, Patrick Kavanagh, Liam O'Flaherty, Frank O'Connor, Flann O'Brien, Ben Kiely, Mary Lavin and John Broderick. In later years it was presided over by Miss King and Miss O'Flaherty. Today many of Dublin's excellent bookshops are clean, well-lit spaces, with coffee shops, exhibition spaces, and children's play areas. Many of the independent booksellers have mostly been taken over by the big corporations, so that the interiors of Waterstones and Hodges Figgis (an old established shop now owned by the same group as Waterstones) are similar to branches of those shops in other cities. They are the best of their kind, because Dubliners love bookshops and would be quick to criticize poor stock and lack of choice. Parson's was a different kind of bookshop, the kind where books are piled from floor to ceiling and where regulars come in and browse for hours looking for treasures. It was a place where writers and people who loved writing bumped into each other and lingered to discuss their latest reading. It was the kind of bookshop, and there used to be many of these, where the booksellers honoured their customers' love of literature. In 2004, to mark Patrick Kavanagh's centenary, a plaque was placed on the site of the former shop to commemorate his connection with it. Among the very good second-hand and antiquarian bookshops in central Dublin are Cathach Books in Duke Street and Greene's Bookshop in Clare Street. Conradh na Gaeilge-An Siopa Leabhar at 6 Harcourt Street (*www.cnag.ie/siopa.htm*) specializes in Irish-language books.

The Queen's Royal Theatre in Great Brunswick Street (Pearse Street) was built in 1844 on the site of an earlier theatre called the Adelphi. It had no special distinction until the 1880s, when, under the management of J. W. Whitbread, it began to present Irish melodramas, some of which were written by Whitbread himself, including the overtly political *Wolfe Tone* (1898), produced in the centenary year of the '98 Rebellion. The most celebrated of the melodramas were those by Dion Boucicault.

In the 1920s the Queen's became a variety theatre, well known for its pantomimes. In those years Jimmy O'Dea was king of the boards. When the Abbey Theatre burned down in 1951, the Abbey Company removed to the Queen's, where it remained until the opening of the new Abbey in 1966. The Queen's was demolished in 1969.

Théodore Géricault's ***The Raft of the Medusa*** (*Le Radeau de la Méduse*) was started in 1818 and completed in 1819. The painting illustrates the crew and passengers of the *Medusa*, a French military ship owned by the government. The *Medusa* ran aground on 2 July 1816 off Africa's west coast and was then battered by a gale. The crew and captain of the ship escaped onto lifeboats hauling an improvised raft that carried 149 passengers. In time the captain and crew set the raft adrift by cutting the rope used for towing. This left the passengers with no provisions and nothing to protect them from the heat. While the boats reached Saint-Louis, Senegal, safely, those on the raft drifted for twelve days in extreme heat with no water, at the end of which there were only fifteen survivors and allegations of cannibalism. A scandal developed in France when it was revealed that the captain of the ship was selected because of political partisanship rather than ability.

In preparation for making the painting Géricault questioned survivors, examined dead bodies, and constructed a raft in his workshop. His representation of the corpses and the bodies in pain falling towards the spectator caused controversy, breaking with previous boundaries of what was considered acceptable. In 1819 the painting was exhibited at the Paris Salon. In 1821 Géricault took the painting to London, where it was shown to great acclaim, and then he brought it to Dublin for a six- week exhibition in the Rotunda.

The Dublin exhibition was not as successful, for nearby the Marshalls' Moving Panorama of the same scene, accompanied by band music, was considerably more popular.

Fifteen years previously Dublin taste had been instructed in the horrors of the French Revolution when Madame Tussaud opened her Grand European Cabinet of Figures at the Shakespeare Gallery in Exchequer Street. The waxwork figures had many faces cast from the heads of guillotined victims of the Terror, and she also had on show models of some contemporary Irish political figures including Henry Grattan.

At the beginning of the twentieth century the young Austin Clarke witnessed the destruction of another panorama:

> One Sunday morning after Mass, my sisters and I went down to the railings of Rutland Square to see the charred remains of the vast marquee which had been struck the night before by a stroke of lightening. Within it had been the Swiss Village, as it was called, this being a panoramic model of the Alps and their valleys. We knew that God sent fire from Heaven because the Exhibition had been open on the previous Sunday.

The **Solomons family** was among the most distinguished of Dublin's Jewish families at the turn of the twentieth century. Maurice Solomons, an optician, came to Dublin from Yorkshire. Among the children of Maurice and Rosa Solomons were Bethel, a prominent physician, and Estella, a painter and printmaker.

Bethel Solomons (1885-1965) was a graduate of Trinity College Dublin and also studied in Paris, Vienna, Berlin, Leipzig, Dresden and Munich. He was Master of the Rotunda, 1926-33, and a gynaecologist who contributed extensively to medical journals on obstetrics and gynaecology. Solomons was working in obstetrics at a very difficult time in terms of the pressures on the profession to conceptualize reproduction in ways that would chime with the interests of the Irish state. Inevitably, he saw women who had attempted illegal abortions, and women for whom childbirth would be fatal but to whom contraception was forbidden. Most of his patients went on to have very large families and he had to develop practices that would balance care for his patient—the mother—with the extraordinary demands made upon her.

His elder sister, Estella (1882-1968) attended finishing school in Germany, studied art at the Royal Hibernia Academy and the Dublin Metropolitan School of Art, as well as in Paris and London. At the beginning of the twentieth century she was one of a number of women artists involved in Hugh Lane's project for a gallery of modern art. She first exhibited with the Young Irish Artists in 1903. A self-portrait, shown at the 1987 Irish Women Artists Exhibition in Dublin, shows a strong, enquiring face, with a striking head of heavy dark hair.

In 1906 Solomons visited Amsterdam, and became enthralled by Rembrandt. She returned to Holland later to study landscape. The Amsterdam visit may have prompted her interest in etching. She worked at least 92 copperplates, mainly of Dublin scenes. Eight of her etchings appear as illustrations to a rather whimsical volume, D. L. Kelleher's *The Glamour of Dublin* (1918, revised and expanded, 1928). She depicts Leinster Market, Carlisle Court, Winetavern Street, The Merchant Tailors' Arch and Hoey Court; the style offers a Dublin *chiaroscuro* of backstreets and alleyways, scenes framed under arches, with very little sky.

Estella Solomons was a member of Cumann na mBan, the women's auxiliary to the Irish Volunteers, founded in April 1914, and both nationalism and feminism remained important to her through her life. During the Troubles her studio was a hiding place for people on the run. She married the poet Seumas O'Sullivan (pseudonym of James Sullivan Starkey, 1879-1958). Unlike some of her women artist friends, she was able to go on painting after marrying and continued to exhibit work into her eighties. There was an exhibition of her landscape paintings at the Crawford Gallery in Cork in 1986.

Before I ever visited Dublin myself, I remember opening the **Tea Time Express** cake box brought to the house by any visitor from the capital. My mother had lived for a year in Dublin and she never heard of a friend going to the city without asking him/her to pass by the shop on Dawson Street and get her a cake. Tea Time Express was founded in 1938 by the Arigho family. The original bakery was located in Usher's Island in Dublin's city centre. Initially the business delivered its cakes door-to-door in the city, using bicycles with sidecars. The familiar sight of bicycles whizzing round the streets of Dublin became affectionately known as the "Tea Time Express". The first and most famous shop was at 51b Dawson Street, where it was common to see people queuing in the street waiting to buy their cakes and pastries. That shop has gone, but the brand thrives.

The **United Arts Club** was founded in 1907 when the essentially middle-class aspiration to bring together people interested in literature, music, painting, drama and good conversation was a respectable pedagogic and liberal project. Among its advertised activities are the holding of exhibitions, concerts, recitals, discussions, lectures, poetry readings, chess and bridge. The election of new members is carried out monthly by the Committee and candidates must be proposed and seconded by members of the club of three years standing. Membership is open to practitioners in all disciples of the arts as well as to people who have a "genuine interest" in the arts. The United Arts Club was envisaged as "combining the unusual advantages of a social club, open to both ladies and gentlemen, with features of special interest to workers in Art, in Music, and in Literature."

The founder was Ellie Duncan, later first curator of the Municipal Gallery of Modern Art, and among the founding members were Augusta Gregory, Casimir Markievicz, Constance Markievicz, George Russell (AE), Jack B. Yeats and W. B. Yeats. The club offered full membership to men and women from the start. In 1911, thanks to

Duncan, the club hosted Dublin's first major post-impressionist exhibition at its premises in Upper Fitzwilliam Street. The Dublin public imagination, alas, failed to be captured by the work of Cézanne, Matisse, Van Gogh and others.

Today the club awards a prize named after Constance Markievicz to encourage young Irish Artists. The competition is run annually and has a different theme and particular artistic discipline each year.

In 1729 a rival to Dublin's Smock Alley Theatre appeared in the booth started in Fownes's Street, between Dame Street and Temple Bar, by **Madame Violante,** a celebrated rope-dancer. Not much is known about Violante's origins, but while the name may well have been adopted for the stage, the presumption in all early references to her is that she was "foreign". With three or four other foreigners she put on entertainments involving rope-dancing, tumbling, acrobatics, pantomime and dance. Although she did not have the necessary patent, Violante began to branch into mainstream drama, and she gathered together a troupe of children whom she termed her "Lilliputian Company". Violante's most celebrated discovery was Margaret Woffington, who joined the troupe as a child and had an early success in the role of Peggy Peachum in John Gay's *The Beggar's Opera*:

> *Peggy Woffington was at her Father's death no more than ten years of Age, and her Sister eight years younger than herself. Even at that tender Age, she discovered Beauties which surprized and enchanted… She had often been seen by the well-known Madame VIOLANTE in the mean Employment of fetching Water from the Liffey for her Mother's Use; who being at that time mistress of a Booth, in Dame Street, and a Person of no small Penetration, thought she could read in PEGGY'S Features, a Mind worthy of better Employment.*

> *(Memoirs of the Celebrated Mrs Woffington, Interspersed with several theatrical anecdotes, the amours of many persons of the first rank; and some interesting characters drawn from real life.* London: 1760*)*

With the success of *The Beggar's Opera*, Madame Violante moved to 53 South Great George's Street, then George's Lane. William Chetwood remarks, in his 1749 history of the Irish theatre, that

Violante's company of young actors "play'd several Dramatic pieces with grotesque entertainments, till stop'd by the Lord Mayor of the City of Dublin, Mrs. Violante, having no Sanction, or proper Authority to exhibit such Entertainment." Lacking a Patent, the George's Lane theatre was closed by order of the Corporation, but Violante opened a regular theatre in Rainsford Street in the Liberty of Donore, outside municipal jurisdiction.

In the 1970s Dublin Corporation decided to develop a site at **Wood Quay** for its new civic offices. Before building work could begin archaeological works were carried out at the site, which had deep, stratified deposits ranging from the early tenth to the early fourteenth century. This provided valuable evidence about the nature of the Viking age settlements in Dublin, showing house plots, town defences, and land reclamation. In 1977 conservationists, led by Professor F. X. Martin, O.S.A., chairman of the Friends of Medieval Dublin, asked for more time for the excavations. Hostility developed between the developers and the conservationists and there was a scandal when some of the site was bulldozed and valuable material destroyed. Some of the artefacts recovered from the Wood Quay excavation are on display at the Dublinia exhibition. In an interview with Dáire Keogh in *History Ireland* in 1997, Fr. Martin described his involvement at the Wood Quay protest:

Wood Quay became a major part of my life. It was a great adventure which we organised very successfully, gathering a crowd of 20,000 to the march in September 1978. We sent out word to the public and people came dressed appropriately; academics in their gowns and many young people dressed as Vikings with horns on! We marched outside the Dáil to show our defiance of authority, but it was all peaceful. We marched ten abreast marshalled by an ex-army captain, J. P. Duggan. He was given authority to give orders to people. Of course the snag was that he gave the orders in Irish and practically nobody understood what he was talking about!

We decided the only way to stop the Corporation was to seize the site. That was a very tricky, because technically by seizing the site we were breaking the law. Nevertheless, I decided without consultation with anybody else, that we would take twenty hostages, prominent people who would become our voluntary captives. At that stage women were not so prominent in Irish public life but we got five or six women including Mary Lavin, a great soul who has gone to her reward, the sculptress Imogen Stewart, Gemma Hussey who has now lapsed into a kind of politics, the poet Eavan Boland and Rita Childers. The others included the outstanding architect Michael Scott and the Lord Mayor of Dublin! It was a very successful demonstration, which also showed that we were not just a hard-nosed male lot.

For better or for worse, I became known as "the Wood Quay priest". The big question was whether I would get into legal trouble. I was saved from the danger of arrest by Mary Robinson, who would say things like, "F.X. don't do that. That'll be contempt of court"! Finally, the courts ruled that "Father Martin and his gang" were to be off the site or else we would face the consequences of going to prison. Mind you it would have been a sardonic joke if they had tried arresting us. Still, I remember Mary Robinson running over from the Four Courts, holding her wig in one hand and her gown flapping around her shoulders warning us to us get off the site immediately.

DK: What do you think you achieved by the whole enterprise?

FXM: I have no personal regrets about seizing the site. We made Dublin, but also Ireland, conscious of its heritage. Personally I regret not being imprisoned, even for a night. It was a great opportunity for me because if you want to be famous, really famous, in Ireland you have to go to prison like de Valera and Michael Collins did in their time! You're not fully honoured unless you've spent some time behind bars.

If I had not been writing an abcdarium, I might have gone many more years without lifting from my shelf *The Whole Story of the X.Y.Z.* by Brinsley MacNamara (published in Belfast in 1951) to see what it is about. It is about Dublin, by happy chance, as I saw as soon as I looked properly at the cover illustration by W. H. Conn, featuring a middle-aged chap in a suit and tie, smoking a cigarette and looking quizzically at the readers, before a panorama of the Liffey and the Four Courts. As a young man MacNamara (1890-1963) was a member of the Abbey Theatre Company. His first novel, *The Valley of the Squinting Windows*, caused considerable offence in his home village, with its attack on the meanness and narrow-mindedness of Irish provincial life. He went on to write comedies for the Abbey and further prose fiction. *The Whole Story of the X.Y.Z.* is a little comic novella about a clerk in a Dublin solicitor's office who invents for himself a distinguished background during the period of the Irish Literary Revival. It spoofs the post-independence tendency for Irish people to brag about their roles as rebels or at least critics of empire pre-1916, and the social tic by which almost all Irish people claimed acquaintance with the great men of the past. X.Y.Z., an allusion to Thomas De Quincey's pseudonym, stands for the Xanadu Young Zozimus Society, by the way. More of Zozimus later.

Chiang Yee (1903-77) was born in China and lived in London before settling in the United States. A painter, calligrapher, poet and travel writer, he produced several volumes in the "Silent Traveller" series as well as the classic textbook *Chinese Calligraphy*. In 1938 he visited Christine and Edward, the Countess and Earl of Longford, at their Leinster Road house. Ten years later he returned, and this second visit is the basis of *The Silent Traveller in Dublin* (1953). The colour illustrations are remarkably lovely. Yee found in Dublin large watery skies and muted colours. He was conscious of water and of the wind in the trees. The line drawings are quirky and gently comic. Yee finds analogies and differences between Irish and Chinese cultures and the arts. In the following passage he is viewing *The Book of Kells* in the library at Trinity College Dublin:

> *Pictorial art, including decorative art, is the chief flower of a nation's culture. The highly developed Irish illuminative art displayed in The Book of Kells must have stemmed from a long way back in Ireland's history. We Chinese should not indulge in the absurd boast that the antiquity of our art exceeds that of any other art... What fascinated and intrigued me most of all was the inimitable yet profuse patterns of the smaller illuminated initials... Looking at reproductions of them, I cannot but think that Irish businessmen should try to incorporate them in their goods—Irish linen, for instance, scarves, handkerchiefs, pillow cases, etc. Customers would be delighted to have their initials printed or worked on their purchases. But doubtless such an idea serves only to prove more clearly that I have an "infanticide" [sic] brain.*

Zozimus (1794?-1846) was born as Michael Moran in Faddle Alley, off Black Pitts, in the Liberties of Dublin. He was probably blind from birth, though some accounts have him struck blind in infancy or childhood. Zozimus was a beggar-poet, who performed his verse as a musician might busk. His favourite sites were reputedly Essex Bridge, Wood Quay, Church Street, Dame Street, Capel Street, Sackville Street, Grafton Street, Henry Street and Conciliation Hall. He began each session with the verse:

Ye sons and daughters of Erin,
Gather round poor Zozimus, yer friend;
Listen boys, until yez hear
My charming song so dear.

He gained the name Zozimus from the poem he recited, the "Life of St. Mary of Egypt", transformed by Moran from a verse version by Bishop Anthony Coyle, which tells the story of a woman—a harlot—converted in the Holy Land and attended by Bishop Zozimus, to whom she makes her confession. Zozimus deserves to be remembered for his "The Finding of Moses in the Bulrushes" if for nothing else:

In Agypt's land, contaygious to the Nile,
Old Pharaoh's daughter went to bathe in style,
She tuk her dip and came unto the land,
And for to dry her royal pelt she ran along the strand:
A bull-rush tripped her, whereupon she saw
A smiling babby in a wad of straw,
She took it up and said in accents mild,
"Tare-an-ages, girls, which o'yees own the child?"

There are, naturally enough, several transcriptions of the song, since Zozimus was not a published poet but worked in the tradition of the gleemen. It is as the last of the gleemen that W. B. Yeats wrote about him in *The Celtic Twilight*, and thus perpetuated his reputation. Yeats makes a couple of references to the tantalizing ways in which Zozimus called into question his own identity, and seems a true contemporary of James Clarence Mangan, but also of James Joyce. For one thing there is

Yeats' suggestion that the verse of "Moses" given above was actually Zozimus' parody of his own poem.

Moran's success spawned a number of imitators on the streets of Dublin, and Yeats also tells a terrific story—clearly the origin of Brinsley MacNamara's novella—about the way in which the real Zozimus one day comes across an actor pretending to be him and collecting money from the crowd. The real blindness of one and the pretend blindness of the other contribute to the uncanny nature of the story. "Is it possible none of yez can know me?" pleads Zozimus. "Don't yez see it's myself; and that's someone else?"

Zozimus was clearly a cult figure, and named after him were the magazine *Zozimus*, 1870-72; also *Zoz, or the Irish Charivari*, 1876-79; and a New York collection of stories, *The Zozimus Papers* (1889).

He died at his lodging at 15 Patrick Street and Yeats gives a description of his funeral.

> *The funeral took place the next day. A good party of his admirers and friends got into the hearse with the coffin, for the day was wet and nasty. They had not gone far when one of them burst out with "It's cruel cowld, isn't it?" "Garra'," replied another, "we'll all be as stiff as the corpse when we get to the berrin-ground." "Bad cess to him," said a third; "I wish he'd held out another month until the weather got dacent." A man called Carroll thereupon produced a half-pint of whiskey, and they all drank to the soul of the departed. Unhappily, however, the hearse was over-weighted, and they had not reached the cemetery before the spring broke, and the bottle with it.*

FURTHER READING

As I was writing this book, the works I consulted most frequently were *The Oxford Companion to Irish History*, ed. S. J. Connolly (Oxford: Oxford University Press, 1998); Fintan Cullen, *Visual Politics: The Representation of Ireland 1750-1930* (Cork: Cork University Press, 1997); D. J. Hickey and J. E. Doherty, *A Dictionary of Irish History 1800-1980* (Dublin: Gill and Macmillan, 1980); Vivien Igoe, *Dublin Burial Grounds and Graveyards* (Dublin: Wolfhound Press, 2001); *The Encyclopaedia Of Ireland*, ed. Brian Lalor (Dublin: Gill & Macmillan, 2003); Christopher Morash, *A History of Irish Theatre, 1601-2000* (Cambridge: Cambridge University Press, 2002).

Bibliography

Jonah Barrington, *Personal Sketches of His Own Time*. First pub. 1827-32; Dublin: Ashfield Press, 1998.

Dermot Bolger (ed.) *Invisible Dublin: A Journey through Dublin's Suburbs*. Dublin: Raven Arts Press, 1991.

Elizabeth Bowen, *Seven Winters*. Dublin: Irish Academic Press, 1972.

Elizabeth Bowen, *The Shelbourne*. New York: Vintage, 2001.

Noel Browne, *Against the Tide*. Dublin: Gill & Macmillan, 1986.

William Bulfin, *Rambles in Eirinn*. Dublin: M.H. Gill, 1907.

Tony Cascarino (with Paul Kimmage), *Full Time: The Secret Life of Tony Cascarino*. London: Scribner, 2002.

Austin Clarke, *A Penny in the Clouds*. London: Routledge & Kegan Paul, 1968.

Austin Clarke, *Twice Around the Black Church: Early Memories*. London: Routledge & Kegan Paul, 1962.

Howard Clarke, Sarah Dent and Ruth Johnson, *Dublinia: The Story of Medieval Dublin*. Dublin: O'Brien Press, 2002.

Richard Cobb, *Promenades*. Oxford: Oxford University Press, 1980.

Tim Pat Coogan, *De Valera: Long Fellow, Long Shadow*. London: Hutchinson, 1993.

Peter Costello, *Dublin Castle: In the Life of the Irish Nation*. Dublin: Wolfhound Press, 2001.

Peter Costello and Peter Van Der Kamp, *Flann O'Brien, An Illustrated Biography*. London: Bloomsbury, 1987.

Maurice Craig, *Dublin, 1660-1860*. London: Cresset Press, 1952.

Anthony Cronin, *Dead As Doornails*. Dublin: The Dolmen Press, 1976.

Anthony Cronin, *No Laughing Matter: The Life and Times of Flann O'Brien*. Dublin: New Island Books, 2003.

Fintan Cullen (ed.), *Sources in Irish Art. A Reader*. Cork: Cork University Press, 2000.

Louis Cullen, *Life in Ireland*. London: B.T. Batsford, 1968.

Fergus D'Arcy, "The Decline and Fall of Donnybrook Fair: Moral Reform and Social Control in Nineteenth-Century Dublin," *Saothar*, vol. 13, 1988: 7-21.

Frank Delaney, *James Joyce's Odyssey: A Guide to the Dublin of Ulysses*. London: Paladin, 1983; 1987.

Éamon de Valera, "Why Ireland Was Neutral." Dublin: pamphlet reprinted from *The Irish Press*, 17 May 1945.

David Dickson (ed.), *The Gorgeous Mask: Dublin 1700-1850*. Dublin: Trinity History Workshop, 1987.

J. P. Donleavy, *J. P. Donleavy's Ireland: In All Her Sins and in Some of Her Graces*. New York: Viking, 1986.

Eamon Dunphy, *Only a Game?: Diary of a Professional Footballer*. London: Penguin, 1987.

Eamon Dunphy, *Unforgettable Fire: The Story of "U2"*. London: Penguin, 1988.

Terry Eagleton, *The Truth About the Irish*. Dublin: New Island Books, 1999.

Richard Ellmann, *James Joyce*. Oxford: Oxford University Press, 1959.

Fergus Finlay, *Mary Robinson. A President with a Purpose*. Dublin: O'Brien Press, 1990.

Christopher Fitz-Simon, *The Boys: A Biography of Mícheál Mac Liammóir and Hilton Edwards*. Dublin: New Island Books, 2002.

Jacques Fontaine, *Mémoires d'une famille huguenote, victime de la révolution et de l'Édit de Nantes*. Paris: Presse de Languedoc, 1995.

Sigmund Freud, *Jokes and their Relation to the Unconscious*. Ed. James Strachey. London: Routledge, 1960.

Sir Peter Froggatt, "John Snow, Thomas Wakley, and *The Lancet*", *Anaesthesia* 57 (7), 667-675.

Peter Gray, "Memory and Commemoration of the Great Irish Famine", in P. Gray and K. Oliver (eds.), *The Memory of Catastrophe*. Manchester University Press, 2004.

John P. Harrington (ed.), *The English Traveller in Ireland: Accounts of Ireland and the Irish Through Five Centuries*. (Dublin: Wolfhound Press, 1997.

Seán Hillen, *www.irelantis.com*

Roy Keane and Eamon Dunphy, *Keane: The Autobiography*. London: Michael Joseph, 2002.

Margaret Kelleher, "Hunger and History: Monuments to the Great Irish Famine", *Textual Practice*, 16:2 (2002), 249-76.

Frieda Kelly, *A History of Kilmainham Gaol: The Dismal House of Little Ease*. Dublin: Mercier Press, 1988.

James Kelly, *"That Damn'd Thing Called Honour": Duelling in Ireland 1570-1860*. Cork: Cork University Press, 1995.

Herbert A. Kenny, *Literary Dublin: A History*. New York: Taplinger Publishing Company, 1974.

Benedict Kiely (compiler), *Dublin*. Oxford: Oxford University Press, 1983.

Peadar Kirby, Luke Gibbons, and Michael Cronin (eds.), *Reinventing Ireland: Culture and the Celtic Tiger*. London: Pluto Press, 2002.

John M. Kirk and Donall P. O. Baoill (eds.), *Travellers and Their Language*. Belfast Studies in Language, Culture & Politics. Belfast: Queen's University Belfast, 2002.

W. R. Le Fanu, *Seventy Years of Irish Life, Being Anecdotes and Reminiscences*. First pub. 1893; London: Edward Arnold, 1914.

Ronit Lentin and Robbie McVeigh (eds.), *Racism and Anti-racism in Ireland*. Dublin: Beyond the Pale, 2002.

Pat Liddy, *Dublin, A Celebration: From the 1st to the 21st Century*. Dublin: Dublin Corporation, 2000.

Belinda Loftus, *Mirrors: William III and Mother Ireland*. Dundrum, Co. Down: Picture Press, 1990.

Maria Luddy, *Hanna Sheehy Skeffington*. Dublin: Historical Association of Ireland, 1995.

Linde Lunney, "The Celebrated Mr. Dinwiddie: An Eighteenth-Century Scientist in Ireland". *Eighteenth-Century Ireland/Iris an dá chultúr* 3, 1988: 69-83.

Sinead McCoole, *No Ordinary Women: Irish Female Activists in the Revolutionary Years, 1900-1923*. Dublin: O'Brien Press, 2003.

Neil McCormick, *I Was Bono's Doppelganger*. London: Michael Joseph, 2004.

J. L. McCracken, "The Fate of an Infamous Informer", *History Ireland*, vol.9, no.2, Summer 2001.

Neil McKenna, *The Secret Life of Oscar Wilde*. London: Century, 2003.

David McKittrick, Seamus Kelters, Brian Feeney and Chris Thornton, *Lost Lives: The Stories of the Men, Women and Children Who Died as a Result of the Northern Ireland Troubles*. Edinburgh: Mainstream Publishing, 1999.

Mícheál Mac Liammóir, *All for Hecuba: An Irish Theatrical Autobiography*. Dublin: Branden Publishing Co., 1967.

James Malton, *Picturesque and Descriptive View of the City of Dublin*. Dublin: Dolmen Press, 1980.

James Clarence Mangan, *Selected Writings*. Ed. Sean Ryder. Dublin: University College Dublin Press, 2004.

F. X. Martin (ed.), *Leaders and Men of the Easter Rising: Dublin 1916*. London: Methuen, 1967.

F. X. Martin, "Wood Quay Warrior", interviewed by Dáire Keogh, *History Ireland*, vol.5, no.2, Summer 1997.

Constantia Maxwell, *Dublin under the Georges*. London: George Harrap, 1946.

Cliona Murphy, "The Religious Context of the Women's Suffrage Campaign in Ireland". *Women's History Review*, vol. 6, no.4., 1997.

Robert Nicholson, *The Ulysses Guide: Tours through Joyce's Dublin*. London: Methuen, 1988.

Sinéad ní Shuinéar, "Apocrypha to Canon: Inventing Irish Traveller History", *History Ireland*, 12:4, Winter 2004, pp. 15-19.

David Nokes, *Jonathan Swift, a Hypocrite Reversed: A Critical Biography*. New York: Olympic, 1985.

Diana Norman, *Terrible Beauty: A Life of Constance Markievicz*. London: Hodder and Stoughton, 1987.

Deirdre O'Brien, *Four Roads to Dublin: The History of Rathmines, Ranelagh and Leeson Street*. Dublin: O'Brien Press, 1995; 2001.

Edna O'Brien, *The Country Girls Trilogy: "The Country Girls", "The Lonely Girl", "Girls in Their Married Bliss"*. London: Penguin, 1988.

Flann O'Brien, *The Various Lives of Keats and Chapman, [and] The Brother*. Ed. Benedict Kiely. London: Hart-Davis, MacGibbon 1976.

Kate O'Brien, *My Ireland*. London: B. T. Batsford, 1962.

Sean O'Casey, *Drums Under the Windows*. London: Macmillan, 1945.

Rúan O'Donnell, *Remembering Emmet: Images of the Life and Legacy of Robert Emmet*. Dublin: Wordwell, 2003.

Rúan O'Donnell, *Robert Emmet and the Rebellion of 1798*. Dublin: Irish Academic Press, 2003.

Stephan Oetterman, *The Panorama: History of a Mass Medium*. New York: Zone Books, 1997.

Edward O'Neill and Barry Whyte, *Two Little Boys: The Dublin and Monaghan Bombings*. Dublin: Currach Press, 2004.

Thomas and Valerie Pakenham, *A Traveller's Companion to Dublin*. London: Constable & Robinson, 1988; 2003.

Susan Parkes, *A Danger to the Men?: A History of Women in Trinity College Dublin 1904-2004*. Dublin: Lilliput Press, 2004.

Peter Pearson, *Decorative Dublin*. Dublin: O'Brien Press, 2002.

Peter Pearson, *The Heart of Dublin: Resurgence of an Historic City*. Dublin: O'Brien Press, 2000.

V. S. Pritchett, *Dublin: A Portrait*. London: Bodley Head, 1967.

Carter Ratcliff, "Sean Scully: The Constitutive Stripe," in *Sean Scully: The Catherine Paintings*. Fort Worth: Modern Art Museum of Fort Worth, 1993.

Herman Reichenbach, "Lost Menageries—Why and How Zoos Disappear (Part 1)", *International Zoo News*, vol. 49/3 (no. 316) April/May 2002.

Ian Campbell Ross (ed.), *Public Virtue, Public Love. The Early Years of the Dublin Lying-In Hospital: The Rotunda*. Dublin: O'Brien Press, 1986.

John Ryan, *Remembering How We Stood: Bohemian Dublin at the Mid-century*. Dublin: Lilliput Press, 1987.

Oliver St. John, *As I Was Going Down Sackville Street* London: Rich & Cowan, 1937.

Esther K Sheldon, *Thomas Sheridan of Smock-Alley: Recording his Life as Actor and Theater Manager in Both Dublin and London, and Including a Smock-Alley Calendar for the Years of his Management*. Princeton: Princeton University Press, 1967.

Lorna Siggins, *Mary Robinson: The Woman Who Took Power in the Park*. Edinburgh: Mainstream Publishing, 1997.

Stella Tillyard, *Citizen Lord: The Life of Edward Fitzgerald, Irish*

Revolutionary. New York: Farrar Straus & Giroux, 1999.

Caroline Walsh, *The Homes of Irish Writers*. Dublin: Anvil Press, 1980.

J. E. Walsh, *Sketches of Ireland Sixty Years Ago*. Dublin: James McGlashan, 1847.

Margaret Ward, *Maud Gonne: A Life*. London: Pandora Press, 1993.

John Waters, *Race of Angels: Ireland and the Genesis of U2*. Belfast: Blackstaff Press, 1994.

Yvonne Whelan, "Contested Geographies of Imperial Power: Interpreting Royal Visits to Ireland at the Turn of the Century", *http://www.esh.ed.ac.uk/urban_history/text/WhelanM3.doc*. 2005.

Harry White, *The Keeper's Recital: Music and Cultural History in Ireland, 1770-1970*. Cork: Cork University Press, 1998.

Pádraig Yeates, "The Dublin 1913 Lockout", *History Ireland*, vol.9, no.2, Summer 2001.

Chiang Yee, *The Silent Traveller in Dublin*. London: Methuen, 1953.

INDEX OF LITERARY & HISTORICAL NAMES

Clarke, Harry 245
Clarke, Kathleen 173
Clarke, Olivia 104
Clarke, Thomas 138, 173, 183
Clayton, Robert 93
Clyn, John 34
Coade, Eleanor 85
Coade, George 85
Cobb, Richard 4
Colbert, Con 185
Colles, Abraham 126
Collins, Michael 87, 269
Comerford, Joe 242
Comyn, John 26
Conn, W. H. 269
Connellan, Owen 130
Connolly, James 7, 138, 158-
9,179-81, 183, 185-6
Connolly, Nora 186
Cook, Judith 222
Cooley, Thomas 57
Copeland, Ralph 153
Corcoran, Séan 14
Corrigan, Dominic 126
Costello, John 214
Costello, Seamus 222
Cousins, James 164
Cousins, Margaret 164
Cox, Watty 77
Coyle, Anthony 271
Crampton, Philip 116
Croarkin, Thomas 220
Cromwell, Oliver 36, 40, 42, 124
Cronin, Anthony 215-7
Crosbie, Richard 86
Crowley, John 232
Cruickshank, Dan 203
Cú Chulainn 248
Cullen, Luke 111
Cullen, Paul 96
Curley, Dan 150

Curran, John Philpot 113-4
Curran, Sarah 113-4
Currie, Austin 224, 226
Cusack, Cyril 230
Cusack, Michael 236

Daly, Edward 185
Dana, see Rosemary Scallon
Dargan, William 84, 91, 143-4
Dargle, John 220
Darwin, Charles 152
Davies, Christian 134-5
Davis, Desmond 231
Davis, Thomas 2, 106, 123
Davitt, Michael 148
Dawson, Joshua 99
Deane, Sir Thomas 80, 102
Deane, Thomas 100, 102
De Clare, Richard, see Richard Fitz
Gilbert
de Gree, Peter 83
de Lacy, Hugh 23
Delaney, Edward 8
Delany, Mary 49
Delany, Patrick 49
de Londres, Archbishop Henry, see
Blund, Archbishop Henry
Dempsey, Concepta 220
Denny, Arabella 258-9
De Quincey, Thomas 73, 270
De Valera, Éamon 2, 138, 185,
206-10, 269
Devlin, Anne 111, 114
Devonshire, William Cavendish,
Seventh Duke of 147
Devonshire, William Cavendish,
Third Duke of 59
Devoy, John 149
Dickens, Charles 100
Dickinson, Thorold 202-3
Digges, West 51-2

INDEX OF PLACES AND LANDMARKS